THE
SECOND BILL
OF RIGHTS

Also by Cass R. Sunstein

Why Societies Need Dissent, 2003

Risk and Reason, 2002

Punitive Damages (with Reid Hastie, John Payne, David Schkade, and W. Kip Viscusi), 2002

Designing Democracy, 2001

Republic.com, 2001

One Case at a Time, 1999

The Cost of Rights (with Stephen Holmes), 1999

Free Markets and Social Justice, 1997

Legal Reasoning and Political Conflict, 1996

Democracy and the Problem of Free Speech, 1993

The Partial Constitution, 1993

After the Rights Revolution, 1990

THE
SECOND BILL
OF RIGHTS

FDR'S UNFINISHED
REVOLUTION
AND
WHY WE NEED IT
MORE THAN EVER

CASS R. SUNSTEIN

BASIC
BOOKS
A Member of the Perseus Books Group
New York

TO THE MEMORY OF MY FATHER

Designed by Reginald R. Thompson

Library of Congress Cataloging-in-Publication Data

Sunstein, Cass R.
   The second bill of rights : FDR's unfinished revolution and why we need it more than ever / Cass R. Sunstein.
      p. cm.
   Includes bibliographical references and index.
   ISBN 0-465-08332-3 (alk. paper)
   1. Human rights—United States—History. 2. United States—Social policy. 3. United States—Economic policy. 4. Labor policy—United States. I. Title.

KF3300.S863 2004
342.7308'5—dc22
                                                          2003025549

04 05 06 / 10 9 8 7 6 5 4 3 2 1

The alms given to a naked man in the street do not fulfil the obligations of the state, which owes to every citizen a certain subsistence, a proper nourishment, convenient clothing, and a kind of life not incompatible with health.

Montesquieu

I ask Congress to explore the means for implementing th[e] economic bill of rights—for it is definitely the responsibility of the Congress to do so.

Franklin Delano Roosevelt

Those who denounce state intervention are the ones who most frequently and successfully invoke it. The cry of laissez faire mainly goes up from the ones who, if really "let alone," would instantly lose their wealth-absorbing power.

Lester Ward

Contents

The Second Bill of Rights

**Proposed by
Franklin Delano Roosevelt
January 11, 1944**

EVERY AMERICAN IS ENTITLED TO:

The right to a useful and remunerative job in the industries or shops or farms or mines of the nation;

The right to earn enough to provide adequate food and clothing and recreation;

The right of every farmer to raise and sell his products at a return which will give him and his family a decent living;

The right of every businessman, large and small, to trade in an atmosphere of freedom from unfair competition and domination by monopolies at home or abroad;

The right of every family to a decent home;

The right to adequate medical care and the opportunity to achieve and enjoy good health;

The right to adequate protection from the economic fears of old age, sickness, accident, and unemployment;

The right to a good education.

Introduction

MY MAJOR AIM in this book is to uncover an important but neglected part of America's heritage: the idea of a second bill of rights. In brief, the second bill attempts to protect both opportunity and security, by creating rights to employment, adequate food and clothing, decent shelter, education, recreation, and medical care. The presidency of America's greatest leader, Franklin Delano Roosevelt, culminated in the idea of a second bill. It represented Roosevelt's belief that the American Revolution was radically incomplete and that a new set of rights was necessary to finish it.

The second bill was proposed in 1944 in a widely unknown speech that was, I believe, the greatest of the twentieth century. The origins of the basic idea can be traced to the earliest days of Roosevelt's New Deal, and even before, to his first campaign for the presidency, when he proposed "an economic declaration of rights" that entailed "a right to make a comfortable living." The second bill was a direct product of America's experience with the desperation and misery of the Great Depression. Rights are a product of wrongs, and after a period of massive unemployment and poverty, it seemed only natural to argue on behalf of a right to economic security. But the immediate impetus for the second bill came from a fusion of New Deal thinking in the early 1930s with the American response to World War II in the early 1940s. The threat from Hitler and the Axis powers broadened the New Deal's commitment to security and strengthened the nation's appreciation of human vulnerability. At the same time, the external threat deepened the need for a fresh understanding of America's defining commitments, an understanding that could have international as well as domestic appeal and could serve as a beacon of hope, an example of what free societies and decent governments offer their people.

There is a direct link between the second bill and Roosevelt's famous speech of 1941, in which he proposed the four freedoms: freedom of speech, freedom of religion, freedom from want, and freedom from fear. The four freedoms were not the work of any speechwriter; they were dictated by Roosevelt himself, who insisted, in direct response to the growing international crisis (and over the opposition of a principal adviser), that these essential freedoms should exist "everywhere in the world." The second bill of rights was meant to ensure the realization of freedom from want—which, in Roosevelt's view, meant "economic understandings which will secure to every nation everywhere a healthy peacetime life for its inhabitants." During World War II, Roosevelt and the nation saw an intimate connection between freedom from want and protection against external threats, captured in the notion of "freedom from fear." In his words, "Freedom from fear is eternally linked with freedom from want."

Roosevelt's emphasis on freedom should be underlined. He was committed to free markets, free enterprise, and private ownership of property. He was not an egalitarian. While he insisted that the wealthiest members of society should bear a proportionately higher tax burden, and while he sought a decent floor for those at the bottom, he did not seek anything like economic equality. He believed in individualism. It was freedom, not equality, that motivated the second bill of rights. Roosevelt contended that people who live in "want" are not free. And he believed too that "want" is not inevitable. He saw it as a product of conscious social choices that could be counteracted by well-functioning institutions directed by a new conception of rights. In World War II, Roosevelt internationalized that belief, arguing that "security" required freedom everywhere in the world.

Although Roosevelt's second bill is largely unknown in the United States, it has had extraordinary influence internationally. It played a major role in the Universal Declaration of Human Rights, finalized in 1948 under the leadership of Eleanor Roosevelt and publicly endorsed by American officials at the time. The Universal Declaration includes social and economic guarantees that show the unmistakable influence of the second bill. And with its effect on the Universal Declaration, the second bill has influenced dozens of constitutions throughout the world. In one or another form, it can be found in countless political and legal documents. We might even call the second bill of rights a leading American export.

We can go further. The United States continues to live, at least some of the time, under Roosevelt's constitutional vision. A consensus underlies several of the rights he listed, including the right to education, the right to social security, the right to be free from monopoly, possibly even the right to a job. When asked directly, most Americans support the second bill, and even say that many of its provisions should be seen not as mere privileges but as rights to which each person is "entitled as a citizen." Some contemporary leaders are committed, in principle, to "freedom from want." But in terms of actual policy, the public commitment is often partial and ambivalent, even grudging. Much of the time, the United States seems to have embraced a confused and pernicious form of individualism. This approach endorses rights of private property and freedom of contract, and respects political liberty, but claims to distrust "government intervention" and insists that people must fend for themselves. This form of so-called individualism is incoherent, a tangle of confusions. It was definitively rejected during the New Deal era, and it has no roots in America's founding period. Its only brief period of success came early in the twentieth century. Roosevelt himself pointed to the essential problem as early as 1932: the exercise of "property rights might so interfere with the rights of the individual that the government, without whose assistance the property rights could not exist, must intervene, not to destroy individualism but to protect it."

Remarkably, the confusions that Roosevelt identified have had a rebirth since the early 1980s, largely because of the influence of powerful private groups. The result is a false and ahistorical picture of American culture and history both at home and abroad. That picture is not innocuous. America's self-image—our sense of ourselves—has a significant impact on what we actually do. We should not look at ourselves in a distorted mirror.

The country seems in the past decades to have lost sight of the very ideas that paved the way toward the second bill. To make a long story short, the second bill was spurred by a recognition that no one is really against government intervention. The wealthy, at least as much as the poor, receive help from government and the benefits it bestows. Those of us who have plenty of money and opportunities owe a great deal to an active government that is willing and able to protect what we have. As Roosevelt stressed, property rights depend on government. Freedom requires not merely national defense but, among other things, a court system, an ample body of law to govern and enforce contracts and prevent civil wrongs, and the police. To provide all these things, freedom requires taxation. Once we appreciate this point, we will find it impossible to complain about "government interference" as such or to urge, ludicrously, that our rights are best secured by getting government "off our backs." Those who insist they want "small government" want, and need, something very large. The same people who object to "government intervention" depend on it every day. Roosevelt was entirely aware of this point and made it during the Depression. When the nation's security was at risk, he made it again—and he used it as a basis for a broadened understanding of what a nation would do if it were genuinely committed to ensuring the "security" of its citizens. The threat to security from abroad was a reason to strengthen and to rethink the idea of security at home.

In addition to recovering the second bill and its rationale, I hope to cast light on a larger issue: Why does the American Constitution lack Roosevelt's second bill? Why hasn't it become a part of our constitutional understandings? To answer that question, I will explore several aspects of American history, including the distinctive nature of our Constitution and culture. I will contend that much of the answer lies in nothing abstract or grand, but in a particular and hardly inevitable event: the election of President Richard M. Nixon in 1968. If Nixon had not been elected, significant parts of the second bill would probably be part of our constitutional understandings today. In the 1960s, the nation was rapidly moving toward accepting a second bill, not through constitutional amendment but through the Supreme Court's interpretations of the existing Constitution. An appreciation of this point will drive home, very clearly, the extent to which the meaning of America's Constitution depends on the commitments of its judges. Even more important, it will show that a belief in the second bill lies beneath the surface of our current constitutional understandings. With a little work of recovery, we can easily uncover it there. Parts of it are widely accepted already.

I also want to ask whether, and in what sense, our Constitution and our culture should be committed to the second bill. Roosevelt did not want to amend the Constitution. He saw the second bill not as a legal document for judges but as a set of public commitments by and for the citizenry, very much like the Declaration of Independence. As Roosevelt deeply hoped, some New Deal reforms have achieved that status. Consider the commitment to social security, probably Roosevelt's proudest achievement. Americans have come to believe that adequate provision for retirement years is a right, not a mere privilege. My guess is that if polled, millions of Americans would say that social security is, in fact, in the American Constitution. Whatever the percentage, and whatever the current reform proposals, the nation is unambiguously and even unalterably committed to some kind of social security system. This commitment is not much less secure than the commitment to protection against unreasonable searches and seizures—even though the latter, unlike the former, is part of the formal bill of rights. In both cases, we dispute what the commitment specifically requires, but we do not dispute the commitment itself.

The second bill of rights should be understood in similar terms—as a catalog defining our most basic principles, recognized and cherished by both leaders and citizens. In the nation that is responsible for its creation, the second bill deserves at least that status.

PART I

ROOSEVELT

1

The Speech
of the Century

He wants to make the boys think he's hard-boiled. Maybe he
fools some of them, now and then—but don't ever let him
fool you, or you won't be any use to him. You can see the
real Roosevelt when he comes out with something like the
Four Freedoms. And don't get the idea that those are any
catch phrases. He believes them! That's what you and I have
got to remember in everything we may be able to do for him.

Harry Hopkins

ON JANUARY 11, 1944, the United States was engaged in
its longest conflict since the Civil War. The war effort was
going well. In a remarkable short period, the tide had
turned sharply in favor of the Allies. In early 1943, the American and
British air forces routed German planes and troops on the frontiers
of Tunisia; with the surrender of the last German unit in May, the Allies controlled all of Africa. By late summer, the Italian people,
pounded by an air campaign, lost their will to resist; on September 3,
Italy withdrew from the conflict by signing an armistice. All that remained were the increasingly crippled forces of Germany and Japan.
Ultimate victory was no longer in serious doubt. The real question
was the nature of the peace.

At noon, America's optimistic, aging, self-assured, wheelchair-bound president, Franklin Delano Roosevelt, had the text of his State of the Union address delivered to Congress. Because he was ill with a cold, Roosevelt did not make the customary trip to Capitol Hill to appear in person. Instead he spoke to the nation via radio—the first and only time a State of the Union address was also a Fireside Chat. Millions of Americans assembled by their radios that night to hear what Roosevelt had to say.

His speech wasn't elegant. It was messy, sprawling, unruly, a bit of a pastiche, and not at all literary. It was the opposite of Lincoln's tight, poetic Gettysburg Address. But because of what it said, it has a strong claim to being the greatest speech of the twentieth century.

Immediately after the Japanese attack on Pearl Harbor, Roosevelt had promised an Allied victory. "No matter how long it may take us to overcome this premeditated invasion, the American people in their righteous might will win through to absolute victory. . . . With confidence in our armed forces—with the unbounding determination of our people—we will gain the inevitable triumph—so help us God." He had often insisted that the ultimate outcome was assured. The president's earliest projections for American military production—tens of thousands of planes, tanks, and antiaircraft guns, 6 million tons of merchant shipping—initially seemed staggering, outlandish, utterly unrealistic. To the many skeptics, including his own advisers, Roosevelt responded offhandedly, "Oh—the production people can do it, if they really try." In a few years, his projections had been greatly exceeded. Yet in the early days of 1944, with victory on the horizon, Roosevelt believed that difficult times lay ahead. Fearing national complacency, he devoted most of his speech to the war effort. He did so in a way that explicitly linked that effort to the New Deal and the other crisis the nation had surmounted under his leadership, the Great Depression.

Roosevelt began by emphasizing that the war was a shared endeavor and the United States simply one participant: "This Nation in the past two years has become an active partner in the world's greatest war against human slavery." The war was in the process of being won. "But I do not think that any of us Americans can be content with mere survival." After victory, the initial task was to prevent "another interim that leads to new disaster—that we shall not repeat the tragic errors of ostrich isolationism—that we shall not repeat the excesses of the wild twenties when the Nation went for a joy ride on a roller coaster which ended in a tragic crash." This sentence immediately connected the war against tyranny with the effort to combat economic distress and uncertainty. Hence "the one supreme objective for the future," the objective for all nations, was captured "in one word: Security." Roosevelt argued that the term "means not only physical security which provides safety from attacks by aggressors," but includes "economic security, social security, moral security." All of the allies were concerned with not merely the defeat of fascism but also improved education, better opportunities, and improved living standards. Roosevelt insisted that "essential to peace is a decent standard of living for all individual men and women and children in all nations. Freedom from fear is eternally linked with freedom from want."

In connecting the two freedoms, he argued first and foremost that America could be free from fear only if the citizens of "all nations" were free from want. External threats are often made by people who face extreme deprivation. But Roosevelt also meant to remind the nation that citizens cannot be free from fear unless they have some protection against the most severe forms of want; minimal security, coming from adequate education and decent opportunity, is itself a safeguard against fear. The threat from Germany and Japan occasioned a renewed emphasis on protecting against the most serious forms of human vulnerability at home.

Then Roosevelt turned to the problem of domestic selfishness and profit mongering. Amid war, some groups were attempting to "make profits for themselves at the expense of their neighbors—profits in money or in terms of political or social preferment." He deplored this "selfish agitation," asserting that "in this war, we have been compelled to learn how interdependent upon each other are all groups and sections of the population of America." Here he laid special emphasis on the difficult position of people who depended on fixed incomes—teachers, clergy, police officers, widows and miners, old age pensioners, and others at risk from inflation. To ensure a fair and stable economy and to protect the war effort, he proposed a number of reforms, including a tax law that would "tax all unreasonable profits, both individual and corporate," and a "cost of food law" designed to protect consumers from prohibitively expensive necessities.

Much more controversially, Roosevelt argued for a national service act. This was only vaguely described, but he contended that it would prevent strikes and ensure that ordinary citizens, no less than soldiers, would contribute to victory in war. As for soldiers themselves, he insisted that legislation be enacted to permit them to vote. "It is the duty of the Congress to remove this unjustifiable discrimination against the men and women in our armed forces—and to do it as quickly as possible."

At this stage, Roosevelt turned to purely domestic affairs. He began by pointing toward the postwar era: "It is our duty now to begin to lay the plans and determine the strategy for the winning of a lasting peace and the establishment of an American standard of living higher than ever before known." He added that the nation "cannot be content, no matter how high that general standard of living may be, if some fraction of our people—whether it be one-third or one-fifth or one-tenth—is ill-fed, ill-clothed, ill-housed, and insecure." Suddenly the speech became far more ambitious. Roosevelt looked back, and not entirely approvingly, to the framing of the Constitution. At its inception, the nation had grown "under the protection of certain inalienable political rights—among them the right of free speech, free press, free worship, trial by jury, freedom from unreasonable searches and seizures."

But over time, these rights proved inadequate. Unlike the Constitution's framers, "we have come to a clear realization of the fact that true individual freedom cannot exist without economic security and independence." As Roosevelt saw it, "necessitous men are not free men," not least because those who are hungry and jobless "are the stuff out of which dictatorships are made." He echoed the words of Jefferson's Declaration of Independence, urging a kind of declaration of interdependence: "In our day these economic truths have become accepted as self-evident. We have accepted, so to speak, a second Bill of Rights under which a new basis of security and prosperity can be established for all—regardless of station, race, or creed." It is worth pausing over the last six words. A decade before the constitutional assault on racial segregation and two decades before the enactment of a general civil rights law, Roosevelt insisted on an antidiscrimination principle.

Then he listed the relevant rights:

- The right to a useful and remunerative job in the industries or shops or farms or mines of the nation;
- The right to earn enough to provide adequate food and clothing and recreation;
- The right of every farmer to raise and sell his products at a return that will give him and his family a decent living;
- The right of every businessman, large and small, to trade in an atmosphere of freedom from unfair competition and domination by monopolies at home or abroad;
- The right of every family to a decent home;
- The right to adequate medical care and the opportunity to achieve and enjoy good health;
- The right to adequate protection from the economic fears of old age, sickness, accident, and unemployment;
- The right to a good education.

Having cataloged these eight rights, Roosevelt immediately recalled the "one word" that captured the world's objective for the future. He argued that these "rights spell security," and hence that the recognition of the second bill was continuous with the war effort. "After this war is won," he said, "we must be prepared to move forward, in the implementation of these rights." There was a close connection between this implementation and the coming international order. "America's own rightful place in the world depends in large part upon how fully these and similar rights have been carried into practice for our citizens. For unless there is security here at home there cannot be lasting peace in the world."

Roosevelt asked "the Congress to explore the means for implementing this economic bill of rights—for it is definitely the responsibility of the Congress to do so." He observed that many of the relevant problems were before congressional committees and added that if "no adequate program of progress is evolved, I am certain that the Nation will be conscious of this fact." He made a special plea on behalf of the nation's "fighting men abroad—and their families at home," many of them far from privileged, who "expect such a program and have the right to insist on it."

He closed by unifying the two disparate topics of his speech, indeed the two disparate topics of his presidency—freedom from fear and freedom from want. "There are no two fronts for America in this war. There is only one front. There is one line of unity which extends from the hearts of the people at home to the men of the attacking forces in our farthest outposts." In so saying, Roosevelt attempted to unify the nation—those at home and those abroad—and thus quell the "selfish agitation" with which he began. He also meant to suggest that security, his organizing theme, could be provided only if the movement for the second bill could be linked with the movement for defeating the Axis powers.

Roosevelt's second bill of rights speech was an effort to integrate the two "doctors" who had occupied his lengthy presidency. Once the fascist threat became serious, Roosevelt's domestic programs were put on what he saw as temporary hold, to the great disappointment of many of his strongest supporters. Roosevelt explained the shift in emphasis in some informal remarks distinguishing between "Dr. New Deal" and "Dr. Win the War." After the attack on Pearl Harbor, he said, the strategies of the first doctor were ill-suited to the new task:

How did the New Deal come into existence? It was because in 1932 there was an awfully sick patient called the United States. He was suffering from a grave internal disorder—he was awfully sick—he had all kinds of internal troubles. And they sent for a doctor. . . . But two years ago, after [the sick patient] had become pretty well, he had a very bad accident. . . . Two years ago on the 7th of December, he got into a pretty bad smash-up—broke his hip, broke his leg in two or three places, broke a wrist and an arm. Some people didn't even think he would live, for a while. Old Doc New Deal didn't know anything about broken legs and arms. He knew a great deal about internal medicine but nothing about this new kind of trouble. So he got his partner, who was an orthopedic surgeon, Dr. Win the War, to take care of this fellow. And the result is that the patient is back on his feet. He has given up his crutches. He has begun to strike back—on the offensive.

The call for the second bill was an attempt to connect these two doctors—to suggest that they shared the single task of ensuring security. The wheelchair-bound Roosevelt, a victim of polio, was never able to give up his crutches or "get back on his feet" (and his metaphor here could not have been entirely coincidental). But in his second bill of rights speech, he was able to take the initiative, both domestically and internationally. The link between Roosevelt's two doctors was understood by his listeners. After the speech, *Time* magazine reported, not approvingly, that "Dr. Win-the-War has apparently called into consultation Dr. Win-New-Rights. . . . Some druggists on Capitol Hill thought the handwriting on the prescription seemed strangely familiar—identical, in fact, with that of the late Dr. New Deal."

The most concrete result of the second bill of rights proposal was the GI bill of rights, which offered an array of housing, medical, educational, and training benefits to returning veterans. The GI bill gave millions of veterans a chance to attend colleges and universities. "GI Bill beneficiaries," according to Stanford historian David Kennedy, "changed the face of higher education, dramatically raised the educational level and hence the productivity of the workforce, and in the process unimaginably altered their own lives." The fate of returning soldiers was a large part of what motivated Roosevelt to attend to domestic issues during the war; he defended the second bill partly by reference to the legitimate expectations of those leaving the military for civilian life. Roosevelt wanted to ensure that returning soldiers would have decent prospects for the future. But the GI bill fell far short of what Roosevelt sought to provide.

Roosevelt's second bill of rights speech captured the extraordinary twentieth-century revolution in the conception of rights in America and elsewhere. It marked the utter collapse of the (ludicrous) idea that freedom comes from an absence of government. It also identified crucial, enduring innovations in American government between 1933 and 1944—innovations that embodied the rise of the modern state. Roosevelt proposed that the second bill should be seen as integral to national security, part of the broader fight against foreign enemies. The basic themes of Roosevelt's speech have echoed throughout American political life to the present day. In some ways he was correct to say that the nation "accepted" such a bill. By 1944 many Americans were undoubtedly prepared to endorse it. Many Americans continue to do so today. But that acceptance has proved highly ambivalent, and it has come under pressure from powerful private groups with an intense interest in burying or delegitimating the second bill—and in recovering the kind of confused, self-serving, and even incoherent thinking that immediately preceded Roosevelt's New Deal.

I will devote considerable attention to the nature of that ambivalence. Roosevelt was entirely aware of it. During his last year, Roosevelt concluded that America's system of political parties needed to be fundamentally altered. He told his principal speechwriter, Samuel Rosenman, that "the time has come for the Democratic party to get rid of its reactionary elements in the South, and to attract to it the liberals in the Republican party. . . . We ought to have two real parties—one liberal and one conservative." To this end, Roosevelt started negotiations with Wendell Wilkie, the 1940 Republican presidential candidate, stating that with "the liberals of both parties Wilkie and I together can form a new, really liberal party in America." Wilkie responded quite favorably, saying that he was "ready to devote almost full time to this." But both men were dead within the year, and the project was orphaned.

In my view, the second bill should be able to command a bipartisan consensus without anything like a realignment of parties. But first let us consider its origins.

2

The Myth of Laissez-Faire

We know now that Government by organized money is just as dangerous as Government by organized mob. Never before in all our history have these forces been so united against one candidate as they stand today. They are unanimous in their hate for me—and I welcome their hatred. I should like to have it said of my first Administration that in it the forces of selfishness and of lust for power met their match. I should like to have it said of my second Administration that in it these forces met their master.

Franklin Delano Roosevelt

IN THE SUMMER OF 1932, with the nation mired in the Depression, Franklin Delano Roosevelt was nominated for the presidency by the Democratic convention in Chicago. He began by violating an established tradition. Throughout the nation's history, it had been the practice of presidential nominees to stay away from the convention and accept the nomination only after formal notification, several weeks after the event itself. Roosevelt departed from precedent and flew from New York to Chicago to address the delegates in person. He began by urging that his action should be symbolic. "Let it be from now on the task of our party to break foolish traditions."

Roosevelt's speech electrified the convention. His declared goal was to "drive out" the "specter of insecurity from our midst." What, he asked, do Americans "want more than anything else?" His answer was simple: "work, with all the moral and spiritual values that go with it; and with work, a reasonable measure of security. . . . Work and security—these are more than words." He complained of leaders who maintained that "economic laws—sacred, inviolable, unchangeable—cause panics which no one could prevent. . . . We must lay hold of the fact that economic laws are not made by nature. They are made by human beings." Roosevelt ended with the promise that millions of hopeful Americans "cannot and shall not hope in vain. I pledge you, I pledge myself, to a new deal for the American people."

The term "new deal" was not intended to signal anything especially important. Sam Rosenman, the adviser who penned those words, said, "I had not the slightest idea" that the phrase "would take hold the way it did, nor did the Governor when he read and revised what I had written. In fact, he attached no importance to the two monosyllables." But to the surprise of all, including Roosevelt himself, those monosyllables came to capture much of his presidency, which indeed involved a kind of reshuffling of the social cards. Writing six years later about the origin of the phrase, Roosevelt engaged in a bit of revisionist history:

> The word "Deal" implied that the government itself was going to use affirmative action to bring about its avowed objectives rather than stand by and hope that general economic laws alone would attain them. The word "New" implied that a new order of things designed to benefit the great mass of our farmers, workers and business men would replace the old order of special privilege in a Nation which was completely and thoroughly disgusted with the existing dispensation.

The second bill of rights was a direct outgrowth of these ideas. To understand them, and to see how Roosevelt and his New Deal altered the American understanding of rights, we must focus on two developments. The first is conceptual and involves a major reassessment of what really happens in a free market economy. The conceptual development amounted to an attack on the whole idea of laissez-faire—a suggestion that government and coercion are not opposed to human liberty but in fact are necessary to it. The second development is practical, involving the Great Depression and the nation's reaction to it. The two developments are closely linked. Standing by itself, a set of conceptual claims is most unlikely to move a nation. But the Great Depression helped drive the conceptual lesson home. The new understanding of rights was a product of a new understanding of wrongs.

In a nutshell, the New Deal helped vindicate a simple idea: No one really opposes government intervention. Even the people who most loudly denounce government interference depend on it every day. Their own rights do not come from minimizing government but are a product of government. The simplest problem with laissez-faire is not that it is unjust or harmful to poor people, but that it is a hopelessly inadequate description of any system of liberty, including free markets. Markets and wealth depend on government.

The misunderstanding is not innocuous. It blinds people to the omnipresence of government help for those who are well-off and makes it appear that those who are suffering and complaining about it are looking for handouts. The New Deal vindicated these basic claims about our dependence on government, and the second bill of rights grew out of them. Unfortunately, under an onslaught of confused rhetoric about government as a "necessary evil," we have lost sight of these claims today. Proposing a sensible system of federal tax credits to promote health insurance coverage, President George W. Bush found it necessary to offer the senseless suggestion that what he was proposing was "not a government program." Doris Kearns Goodwin writes sensitively and acutely about Roosevelt, but she entirely misses the point when she says of the second bill: "Nor had he ever been so explicit in linking together the negative liberty from government achieved in the old Bill of Rights to the positive liberty through government to be achieved in the new Bill of Rights." This opposition between "liberty from government" and "liberty through government" misconceives what Roosevelt's presidency was all about.

LEGAL REALISM AND REAL LAW

Roosevelt's attack on the idea of laissez-faire had a long legacy. Jeremy Bentham, the father of utilitarianism, was a great believer in private property. But he also said that "there is no natural property" because "property is entirely the creature of law." Above all, property creates expectations, and firm expectations "can only be the work of law." Thus "it is from the law alone that I can enclose a field and give myself to its cultivation, in the distant hope of the harvest." In Bentham's account, "property and law are born and must die together. Before the laws there was no property; take away the laws, all property ceases."

This basic claim was an important strain of *legal realism*, the most influential movement in early-twentieth-century American law. The realists, most notably law professors Robert Hale and Morris Cohen, insisted that markets and property depend on legal rules. What people have is not a reflection of nature or custom, and voluntary choices are only a part of the picture. Government choices are crucial. This is so always, and simply as a matter of fact. Ownership rights are legal creations. In the New Deal, the realists were vindicated. Many of the legal realists found prominent positions in the Roosevelt administration.

For the realists, the most serious problem with laissez-faire was that the basic idea was simply a myth, a tangle of confusion. As Hale wrote, "The dependence of present economic conditions, in part at least, on the government's past policy concerning the distribution of the public domain, must be obvious. Laissez-faire is a utopian dream which never has been and never can be realized." Supreme Court Justice Oliver Wendell Holmes Jr., in some ways the first legal realist, wrote in a profound, haiku-like aphorism: "Property, a creation of law, does not arise from value, although exchangeable—a matter of fact." Holmes proclaimed that property and value are a product of legal rules, not of purely private interactions and still less of nature. Economic value does not *predate* law; it is *created* by law. All of this, wrote Holmes, was simply "a matter of fact."

The realists urged that government and law are omnipresent—that if some people have a lot and others a little, law and legal coercion are a large part of the reason. Of course many people work hard and many others do not. But the distribution of wealth is not simply a product of hard work; it depends on a coercive network of legal rights and obligations. The realists complained that we ignore the extent to which we have what we have and do what we do because of the law. They contended that people tend to see as "voluntary" and "free" interactions that are shot through with public force. In their view, the laws of property, contract, and tort are social creations that allocate certain rights to some people and deny them to others. These forms of law represent large-scale government "interventions" into the economy. They are coercive to the extent that they prohibit people from engaging in desired activities. If homeless people lack a place to live, it is not because of God's will or nature. It is because the rules of property are invoked and enforced to evict them, if necessary by force. If employees have to work long hours and make little money, it is because of the prevailing rules of property and contract. The realists believed that private property is fine, even good, but they denied that the rules of property could be identified with liberty. Sometimes those rules disserve liberty.

Robert Hale set forth these ideas with particular clarity. Hale wrote against the background of the political struggle over government efforts to set minimum wages and regulate prices, a struggle he believed was being waged on false premises. His special target was the view that governmental restrictions on market prices should be seen as illegitimate regulatory interference in the private sphere. This, said Hale, was an exceedingly confused way to describe the problem. Regulatory interference was already there. Hale wrote that a careful look would "demonstrate that the systems advocated by professed upholders of laissez-faire are in reality permeated with coercive restrictions of individual freedom and with restrictions, moreover, out of conformity with any formula of 'equal opportunity' or 'preserving the equal rights of others.' Some sort of coercive restriction of individuals, it is believed, is absolutely unavoidable."

Consider the situation of someone who wants to eat but lacks funds. Hale acknowledged, with apparent bemusement, that "there is no law against eating in the abstract," but stressed that "there is a law which forbids him to eat any of the food which actually exists in the community—and that law is the law of property." No law requires property holders to give away their property for nothing. Here "it is the law that coerces" a person without resources "into wage-work under penalty of starvation—unless he can produce food. Can he?" Of course no law prevents the production of food. But in every advanced nation, the law does indeed ban people from cultivating land unless they own it. "This again is the law of property," and the owner is not likely to allow cultivation unless he can be paid to do so. For those who need to eat and lack money, "that way of escape from the law-made dilemma of starvation or obedience" to the demands of owners "is closed."

With this argument, Hale did not mean to argue that property rights should be abolished; he was hardly a socialist. Nor did Hale mean to argue that in a free market system, many people lack ways of avoiding starvation. His goal was to draw attention to the pervasive effects of law and public coercion in structuring economic relationships. More generally, Hale claimed, "laissez faire is not such, but really governmental indifference to [the] effects of artificial coercive restraints, partly grounded on government itself." Thus "the distribution of wealth at any given time is not exclusively the result of individual efforts under a system of government neutrality." Constraints on the freedom of nonowners were an omnipresent result of property law. What would it mean to say, as many people did in the early twentieth century (and as many do now), that "a free American has the right to labor without any other's leave"? Hale answered that if taken seriously, this claim would "insist on a doctrine which involves the dangerously radical consequence of the abolition of private ownership of productive equipment, or else the equally dangerous doctrine that everyone should be guaranteed the ownership of some such equipment." In a free market, people do not really have the right to work "without any other's leave." Because of property rights, people can work only with the "leave" of others.

What, concretely, does it mean to own a manufacturing plant? Hale answered that under the law, ownership entails "a privilege to operate the plant, plus a privilege not to operate it, plus a right to keep others from operating, plus a power to acquire all the rights of ownership in the products." But this was not Hale's central point. Above all, he meant to emphasize that this "power is a power to release a pressure which the law of property exerts on the liberty of others. If the pressure is great, the owner may be able to compel the others to pay him a big price for their release; if the pressure is slight, he can collect but a small income from his ownership. *In either case, he is paid for releasing a pressure exerted by the government—the law. The law has delegated to him a discretionary power over the rights and duties of others*" (emphasis added).

In a remarkable step, Hale argued that property rights were in effect a delegation of public power—to private people by government. In so arguing, Hale did not argue against property rights. Instead he sought to draw attention to the fact that property owners are, in effect, given a set of powers by law. If you have property, you have "sovereignty," a kind of official power, vindicated by government, over that property. In these circumstances, Hale found it almost comical that some people complained that government should never restrict property rights. In his view, a limitation on the delegation of power—in the form, for example, of a curtailment of "the incomes of property owners"—is "in substance curtailing the salaries of public officials or pensioners." Or consider these startlingly unambiguous words, from an unsigned student essay written in 1935: "Justification for this purported refusal to supervise the ethics of the market place is sought in doctrines of laissez-faire. . . . In general, *the freedom from regulation postulated by laissez faire adherents is demonstrably nonexistent and virtually inconceivable. Bargaining power exists only because of government protection of the property rights bargained,* and is properly subject to government control."

The same point lies behind the following suggestion: "Those who denounce state intervention are the ones who most frequently and successfully invoke it. The cry of laissez faire mainly goes up from the ones who, if really 'let alone,' would instantly lose their wealth-absorbing power."

In making these claims, the legal realists did not deny the possibility that some rights are, in a sense, natural or even God-given. Nothing in their arguments should be seen as taking a stand on that question. They were not urging that as a matter of fundamental principle, rights come from government. They were arguing instead that in actual life, people are able to have rights, and enjoy them, only if law and government are present. We can speak as confidently as we like of natural or God-given rights, but without public protection of private property, people's holdings are inevitably at great risk. Whatever the source of rights in principle, legal protection is indispensable to make rights real in the world. Those who complain of "government," arguing that they want merely to fend for themselves, ignore this point at their (literal) peril.

The realists' claims on this count were extremely prominent in America between 1910 and 1940. They can even be found in the work of socialism's greatest critic, Nobel Prize winner F. A. Hayek, a firm believer in free markets. In his most famous work, Hayek reminded his readers that the functioning of competition "depends, above all, on the existence of an appropriate legal system, a legal system designed both to preserve competition and to make it operate as beneficially as possible." He argued that it "is by no means sufficient that the law should recognize the principle of private property and freedom of contract; much depends on the precise definition of the right of property as applied to different things." Echoing the claim of the legal realists, Hayek wrote that "in no system that could be rationally defended would the state just do nothing. An effective competitive system needs an intelligently designed and continuously adjusted legal framework as much as any other." The real battle was not between those who favor "government intervention" and those who reject it. The question was how the legal framework should be "intelligently designed and continuously adjusted." Opposition to government intervention is a smoke screen concealing that question.

Do these points illuminate current problems? Consider the analysis of famines and poverty by economist and Nobel Prize recipient Amartya Sen. He emphasizes that hunger is not a simple product of the unavailability of food. On the contrary, people are hungry if they lack "entitlements" that enable them to eat. Sen urges that an understanding of this point "has the effect of emphasizing legal rights. Other relevant factors, for example market forces, can be seen as operating through a system of legal relations (ownership rights, contractual obligations, legal exchanges, etc.)." Thus Sen's striking claim: "The law stands between food availability and food entitlement. Starvation deaths can reflect legality with a vengeance." In stressing that "law" is what makes the difference between the availability of food and an entitlement to it, and that starvation reflects "legality with a vengeance," Sen is reiterating the realists' most important claim.

ROOSEVELT'S REALISM

The attack on laissez-faire ultimately made its way into the White House. Roosevelt made the point indirectly in his illuminating 1934 critique of the idea of "the self-supporting man." He stressed that "without the help of thousands of others, any one of us would die, naked and starved. Consider the bread upon our table, the clothes upon our backs, the luxuries that make life pleasant; how many men worked in sunlit fields, in dark mines, in the fierce heat of molten metal, and among the looms and wheels of countless factories, in order to create them for our use and enjoyment." Still, this reminder of human interdependence did not refer to law and government. That point was made explicit in Roosevelt's early complaint, in accepting the Democratic nomination, that some leaders refer to "economic laws—sacred, inviolable, unchangeable," and his pragmatic response that "while they prate of economic laws, men and women are starving." Hence his plea that we "must lay hold of the fact that economic laws are not made by nature. They are made by human beings." When people starve, it is a result of social choices, not anything sacred or inevitable.

Or consider Roosevelt's Commonwealth Club address in 1932. He emphasized the view, which he attributed to Thomas Jefferson, "that the exercise of . . . property rights might so interfere with the rights of the individual that the government, without whose assistance the property rights could not exist, must intervene, not to destroy individualism but to protect it." The key point here is that without government's assistance, property rights could not exist. When those governmentally conferred rights turn out to "interfere with the rights of the individual," governmental intervention is necessary to protect individualism itself. The legal realists could not have said it better.

Consider as well Roosevelt's emphasis on "this man-made world of ours" in advocating social security legislation. He is arguing that poverty is a by-product of a humanly created system, not a natural fact. "I decline to accept present conditions as inevitable or beyond control." The same position was codified in the preamble to the most important piece of New Deal labor legislation, the Norris-LaGuardia Act: "Whereas under prevailing economic conditions, *developed with the aid of governmental authority for owners of property to organize in the corporate and other forms of ownership association,* the individual worker is commonly helpless to exercise actual liberty of contract and to protect his freedom of labor, and thereby to obtain acceptable terms and conditions of employment" (emphasis added).

To the extent that property rights played a role in market arrangements—as they inevitably did—those arrangements were creatures of law, including most notably property law, which gave some people a right to exclude others from "their" land and resources. Market wages and hours were a result of legal rules conferring rights of ownership. Considered in this light, minimum wage legislation, which Roosevelt strongly supported, should not be seen as superimposing regulation on a realm of purely voluntary interactions. On the contrary, such legislation merely substituted one form of regulation for another. In this sense the notion of laissez-faire stands revealed as myth. A system of free markets rests on a set of legal rules establishing who can do what, and enforcing those principles through the courts.

The New Dealers thought this was a simple descriptive point—as Holmes put it, "a matter of fact." To say that government intervention is pervasive and that no one is against it is not to say that any particular form of intervention is good or bad. Along with the legal realists, Roosevelt believed that the real questions were the pragmatic ones: What form of intervention best promotes human interests? What form of regulation makes human lives better? If a new regulatory system is superimposed on another, we should evaluate the new system for its effectiveness in diminishing or increasing human liberty. A system of private property is good for individuals and for societies, and the fact that it is created by law does not suggest otherwise.

But in the face of the Great Depression, it seemed a kind of cruel joke to maintain that free markets were sufficient to ensure either liberty or prosperity. As Roosevelt pointed out, people in desperate conditions lack freedom. Fresh initiatives, responding to the problem of pervasive deprivation, seemed indispensable. The question was whether they would work, and this could not be answered by dogmas and abstractions. It was worse than unhelpful to respond to the critics by complaining about "government." As Hale wrote, "the next step is to . . . realize that the question of maintenance or the alteration of our institutions must be discussed on its pragmatic merits, not dismissed on the ground that they are the inevitable outcome of free society." The legal realist Morris Cohen, writing just before the New Deal, put the point similarly: "The recognition of private property as a form of sovereignty is not itself an argument against it. . . . [I]t is necessary to apply to the law of property all those considerations of social ethics and enlightened public policy which ought to be brought to the discussion of any just form of government."

To Roosevelt, that evaluation would be unabashedly empirical and experimental. It would avoid theories and dogmas. It would look to see what sorts of programs actually worked in the world. Its character is reflected in an apparently offhand but revealing comment Roosevelt made during a press conference: "Obviously a farm bill is in the nature of an experiment. We all recognize that . . . if the darn thing doesn't work, we can say so quite frankly, but at least try it." In light of this pragmatic reassessment, it is possible to understand the New Dealers' belief that certain measures that reduced the wealth of rich people were not an intrusion on rights—and that other measures, increasing the opportunities and wealth of poor people, might be necessary to protect rights. Wealth did not come from nature or from the sky; it was made possible by legal arrangements. If new legal arrangements diminished the wealth of some, they were not objectionable for that reason. In Roosevelt's words, "The thing that matters in any industrial system is what it does actually to human beings . . . "

CONCEPTUAL CHANGE AND CONSTITUTIONAL CHANGE

Once the existing distribution of wealth and opportunities was seen as a product of social choices, and once policies were evaluated in terms of how they actually affected human beings, it became much harder to argue that rights should be defined as freedom from government intrusion or to insist on a strong distinction between "negative" and "positive" rights. Even the "negative" right to property requires government's presence. Of course social change is not driven solely or even mostly by conceptual claims. Experience makes all the difference, and the second bill of rights would not have been possible without the experience of the Depression. I will return to this point below, but for the moment let us simply notice that the arguments I have just traced had an impact not merely on politics but also on the Supreme Court.

When Roosevelt was elected, the Supreme Court had, for several decades, interpreted the Constitution to forbid many of the initiatives the New Dealers hoped to implement. An important set of decisions involved the idea of "freedom of contract." The Court ruled against minimum wage and maximum hour laws, saying that government could not "interfere" with voluntary interactions between employers and employees. In an especially striking decision in 1915, the Court ruled that governments could not forbid the "yellow dog contract," by which employers required employees to promise, as a condition of hiring, that they would not join a union. Efforts to forbid these agreements, the Court said, interfered with the rights of employers and employees to contract on whatever terms they chose.

In protecting freedom of contract, the Court emphasized the value of laissez-faire—the need to immunize contracting parties from government intrusion. The clearest statement of this position can be found in *Adkins v. Children's Hospital*, a 1923 decision invalidating minimum wage legislation for women and children. In his majority opinion, Justice George Sutherland wrote: "To the extent that the sum fixed [by the minimum wage statute] exceeds the fair value of the services rendered, it amounts to a compulsory exaction from the employer for the support of a partially indigent person, for whose condition there rests upon him no peculiar responsibility, and therefore, in effect, arbitrarily shifts to his shoulders a burden which, if it belongs to anybody, belongs to society as a whole."

Thus the Court ruled that a minimum wage law interfered with voluntary agreements between employers and employees, creating a "compulsory exaction from the employer" by forcing him to support a poor person. But compare that to the Court's decision in 1937, *West Coast Hotel v. Parrish*, in which it upheld a minimum wage law for women—and in the process essentially ratified the New Deal. In one of the most important opinions in its entire history, the Court spoke in terms that could easily be found in a Roosevelt speech. The liberty protected by the Constitution, wrote Chief Justice Charles Evans Hughes for the majority, "is liberty in a social organization which requires the protection of law against the evils which menace the health, safety, morals and welfare of the people." Hughes suggested that liberty could even argue on behalf of that protection: "the proprietors lay down the rules and the laborers are practically constrained to obey them." The legislature could consider the fact that women's "bargaining power is relatively weak, and that they are the ready victims of those who would take advantage of their necessitous circumstances." The opinion complained of "the exploiting of workers at wages so low as to be insufficient to meet the bare cost of living, thus making their very helplessness the occasion of a most injurious competition."

In a remarkable passage, Hughes added a "compelling consideration which recent economic experience has brought into a strong light." This consideration had to do with the social effects of poverty. "The exploitation of a class of workers who are in an unequal position with respect to bargaining power and are thus relatively defenseless against the denial of a living wage . . . casts a direct burden for their support upon the community. What these workers lose in wages the taxpayers are called upon to pay. The bare cost of living must be met. We may take judicial notice of the unparalleled demands for relief which arose during the recent period of depression and still continue to an alarming extent despite the degree of economic recovery which has been achieved. . . . *The community is not bound to provide what is in effect a subsidy for unconscionable employers*" (emphasis added).

In the fifteen-year period between *Adkins* and *West Coast Hotel,* the constitutional universe changed. Before Roosevelt, a minimum wage law was an unacceptable interference with liberty, a constitutionally intolerable "subsidy" mandated by a coercive state from employers to employees. By 1937 a minimum wage law protected people from "exploitation" in a situation in which "their very helplessness" created competition among workers that drove wages down. In fact, by 1937 a minimum wage law could be seen as an effort to ensure that the community was not forced to subsidize "unconscionable employers." What is most striking here is the reversal of what is considered a subsidy. In 1923 a minimum wage law was seen as forcing employers to subsidize the community; fifteen years later, the absence of a minimum wage law was forcing the community to subsidize employers.

What accounts for this shift? The answer lies in an understanding of who is entitled to what. Without an opinion on that question, we cannot decide whether a "subsidy" is involved at all. A thief does not "subsidize" his victim when he is required to return stolen property. In *West Coast Hotel,* workers have something like a right to a decent wage ("remunerative employment")—so that wages below that amount were effectively asking the community to pick up the tab for their living costs. Hence there was nothing sacred or natural or inevitable in the low wages that the market sometimes produced. The government was permitted to raise them to a decent minimum if it chose.

In the late 1930s and 1940s, the Court ceased to emphasize the voluntary nature of private agreements or to treat them as constitutionally sacrosanct. It emphasized that they were a product of legal rules—and that one or another policy was inevitably a choice, by law and government. The attack on laissez-faire helped produce a fundamental change in constitutional understandings.

Deliberative Democracy

In an important sense, Roosevelt and the New Deal deepened a central constitutional commitment, which involved the system of deliberative democracy. For the Constitution's original framers, it was exceedingly important to produce a political order that combined reflectiveness and reason giving with a degree of popular responsiveness. Public officials were accountable, to be sure, and could be removed by elections; the framers were democrats in that sense. But they feared majorities and wanted to prevent government from being moved by the "interest" or "passion" of private groups, even large ones. Under the constitutional system majorities were not permitted to rule simply because they were majorities. On the contrary, the Constitution created a kind of *republic of reasons*—a system of checks and balances that would increase the likelihood of reflective judgments. Alexander Hamilton spoke most clearly on the point, urging that the "differences of opinion, and the jarring of parties in [the legislative] department of the government . . . often promote deliberation and circumspection; and serve to check the excesses of the majority."

The commitment to deliberative democracy emerges from one of the most illuminating debates in America's early years, raising the question whether the Bill of Rights should include a "right to instruct" representatives. That right was defended with the claim that citizens of a particular region ought to have the authority to bind their representatives about how to vote. This argument might appear reasonable as a way of improving the political accountability of representatives. And so it seemed to many at the time. I suspect that many people, in America and elsewhere, would favor the "right to instruct" today. Shouldn't representatives follow their constituents' wishes? But there is a problem with this view, especially in an era in which political interest was closely aligned with geography. A right to instruct eliminates deliberation within the national legislature. It is all too likely that the citizens of a particular region, influenced by one another's views, might end up with indefensible positions, very possibly resulting from its own insularity. In rejecting the right to instruct, Roger Sherman emphasized the importance of political deliberation:

> The words are calculated to mislead the people, by conveying an idea that they have a right to control the debates of the Legislature. This cannot be admitted to be just, because it would destroy the object of their meeting. I think, when the people have chosen a representative, it is his duty to meet others from the different parts of the Union, and consult, and agree with them on such acts as are for the general benefit of the whole community. If they were to be guided by instructions, there would be no use in deliberation.

Sherman's words reflect the founders' general enthusiasm for deliberation among people who are quite diverse and disagree on issues both large and small. Indeed, it was through deliberation among such people that "such acts as are for the general benefit of the whole community" would emerge. In this light we can better appreciate the framers' preference for a republican system, involving deliberation among elected officials, over a more populist system, in which citizen desires would be less "filtered" through representatives. The framers hoped that their design would simultaneously protect against unjustified passions and ensure a large measure of diversity in government. In this way, they hoped to structure public discussion to ensure better decisions. This explains their enthusiasm for republican institutions.

The Constitution was of course written against the legacy of English monarchy. A little-noticed provision of the document reveals a great deal about its general goals: It forbids the government to grant "titles of nobility." In the framers' generation, preexisting notions of natural hierarchy came under siege, with a novel and revolutionary insistence that culture was, as the historian Gordon Wood put it, "truly man-made." For the American revolutionaries, the problem with the monarchical legacy consisted in its acceptance, as natural, of practices and injustices that were actually "man-made." American republicanism, in the Revolution and the founding period, consisted largely in the identification of this problem. The American founders believed that social practices should be evaluated by the light of reason. Thus the extraordinary start to the first of the Federalist papers, written by Hamilton:

> It has been frequently remarked, that it seems to have been reserved to the people of this country, by their conduct and example, to decide the important question, whether societies of men are really capable or not, of establishing good government from reflection and choice, or whether they are forever destined to depend, for their political constitutions, on accident and force. If there be any truth in the remark, the crisis, at which we are arrived, may with propriety be regarded as the era in which that decision is to be made; and a wrong election of the part we shall act, may, in this view, deserve to be considered as the general misfortune of mankind.

Roosevelt and the New Dealers greatly deepened the commitment to deliberative democracy. They did this by insisting that no less than a monarchical system, the existing distributions of wealth and opportunities were man-made, and that economic facts were not dictated by nature. Roosevelt himself made the link quite clear. He stressed that the American Revolution was fought to ensure "freedom from the tyranny of political autocracy—from the eighteenth-century royalists who held special privileges from the crown" and attempted to "perpetuate their privilege" by denying political rights. But he claimed that in the twentieth century, a form of "economic tyranny" had been exposed, and thus for "too many of us life was no longer free; liberty no longer real." The New Deal attempted to end this form of tyranny.

"The royalists of the economic order have conceded that political freedom was the business of the government, but they have maintained that economic slavery was nobody's business." While accepting the right to vote, "they denied that the government could do anything to protect the citizen in his right to work and his right to live." Thus Roosevelt's new conception of rights was closely connected with his claim that the existing economic order was a product of human beings, not nature.

The New Dealers contended that respect for existing practices and current distributions must depend on the reasons that could be brought forward on their behalf. The process of deliberation through democratic organs would therefore include an assessment of whether the legal rules already in place served liberty, welfare, or democracy itself. In this way, the New Deal period carried forward and renewed one of the oldest themes in American history. Enormous changes followed from these understandings. In his earliest days on the campaign trail, Roosevelt spoke of "an economic declaration of rights, an economic constitutional order"—a clear precursor of the second bill. To understand what happened here, it is necessary to explore the Great Depression and how Roosevelt dealt with it.

3

Rights from Wrongs:
Roosevelt's Constitutional
Order

In this nation I see tens of millions of its citizens—a
substantial part of its whole population—who at this very
moment are denied the greater part of what the very lowest
standards of today call the necessities of life. . . .

I see millions denied education, recreation, and the
opportunity to better their lot and the lot of their children.

I see millions lacking the means to buy the products of
farm and factory and by their poverty denying work and
productiveness to many other millions.

I see one-third of a nation ill-housed, ill-clad, ill-
nourished.

It is not in despair that I paint you that picture. I paint it
in hope—because the Nation, seeing and understanding the
injustice of it, proposes to paint it out. . . .

Franklin Delano Roosevelt

WHERE DO RIGHTS COME FROM? If this is taken as a
philosophical question, many answers might be imagined.
But in practice, rights are a product of concrete historical

experiences with wrongs. The United States Constitution in its original form was borne directly out of two experiences: the tyranny of English rule and the inadequacy of the decentralized system created by the Articles of Confederation that preceded the Constitution. The vivid memory of the American Revolution inspired the effort to ensure the preconditions for republican self-government. The experience under the Articles helped inspire a more centralized system that was genuinely capable of governance. As another example, consider the most significant period of constitutional change in nineteenth-century America, the one that produced the constitutional amendments after the Civil War. This was a direct outgrowth of experience with human slavery and the social subordination of African Americans.

The immediate source of the second bill of rights was the Great Depression, as inadequate education, hunger, and unemployment emerged not as inevitable features of free market societies but as human rights violations. The influence of the Great Depression on the nature and direction of the post-1932 American government was closely parallel to the influence of the Civil War on the post-1865 government. In many respects, the resulting changes were even more fundamental.

FACTS, FIGURES, AND MORE

Even for a nation that had lived through recurrent financial panics, the Depression of the 1930s was something entirely new. Consider some key facts and figures:

- Unemployment skyrocketed. In 1929, only 3 percent of the workforce, or 1.5 million workers, was unemployed. By 1930 the percentage and the number had nearly tripled. By 1931, 7 million workers, fully 14 percent of the workforce, lacked jobs. By late 1932, the percentage had grown to 25 percent of American workers. In Chicago, half of the workers were unemployed. African Americans suffered disproportionate harm. In Memphis they were 38 percent of the total population but 75 percent of the unemployed; in Chicago, 4 percent of the population but 16 percent of the unemployed.

- National income declined precipitously. Total income was $87.4 billion in 1929, $75 billion in 1930, $58.9 billion in 1931, $41.7 billion in 1932, and $39.7 billion in 1933—less than half of what it had been just four years earlier.

- Income from salaries and wages showed a similar trend, declining from $50.8 billion in 1929 to $29.3 billion in 1933. At the end of 1932, the weekly wage in iron and steel industries was only 37 percent of what it had been in 1929. In 1931, a large-scale survey in Detroit found that average weekly earnings had plummeted by two-thirds since 1929. Only about one-third of family heads were employed. The Pennsylvania Department of Labor found that wages were $0.05 an hour in brick and tile manufacturing, $0.05 an hour in sawmills, and $0.075 an hour in general contracting. For months, municipal employees could not be paid.

- Thousands of banks went out of business, and depositors often lost their money. The United States had over 25,000 banks in 1929, but fewer than 15,000 in 1933. In 1931 alone, depositors lost a total of $391,000,000 from bank failures; 9 million accounts were lost as well.

- Net investment in 1931 was −$358 million. In 1932, it was −$5.8 billion.

- Farmers were hit particularly hard, a national problem in light of the fact that agriculture employed 30 percent of the workforce. In 1929, farmers had an unusually difficult year, with an aggregate national income of $6 billion. But by 1932, that figure was just $2 billion.

- The system of economic relief was in serious trouble. In 1932, three-quarters of those eligible for assistance were unable to obtain it. The remaining one-quarter received some food, a little cash, and on occasion some fuel. In New York City, recipients averaged $2.39 per family per week. Charity did very little to fill the gap.

- Suicide rates increased. In 1932 the national rate was 17.4 suicides per 100,000 people, an increase of 24 percent from 1929.

Behind these cold numbers lay millions of individual tragedies. As one observer wrote of Chicago in 1932, "One vivid, gruesome moment of those dark days we shall never forget. We saw a crowd of fifty men fighting over a barrel of garbage which had been set outside the back door of a restaurant. American citizens fighting for scraps of food like animals." Lorena Hickok, appointed by the Roosevelt administration to assess the effects of the Depression on southern farm workers in Georgia, described the situation in this way:

Half starved Whites and Blacks struggle in competition for less to eat than my dog gets at home, for the privilege of living in huts that are infinitely less comfortable than his kennel. . . . If there is a school system in the state, it simply isn't functioning. It can't. The children just can't go to school, hundreds of others don't send them. As a result you've got the picture of hundreds of boys and girls in their teens down here in some of these rural areas who can't read or write. I'm not exaggerating. . . . Why, some of them can barely talk!

A newspaper in Chicago said of the Roseland garbage dump:

About twenty-five men and boys and one woman stood in two rows all day, all the way down to the garbage hill waiting for that load to come down. And then, like a flock of chickens, they started to scratch in that smelly pile, and pick out certain things, which they deposited in baskets they had with them. Apples seemed most popular even when half rotted away. Carrots, potatoes, and bread also found their way into the baskets. . . . Some claimed they were taking the stuff for rabbits and chickens, but I noticed that a pile of lettuce and spinach leaves, which would have been ideal feed, were left untouched. Most of them admitted that it was for their supper.

Nor was this so unusual. In regions of Kentucky and West Virginia, the overwhelming majority of children suffered from malnutrition.

By 1931, adults and children were digging in St. Louis and New York garbage dumps. Orderly lines formed at some dumps as people waited their turn to hunt for food; elsewhere they rushed to each new pile of refuse. In Harlan County, Kentucky, families lived off of dandelions and blackberries. In Appalachian mining communities, some families resorted to eating every other day.

People in Kentucky subsisted on wild onions, weeds, and violet tops, and children went to school lacking underclothes, shoes, and coats. In 1932 the *New York Times* reported:

Fifty four men were arrested yesterday morning for sleeping or idling in the arcade connecting with the subway through 45 West Forty-second Street, but most of them considered their unexpected meeting with a raiding party of 10 policemen as a stroke of luck because it brought them free meals yesterday and shelter last night from the sudden change in the weather. . . . The work of fingerprinting and making necessary comparisons with police records required so much time that Magistrate Renaud postponed the men's trials on disorderly conduct until this afternoon. This insured them sleeping quarters for the night and more free meals today.

Another newspaper offered this account:

When you drive through the Middle West drought country you try not to look at the thrusting out ribs of the horses and cows, but you get so you can't see anything else but ribs, like hundreds of thousands of little beached hulks. It looks like the bones are rising right up out of the skin. Pretty soon, quite gradually, you begin to know that the farmer, under his rags, shows his ribs, too, and the farmer's wife is as lean as his cows, and his children look tiny and hungry.

Democracy itself seemed anachronistic to many, even doomed. Schools were closing in large numbers, as local and state governments were unable to pay teachers. Communist organizers were meeting receptive audiences throughout the country, particularly among the unemployed. Other Americans were drawn to fascism, believing that it promised to provide social order in the midst of chaos. "The fog of despair," historian Arthur Schlesinger Jr. wrote, "hung over the land." Chicago's mayor argued that it would be better for Washington to send $150 million to the city immediately than to send federal troops at a later date. During a congressional hearing, a member of the House of Representatives said, "I would steal before I would starve," and the witness, a Quaker, responded, "I think all of us would probably. I don't know whether you want that in the record."

An Alabama planter, head of the Farm Bureau Federation, warned a Senate committee, "Unless something is done for the American farmer we will have revolution in the countryside within less than twelve months." Pennsylvania's Senator Reed confessed, "I do not often envy other countries their governments, but I say that if this country ever needed a Mussolini, it needs one now." A conservative economist, Virgil Jordan, spoke in similar terms: "An economic Mussolini, before many months have passed, could have them parading in red, white and blue shirts, and saluting some new symbol." Reinhold Niebuhr, the great theologian, wrote an essay on the death of liberal society, urging that "capitalism is dying" and that "it ought to die." A dangerous bitterness grew, especially against the rich.

This was the situation when wheelchair-bound Franklin Delano Roosevelt assumed the presidency and told the nation: "Let me assert my firm belief that the only thing we have to fear is fear itself—nameless, unreasoning, unjustified terror which paralyzes needed efforts to convert retreat into advance." Roosevelt proclaimed, "We do not distrust the future of essential democracy. The people of the United States have not failed. In their need they have registered a mandate that they want direct, vigorous action."

Practice and Theory

The New Deal provided that action. In an astonishingly short period, the national government was dramatically expanded and reformed with the addition of a remarkable range of new programs and agencies. No fewer than five agencies were created in 1933 to give people jobs: the Civil Works Administration, the Civilian Conservation Corps, the Federal Emergency Relief Administration, the Public Works Administration, and the Tennessee Valley Authority. Of the several new laws designed to protect workers, the most important was the National Labor Relations Act, enacted in 1935, which gave workers the right to organize and provided a range of protections to unions and union organizers. The Fair Labor Standards Act, enacted in 1938, created minimum wage and maximum hour protections. A number of statutes, including most significantly the 1935 Social Security Act, were designed to provide assistance for the nonworking poor.

The blizzard of activity had a wide range of diverse themes. The "first New Deal" is sometimes distinguished from the "second New Deal." On the conventional view, the Roosevelt administration sought from 1933 to 1935 to promote cooperative action within industry to prevent falling prices and increase employment. It also sought to provide multiple forms of short-term economic relief, sometimes through jobs, sometimes through financial assistance. Many of the early agencies—most notably the Civilian Conservation Corps, the Federal Emergency Relief Administration, and the Works Progress Administration—were attempts to provide employment and economic assistance to those who most needed it.

The second New Deal, from 1935 to 1937, largely abandoned the effort to promote industry cooperation and emphasized antitrust policy instead. Between 1935 and 1937, the goal was to provide long-term protection for the vulnerable through larger reforms. Here the New Dealers were more ambitious, as reflected in Harry Hopkins's suggestion after the 1934 elections: "Boys, this is our hour. We've got to get everything we want—a works program, social security, wages and hours, everything—now or never. Get your minds to work on developing a complete ticket to provide security for all the folks of this country up and down and across the board." An early step was the Emergency Relief Appropriation Act, which gave the Works Progress Administration $4.8 billion, at the time the highest peacetime allocation in the nation's history. Subsequent measures included not only the Social Security Act and National Labor Relations Act but also the Wealth Tax Act (aimed mostly at the very rich) and the Banking Act, creating the Federal Reserve Board.

There was no simple or consistent theme to Roosevelt's domestic policies. In the words of Robert Jackson, one of Roosevelt's close advisers, "The New Deal was not a reform movement. It was an assembly of movements—sometimes inconsistent with each other." As the historian Ellis Hawley explains, "The New Deal began with government sponsorship of cartels and business planning; it ended with the antitrust campaign and the attack on rigid prices; and along the way, it engaged in minor excursions into socialism, public utility regulation, and the establishment of 'government yardsticks.'" After 1937 there were further shifts, with an interest in new regulatory strategies and especially in the use of fiscal policy to stabilize the economy. Roosevelt was an experimenter, a pragmatist interested in results and solutions rather than theories and themes. "Take a method and try it. If it fails admit it frankly and try another. But above all, try something."

This willingness to experiment should not obscure the broader effects of Roosevelt's presidency. He challenged the framework of government in three different ways, first and most importantly with a new conception of rights. The New Dealers viewed the preexisting understanding of rights as including both too much and too little— excessive protection of established property interests and insufficient protection of the interests of the poor, the elderly, and the unemployed. In his speech accepting the Democratic presidential nomination in 1936, for instance, he argued that although the constitutional framers were concerned only with political rights, new circumstances required the recognition of economic rights as well because "freedom is no half-and-half affair." Hence the New Deal reformers called for substantial changes that would recognize new interests as entitle-

ments and redistribute resources. With respect to the enlarged conception of freedom, Roosevelt's means shifted, but his ends did not.

The second element of Roosevelt's challenge focused on the separation of powers. According to the New Dealers, a system of sharply
separated functions prevented the government from reacting flexi-
bly and rapidly to stabilize the economy and protect the disadvantaged
from fluctuations in the market. In addition, the distribution of powers
among the three branches of government created political struggles
that disabled officials in the executive branch from responding to serious problems on its own. A more unified set of powers was necessary
to allow dramatic and frequent governmental action. Moreover, the
complicated character of modern regulation vastly increased the need
for technical expertise and specialization in making governmental
decisions. Hence the New Dealers argued (successfully in both cases)
for enhanced presidential authority and new regulatory agencies able
to provide both work and security. The New Deal conception of
administration regarded regulatory agencies as politically insulated,
self-starting, and technically sophisticated. Roosevelt himself proclaimed that "the day of enlightened administration has come."

The third element in the New Deal challenge resulted in a shift in
the relationship between the federal government and the states,
greatly expanding the power of the former. Competition among the
states sometimes produced paralysis on problems that called for a
uniform national remedy. States were often arenas for factional strife
and parochialism. The dominance of well-organized private groups
in the states made it difficult to accept the traditional belief that state
autonomy really served local self-determination. To the New Dealers,
the states were weak and ineffectual, unable to protect rights or deal
with serious social problems; they seemed too large to provide a
forum for genuine self-determination. The time-honored idea that
the states would check the federal government appeared perverse in
light of the need for national action. Most of all, the newly recognized rights catalogued by the second bill could not be guaranteed at
the state level. In these circumstances, the call for a dramatic increase
in the exercise of federal regulatory power was quite natural.

Many previous efforts at reform relied on state and local institutions, in part because of the tenacity of the Jeffersonian belief in an engaged citizenry operating through something like face-to-face democracy. By contrast, the New Dealers made the presidency, rather than states and localities, the focal point for self-government. In so doing, the New Deal reformers in a single stroke linked Alexander Hamilton's belief in an energetic national government with Thomas Jefferson's endorsement of citizen self-determination. Roosevelt thus democratized Hamiltonian notions of energetic government through a new conception of the presidency and administration.

But all this is far too abstract. What did the new agencies actually do? In a message to Congress in 1934, Roosevelt explained the goals of his programs:

> These three great objectives—the security of the home, the security of a livelihood, and the security of social insurance—are, it seems to me, a minimum of the promise that we can offer to the American people. They constitute a right which belongs to every individual and every family willing to work. They are the essential fulfillment of measures already taken toward relief, recovery, and reconstruction.

Under Roosevelt, the national government largely attempted to promote work and security. His method was deliberately and self-consciously experimental. As individual programs succeeded or failed throughout the 1930s, agencies were created, altered, and dismantled. I emphasize here the agencies that were specifically designed to create work and security.

WORK AND SECURITY

Roosevelt was singularly unenthusiastic about welfare as such, which he disparaged as "the dole." Believing that government handouts were demoralizing and contrary to national ideals, he sought to find ways to provide relief to the masses of the unemployed that did not compromise the recipients' pride and self-respect. "The Federal Government," he said, "has no intention or desire to force either upon the country or the unemployed themselves a system of relief which is repugnant to American ideals of individual self-reliance." In his 1935 State of the Union address, he argued that "continued dependence upon relief induces a spiritual disintegration fundamentally destructive to the national fiber. To dole out relief in this way is to administer a narcotic, a subtle destroyer of the human spirit. . . . Work must be found for able-bodied but destitute workers."

Employment relief, although often more costly than cash payments, was preferred by the administration and recipients alike. Thus the New Dealers "expected government jobs programmes and social insurance to banish forever the degrading spectre of public assistance based on a means test." They wanted to ensure against mass unemployment with work programs and to protect, through specific programs, "against the ordinary insecurities of age, disability, ill-health, and joblessness." Consider a few examples.

The Civilian Conservation Corps

Roosevelt's first attempt to provide work relief on the federal level was the Civilian Conservation Corps. The CCC was created in early 1933. Its focus on work and conservation made this initiative especially important to Roosevelt personally. Within three months, the CCC had enrolled over 200,000 young men; it eventually employed over 3 million. The programs engaged young men largely in forestry work, paying them a dollar a day plus room, board, and clothing. The work of the CCC included erecting telephone lines, preserving endangered species such as the whooping crane, building truck trails and ranger stations, improving parks and beaches, planting trees, and fighting fires. The "Corps" in the agency name derived from the support the army provided to the project, which included trucks, tents, equipment, and even reserve officers to supervise the workers. The program was implemented with the assistance of disparate branches of government, including the Labor, War, Interior, and Agriculture

Departments. By drawing workers from families on relief and families of wartime veterans, the CCC reduced the overburdened state relief roles.

Many of these workers received instruction in reading and writing at the camps. Though they were racially segregated, the CCC camps provided opportunities for many young African American men, who were given positions in the CCC roughly equivalent to their proportions in the general population. The CCC lasted until 1942, when the wartime army could no longer spare the personnel or resources. Many of the millions of CCC employees went on to join the civil service.

The Federal Emergency Relief Administration

Created during the first hundred days of Roosevelt's first term, FERA was established by a bill originally granting $500 million to the states for relief efforts and temporary employment; over the next two years, six times that amount was distributed. In pushing for the agency, Roosevelt declared that the nation should ensure that none of its citizens would starve. FERA was set up to deal directly with the state agencies. The amount of grant money each state received was tied to its relief expenditures, an attempt to encourage states to provide more help. The FERA administrator was to retain the funds to allocate on the basis of need. Roosevelt appointed Harry Hopkins, one of his chief advisers, as the administrator in May 1933.

Applicants for FERA relief had to submit to a means test in order to qualify for assistance, often in the form of vouchers for food, rent, or fuel. Cash grants were sometimes distributed, as was work relief if projects were available. Because there were restrictions on the use of FERA funds for purchasing materials, a fair amount of work relief consisted of "leaf raking." But most FERA funds were spent on direct relief, either cash or vouchers for basic necessities. One of the most important projects instituted under FERA was a college work scheme that offered students grants in exchange for work. Following the success of the Civil Works Administration in the winter of 1934 and similar work programs under the FERA, these relief programs were replaced in 1935 by a broader program, the Works Projects Administration.

Civil Works Administration

The CWA was established in November 1933 to provide relief for the unemployed during the winter months. To promote that end, the agency did not subject those who applied for work to means testing. The agency lasted only through the winter, as planned, and its total expenditure was $933 million, 10 percent of which was contributed by the states. Eighty percent of the agency's budget went toward wages. At its peak, in February 1934, the CWA employed 4 million workers. By late April, the last of the work crews had been discharged. The CWA constructed or improved 500,000 miles of roads, 40,000 schools, 3,500 parks, playgrounds, and athletic fields, and 1,000 small airports. It employed 50,000 teachers and 3,000 artists and writers. The agency's short life served as a powerful example of the potential for mass work relief programs, and its accomplishments were an impetus for the establishment of a more ambitious work relief program, the Works Projects Administration.

Works Projects Administration

The transition from FERA direct relief to WPA work relief was due in large part to Roosevelt's continuing belief that "to dole out [cash] relief in this way is to administer a narcotic, a subtle destroyer of the human spirit." After 1934 the federal government sought to provide for the massive numbers of unemployed workers, leaving state and local governments to support those who were unable to work. The WPA was established with the passage of the Emergency Relief Appropriation Act, which set aside $4.8 billion dollars for work relief. In its eight-year history, the WPA employed over 3.5 million Americans, who built 651,087 miles of highways, roads, and streets, and constructed or improved 124,031 bridges, 2,500 hospitals, 125,110 public buildings, 8,192 parks, over 3,000 schools, and 853 airport landing fields. Its work can be found all over the United States. WPA projects include LaGuardia Airport in New York City, Lake Shore Drive in Chicago, Huntington Avenue Subway in Boston, and the San Antonio Zoo.

A great deal of controversy initially surrounded the nature and scale of the WPA work projects. Harold Ickes favored large construction efforts, while Harry Hopkins, the administrator of FERA and the CWA, pressed for smaller projects that would allow the agency to spend the majority of its funds on wages. Because the smaller projects allowed the agency greater flexibility and provided a quicker stimulus, Roosevelt ultimately sided with Hopkins, appointing him as administrator of the agency. As with FERA, applicants for work relief under the WPA had to submit to a means test. Successful applicants were paid a wage that was below the prevailing rates but more than the relief stipend. Because the wages and hours of WPA employees were limited, the agency was able to avoid competition with private employers. Thus workers had incentive to leave their WPA jobs if they were able to find employment in the private sector.

The National Youth Administration, a division of the WPA, was created in June 1935 through executive order to assist young people both in and out of school. The program granted financial aid to high school and college students to keep them in school and out of the saturated labor market. For those not in school, the NYA provided vocational training as well as temporary financial aid. It was particularly responsive to the needs of African American youth and included a special fund for African American students in college and a Negro Division created in 1936. From 1935 to 1943, when it was discontinued, the NYA provided relief to over 2 million young people. The WPA supported, on average, close to 30 percent of the unemployed who were able to work. It ensured employment of not only ordinary workers but also actors, teachers, writers, and artists, yielding a wide range of cultural and social benefits.

Farm Security Administration

In 1935 Roosevelt established the Resettlement Administration to assist the rural poor. The agency aimed to move occupants of submarginal land, as well as dispossessed tenant farmers and sharecroppers, onto better land or government-created suburbs. The agency also lent funds to small farmers to purchase equipment and experimented with cooperative farms and long-term leases. Because of a lack of funding and political support, the Resettlement Administration provided very little relief to the rural poor. In 1937 Congress created the Farm Security Administration in the Department of Agriculture. The FSA took over the responsibilities of the Resettlement Administration, shifting the focus from resettlement to the preservation of small family farms.

The FSA provided funds to small landowners for debt repayments and land improvements, and also provided tenants with loans to purchase land. The number of small farmers who received assistance from the FSA was a tiny fraction of those who sought relief. The agency faced the same difficulty procuring funds as its predecessor, since the political will to help the rural poor remained relatively weak. The Farm Credit Administration provided some relief to those who were unable to make payments on their farms by extending loan programs. Since many small farmers did not own the land they worked, this relief too was slight. The FSA was ultimately replaced during the war with the Farmers Home Administration.

Public Works Administration

Funding for public works was passed as part of the National Industrial Recovery Act during the New Deal's first Hundred Days. The Public Works Administration was a large-scale construction program headed by Harold Ickes, Roosevelt's secretary of the Interior. Among the projects undertaken by the PWA were the Bonneville Dam, the completion of the Hoover Dam, the Triborough Bridge in Manhattan, Lake Shore Drive in Chicago, and many of the projects planned under the Tennessee Valley Authority. Though the project provided work relief to some, its central aim was to support private industry, especially the building materials and construction industry. The agency promoted massive, expensive construction projects, such as bridges, dams, roads, and buildings. The bulk of these were undertaken by local governmental entities that received either grants or loans from the PWA, though some projects were actually carried out by federal agencies. The PWA financed over $6 billion worth of projects, employing some 500,000 people a year. The National Industrial Recovery Act created the Housing Division within the PWA in June 1933. It initially provided loans to private, limited-dividend corporations to finance the construction of individual dwellings and housing projects, as well as the clearance of slums.

Rural Electrification Administration

Because low population density made power lines unprofitable in rural areas, only one in ten farms received electricity in 1930. Thus most farms could not use many labor-saving devices. To rectify the disparity, Roosevelt created the Rural Electrification Administration in 1935. The agency first tried to encourage private utility companies to bring service to rural areas by offering them low-interest loans. In 1936 it changed course and established farmer cooperatives, and offered the low-interest loans to them. The cooperatives built the lines and manufactured or purchased power. The REA also provided loans for house wiring and the purchase and installation of electrical appliances and equipment. By 1939, one-fourth of the farms in the country were receiving electricity, an enormous change in the lives of rural Americans.

National Labor Relations Board

The National Labor Relations Board was established in 1935 with the passage of the Wagner Act, an exceptionally ambitious effort to alter the relationship between workers and employers and improve both wages and working conditions. One goal was to increase the collective organization of workers, since it was thought that organized labor would improve the lives of working people. The New Dealers also believed that the very possibility of unionization would lead to a better deal for workers. If managers were aware that workers could choose to unionize, a measure of compromise was highly likely, leading to more cooperation, higher wages, and better benefits.

The Wagner Act empowered the NLRB to enforce a number of provisions forbidding widespread employer practices and giving employees rights that were entirely foreign to preexisting law. Workers were authorized to organize—to join unions and to participate in pro-union activities. The act outlawed "yellow dog" contracts, by which employees agreed, as a condition of employment, not to join a union. It also banned "company unions," labor organizations that were created by the employer or under its influence, and obliged employers to bargain with unions in good faith. In some ways, the Wagner Act amounted to a workers' bill of rights.

Social Security Administration

The large-scale unemployment following the stock market crash of 1929 highlighted the need for some form of old age insurance, and the idea gained popular support as the situation of the elderly continued to worsen in the first years of the Depression. The Social Security Act of 1935 provided a pension for retired workers that was self-funded through a payroll tax to be split evenly between the employer and the employee, with no contributions coming from the government. In 1939 the act was amended to include benefits for the dependents and survivors of retired workers. It contained no provisions for universal health insurance but did provide for unemployment compensation, funded by both state and federal governments. The program also provided federal grants to states for aid to dependent mothers and children, the blind, and the disabled, and for public health services. The Social Security Administration went some distance toward Roosevelt's ultimate goal of providing a social safety net for all citizens.

Home Owners Loan Corporation

Responding to the massive increase in home foreclosures, Roosevelt sought legislation to assist small home owners. The result was the Home Owners Loan Corporation, instituted to assist homeowners who could not pay their mortgages. By refinancing mortgages with deferred payments and at lower interest rates, the HOLC allowed homeowners to keep their houses while helping the lending agency avoid a loss. This agency was a response to Roosevelt's commitment to the right to housing. Within a year, the HOLC had "conducted a vast rescue job, making over a million loans to mortgage-ridden home owners."

What is most striking about these various agencies is that they were concrete expressions of the emerging conception of rights. If a national government took the second bill seriously, it might well begin with enterprises of exactly this sort. The Roosevelt administration's commitment was evident in the shifts in social spending. In 1933 social welfare expenditures were 7.9 percent of the gross national product (GNP). By 1936 they were 13.2 percent of GNP, with significant jumps in spending for social insurance, public aid, health and medical programs, and housing assistance. Increases in public aid were especially dramatic, showing a fourfold increase. And the programs made a real difference to numerous lives. The Works Progress Administration alone employed millions of people, allowing them to work on programs involving slum clearance, reforestation, rural rehabilitation, and highway construction. Some of its specialized projects had broad cultural importance. The Federal Arts Project employed artists to decorate hundreds of post offices, schools, and other public buildings with sculptures and murals. Musicians organized symphony orchestras and community singing. Under the Federal Theatre Project, stock companies toured the country with repertories of old and new plays, bringing professional drama to many communities for the first time.

Participants in the Civilian Conservation Corps earned their money by renewing the nation's decimated forests, planting an estimated 3 billion trees between 1933 and 1942—and also building 30,000 wildlife shelters, creating or improving beaches and parks, and controlling floods. Equally important was the effect of the New Deal on the nation's morale. The burst of activity, designed to help those who needed it, gave the country a sense that it was moving in the right direction. A woman from Florida wrote of Roosevelt, "I love him for all he has done, and I love him for all he wanted to do and could not." A man from Seattle echoed the sentiment: "God bless him. He is doing all he can to relieve the suffering."

This is not to say that all or even most of Roosevelt's programs were successful or that they provide a good model for today. The overall effects of the New Deal are greatly disputed, and it cannot be seriously argued that Roosevelt's steps were sufficient to produce prosperity or even to eliminate widespread unemployment. Of course there was progress. The unemployment rate dropped from 24.9 percent in 1933 to 21.7 percent in 1934, 20.1 percent in 1935, 16.9 percent in 1936, and 14.3 percent in 1937. But it rose to 19 percent in 1938 and started to drop again only in the 1940s, from 9.9 percent in 1941 to 4.7 percent in 1942, to under 2 percent from 1943 through 1945. Changes in gross national product show a similar pattern. The low was $55.6 billion in 1933, rising steadily to $90.4 billion in 1937, falling to $84.7 billion in 1938, and rising significantly only in the 1940s. War production, rather than the New Deal, was the major impetus toward recovery. In fact a serious economic recession in 1937 created large problems for the New Dealers.

Past decades have taught the nation a great deal about how to increase employment and reduce poverty. Many New Deal measures were crude and ineffective. The largest and most enduring achievements were the Social Security Act and the National Labor Relations Act, both of which underwent significant changes in the decades that followed; neither should be immune from rethinking today. We know that government should rely, whenever it can, on flexible, market-friendly reforms, in the form of approaches that take incentives seriously and are alert to the risk of unintended adverse consequences. The central point is not that Roosevelt chose the right methods, but that the second bill was an outgrowth of a particular set of social wrongs and an identifiable set of public responses.

Of course Roosevelt did much more than I have described here. He greatly expanded the power of the Federal Trade Commission, designed to promote competition and protect consumers. He increased the authority of the Food and Drug Administration, intended to ensure product safety. He engaged in a series of measures, most notably the National Industrial Recovery Act, designed to stabilize the economy and promote business confidence. He did a great deal to protect banks and banking. His new regulatory state went far beyond the areas of work and security and altered preexisting understandings of the three pillars of the constitutional order: individual rights, checks and balances, and federalism. That alteration raises a natural question.

WAS THE NEW DEAL UNCONSTITUTIONAL?

I have mentioned the idea of freedom of contract and the Court's insistence, before the New Deal, that this idea imposed sharp limits on regulatory legislation. The 1930s saw an intense struggle between the Supreme Court and the Roosevelt administration. Before Roosevelt assumed office, the Court had erected a series of barriers to the kinds of initiatives Roosevelt hoped to undertake. First, the Court ruled that the power of Congress under the commerce clause of the Constitution was sharply limited, in a way that would make it difficult for the national government to do much of what Roosevelt sought to do: forbid child labor, impose maximum hour and minimum wage laws, and take steps to govern labor-management relations. Second, the Court had suggested that Congress could not "delegate" its power to the president and federal agencies, thus indicating that much of New Deal legislation would be in grave constitutional difficulty if it authorized the president and regulatory institutions to exercise discretion to solve the problems at hand. Third, the Court held (e.g., in the *Adkins* decisions mentioned in Chapter 2) that the Constitution protected "liberty of contract" and thus would not allow government, whether state or federal, to regulate the relationship between employers and employees.

Taken as a whole, these rulings put the New Deal on shaky constitutional ground, as the Court repeatedly ruled in the early years of Roosevelt's administration. When the New Deal suffered a set of large defeats in the Court, Roosevelt concocted his infamous "court-packing" plan, which would allow him to add an additional member to the Court for each justice who had reached the age of seventy, thus gaining a sympathetic majority.

It was only in 1937, in *West Coast Hotel,* that the Court capitulated to Roosevelt amid the threat of a genuine constitutional crisis. We have seen that *West Coast Hotel* rejected the Court's previous protection of freedom of contract. Since that decision, the Court has *never* struck down federal action on the ground that it interferes with that freedom. Two other developments were crucial. The first involved the increased power of the president. After signaling that it might discipline "delegations" of congressional authority from Congress to the president, the Court promptly retreated. It concluded that as long as Congress set out an "intelligible principle," it could give the president and his agencies a great deal of discretion to set regulations as they saw fit. In modern government, both the president and federal agencies are often permitted to choose policy under vague laws, saying, for example, that regulation of telecommunications should be in "the public interest" and that controls on occupational hazards should be imposed "to the extent feasible." Since the New Deal, the Supreme Court has permitted Congress to grant quite open-ended power to the executive branch.

The final development expanded the powers of Congress itself. In short order, the Court ruled that the national government had broad authority to regulate the economy under the commerce clause. Accepting Roosevelt's own arguments, the Court emphasized that because of interdependencies in the national economy, problems in one state are highly likely to affect interstate commerce. For example, a strike in one state would likely affect others, and hence the national government could reasonably decide that national protection of labor–management relations was necessary to protect interstate commerce. Going even further, the Court ruled that companies whose economic activities are apparently limited to one state might be taken to have interstate effects, if only because they tend to purchase products from elsewhere. As a result, the Court refused to strike down *any* exercise of congressional power as beyond the commerce clause for nearly sixty years. Not until 1995 did the Court invalidate congressional action under the commerce clause, when it invalidated a congressional effort to ban the possession of firearms near schools.

How should we assess these changes in constitutional understanding? Did Roosevelt actually violate or amend the Constitution? When the Court capitulated to Roosevelt, did it allow a kind of unwritten constitutional amendment, akin to the written ones that followed the Civil War? This is the view of some of Roosevelt's greatest admirers— and critics. Yale law professor Bruce Ackerman, for example, argues that the United States has had three "constitutional moments": the founding, the Civil War, and the New Deal. In Ackerman's view, each of these moments stimulated a large-scale rethinking of the nation's commitments in a way that fundamentally altered the basic design and goal of the Constitution. The New Deal was unique among the three periods in that it did not involve any textual change in the Constitution. But Ackerman believes that by 1937, the meaning of the Constitution had changed greatly from its meaning in 1932. He argues that the change came from a massive popular movement that did the same work as a literal constitutional change. Because the New Deal was ratified by the public, no less than the Civil War had been, Ackerman believes that it was entirely legitimate.

Other people agree with Ackerman's assessment of what happened but do not share his approval. In their view, the New Deal was an illegitimate departure from the constitutional framework, giving the national government unprecedented powers, allowing Congress to delegate those powers, and intruding on constitutionally protected liberty. This view is widely held today and helps explain some of the work of the Supreme Court under Chief Justice William Rehnquist, which has, in some respects, attempted to reinvigorate the pre–New Deal Constitution. In its most extreme form, this view suggests that there is a "Constitution in Exile"—a real document that the Court abandoned when it capitulated to Roosevelt. Douglas H. Ginsburg, an especially able, fair-minded, and distinguished appellate judge, writes that "respect for the text of the Constitution was the norm . . . through the first third of the twentieth century," but that the "great Depression and the determination of the Roosevelt Administration placed the Supreme Court's commitment to the Constitution as written under severe strain in the 1930s, and it was then that the wheels began to come off." Judge Ginsburg challenges a number of decisions in which the Court allowed the Roosevelt administration to do what it wanted; he singles out the Court's decision to uphold the National Labor Relations Act as a legitimate exercise of congressional power.

Many critics believe it is both possible and important to restore the true Constitution. Less radically, numerous current American judges appear to believe that the courts should make incremental movements toward restoring the constitutional understandings that preceded Roosevelt. In their view, Roosevelt's Constitution lacks full constitutional legitimacy.

This view also exists outside of the judiciary. In fact the early twenty-first century has witnessed a remarkable shift in conservative legal thought. In the 1980s, conservative legal scholars reacted against the liberal decisions of the Warren Court by urging a principle of judicial restraint. They wanted courts to back off—to allow restrictions on abortion, aggressive practices by the police, and a degree of public assistance to religious organizations. These criticisms of the Warren Court were founded on an understandable desire to let the people rule themselves, with limited judicial oversight. But there is no question that among some contemporary Republicans, the New Deal has now become a principal target. For them, Roosevelt is the villain, not Earl Warren, and they find it appropriate to attack Roosevelt's initiatives through politics and law, in courts as well as legislatures. For some of these people, Roosevelt's proudest accomplishments (e.g., the Social Security Act) are nothing to celebrate. One of their major goals is to move toward the constitutional system that preceded Roosevelt—a system with a weaker federal government, fewer regulatory agencies, and a narrower conception of rights. The administrations of Ronald Reagan, George H. W. Bush, and George W. Bush have included many who are skeptical of the New Deal.

The New Deal was grounded in a set of ideas that were concretized late in Roosevelt's presidency as the second bill of rights. Those who reject the New Deal are rejecting the conception of rights that Roosevelt intended to promote. I will discuss the resulting debates in Part III. For now, let us simply return to the Constitution. In my view, Roosevelt's admirers and antagonists are quite wrong to suggest that his initiatives were unconstitutional. Judge Ginsburg misreads both constitutional history and the Constitution as written. To be sure, the Supreme Court issued a series of decisions protecting freedom of contract. But those decisions were illegitimate, lacking any basis in the nation's founding document. The Constitution was not in the least offended by New Deal initiatives that attempted to protect workers from some of the pressures of the marketplace. It was the Court, not Roosevelt, that was acting in violation of the Constitution. Nor does the Constitution forbid Congress from giving a degree of discretion to the president. It is true that under the Constitution, Congress makes the laws. But nothing in the Constitution forbids Congress to "make" a law that allows the president a wide range of choices.

Contrary to a widely held view, regulatory agencies are hardly foreign to the American constitutional framework. Major departments, including those at the cabinet level, existed from the beginning. It is true that the federal government has limited powers and that Congress cannot regulate whatever topics it chooses. But Congress does have the power to regulate "commerce among the several states," to tax, and to spend. Most of the New Deal legislation fit comfortably within these authorities. In our highly interdependent economy, acts in Texas might well affect people in California and New York. It follows that the power to regulate "commerce" among the states naturally allows more federal action than it did when states were more like separate islands. Labor–management strife in one state is very likely to affect interstate commerce. Contrary to Judge Ginsburg's suggestion, the Court was entirely right to uphold the National Labor Relations Act; this was not even a difficult question.

There is an additional consideration. In a democratic system, courts are not our rulers. Judges owe the elected branches of government a large measure of deference and respect. In the face of reasonable doubt, courts should accept any plausible claim that an action is within the constitutional authority of Congress and the president. At least this is the best general rule. Before the New Deal, the Court repeatedly violated that rule, rejecting wholly reasonable judgments by the states and the national government. The most serious acts of unconstitutionality came not from the Roosevelt administration, but from the decisions of the early-twentieth-century Supreme Court, striking down minimum wage and maximum hour legislation and narrowly limiting the power of Congress under the commerce clause.

I do not deny that Roosevelt and the New Deal had a massive effect on the nation's understanding of what the president and Congress could legitimately do. Ackerman's claim that the New Deal was a "constitutional moment" is plausible for one reason: In 1937 American government was dramatically different from what it was in 1932. A large part of my goal here has been to capture the nature of these differences. But the transformation involved no violation of constitutional principles. The American Constitution is a flexible instrument, one that allows for a great deal of change over time. It does not forbid experiment and adjustment. To some extent, it allows for new understandings of rights. It permits changes in institutional arrangements. This is part of its genius.

4

The Birth
of the Second Bill

If you had spent two years in bed trying to wiggle your big
toe, after that anything else would seem easy!

Franklin Delano Roosevelt

ROOSEVELT SOUGHT, and obtained, constitutional change;
he wanted the founding document to be interpreted so as to
permit his programs. Roosevelt did not argue that the Constitution should be amended to include a second bill of rights. In speaking of the second bill, he did not even mention constitutional
amendment. What, then, was Roosevelt proposing? To answer that
question we need to distinguish between constitutional rights and
what I shall call a nation's *constitutive commitments*. Roosevelt was attempting to redefine the latter without affecting the former.

Some rights can be located in a founding document; they are
constitutional rights in the sense that the prevailing interpretation of
the document finds them there. Some of these rights, like the right
to free speech, are explicitly mentioned in the American Constitution. Other constitutional rights are not mentioned expressly, but
they are understood to be encompassed by the Constitution's terms.
Consider the right to travel from one state to another or the right be
free from discrimination on the basis of sex—neither explicitly in

the Constitution, but both found there by way of interpretation. Still other rights lack any kind of constitutional status. The founding document does not refer to them, and it is not seriously argued that they are encompassed by anything in the Constitution. But these rights are nonetheless constitutive commitments. They have a special place in the sense that they are widely accepted and cannot be eliminated without a fundamental change in social understanding. These rights are genuinely constitutive in the sense that they help create, or constitute, a society's basic values. They are also commitments in the sense that they are expected to have a degree of stability over time. A violation would amount to a kind of breach—a violation of a trust.

Both constitutional rights and constitutive commitments should be distinguished from the interests and rights protected through ordinary law and policy. Major league baseball, for example, has the right to be free from the antitrust law, and any effort to apply that law to professional baseball would cause a great stir (including some applause). But such an effort would not count as a breach of anything fundamental.

Compare, for example, the right to join a labor union without losing your job—a right created in the Roosevelt administration. Congress could abolish this right tomorrow, since the American Constitution does not protect it. But the right to join a labor union is so deeply ingrained that its elimination would require a large-scale change in public judgments—something akin to a constitutional amendment. Or consider the right to be free from racial discrimination by private employers, a right created by the Civil Rights Act of 1964. Because the Constitution applies only to government, private employers are free to discriminate as they wish under the Constitution. But the right to be free from private racial discrimination is now part of America's constitutive commitments. Yet another example, perhaps the simplest, is the right to social security. The Constitution does not mention this right, and public officials are permitted to disagree about how to respect it. But it is widely agreed that the nation is committed to the social security system in some form that fundamentally protects the economic expectations of its beneficiaries.

Columbia law professor Louis Henkin notes that "the United States is not a welfare state by constitutional compulsion." But he goes on to say, correctly, that the "welfare system and other rights granted by legislation (for example, laws against private racial discrimination) are so deeply embedded as to have near-constitutional sturdiness. . . . And Americans have begun to think and speak of social security and other benefits as matters of entitlement and right." This "near-constitutional sturdiness" and a sense of entitlement and right were what Roosevelt sought. "We put those payroll contributions there," he explained, "so as to give the contributors a legal, moral, and political right to collect their pensions and unemployment benefits. With those taxes in there, no damn politician can ever scrap my social security program."

Americans are perfectly able to distinguish between rights and privileges. In 1991 a sample of the nation's citizens was asked whether certain goods were "a privilege that a person should have to earn," or instead "a right to which he is entitled as a citizen." By strong majorities, the respondents answered that a college education, a telephone, and an annual salary increase are privileges, not rights. But by equally strong majorities, they said that the following were rights: adequate housing, a reasonable amount of leisure time, adequate provision for retirement years, an adequate standard of living, and adequate medical care. Strong majorities endorsed many of the items on the second bill. In 1990 Americans were asked whether the government "should provide a job for anyone who wants one." Of those who expressed an opinion, an overwhelming 86 percent agreed. In 1998, 64 percent of Texans agreed that the "government should see to it that everybody who wants to work can find a job."

Constitutional rights should be seen as a subset of the broader category of constitutive commitments. Some of a nation's constitutive commitments appear in its founding document, but many do not. In any case, the set of constitutional rights is not fixed over time. If the nation becomes committed to certain rights, they may migrate into the Constitution itself. Consider the ban on sex discrimination. Nothing in the Constitution explicitly forbids discrimination on the basis of sex, and it is ludicrous to think that those who ratified the bill of rights sought to forbid that form of discrimination. Nonetheless, the due process clause of the Fifth Amendment is now understood to ban government from treating women worse than men. This interpretation of the Constitution is a product of changes in the nation's constitutive commitments.

In proposing the second bill, Roosevelt was not arguing for any change in constitutional interpretation but for new constitutive commitments. Drawing on the nation's experience in the first four decades of the century, he believed that the public had accepted a new set of principles, now understood as rights. In the words of Roosevelt's adviser Charles Merriam, "Hunger, sickness, unemployment, insecurity, dog-housed dwelling places, inadequate educational, recreational, cultural advantages, unfair shares of production—these are wrongs of our day, which will not in the long run be denied a remedy in the common judgment of mankind. These conditions are wrong, but they have their complementary rights." This was the spirit in which Roosevelt urged the second bill—not as an effort to alter the founding document but as a concrete account of the nation's understanding of what citizens were entitled to expect. Roosevelt sought to hold up the second bill as a kind of test of the nation's fulfillment of its responsibilities. As we shall see, his effort drew on a central goal of those who wrote the original bill of rights.

Roosevelt was hardly the first to suggest that social and economic guarantees should have special status. In the early decades of the twentieth century, the idea was very much in the air. For example, the German Constitution of 1919 provided a right to a free public education; it also said that every citizen was to be given an opportunity to work and that if no such opportunity could be provided, provision must be made to supply his basic needs. The constitution of Iceland, ratified in 1920, provided that "anyone who is unable to support himself or his family . . . is entitled to receive relief from public funds," and goes on to provide a guarantee of education. The constitution of Spain, ratified in 1931, said that the nation "shall assure to every worker the conditions necessary for a fitting existence," and that legislation would be provided for "cases of insurance for illness, accident, unemployment, old age, invalidity and death," and also to provide "annual holidays with pay." The 1919 constitution of Finland and the 1922 constitution of the Netherlands required the government to provide education for all; the Netherlands constitution went on to say that "poor relief shall be an object of constant solicitude on the part of the Government, and shall be regulated by law."

Notably, however, some of these provisions did not speak in terms of rights. They referred to the responsibilities and tasks of government without specifying that citizens have a right to the protection of certain interests. Moreover, there is no evidence that provisions of this kind had the slightest influence on Roosevelt. The origins of the second bill and Roosevelt's conception of the path of American history lie in Roosevelt's first campaign for the presidency. The idea of security played a central role, and Roosevelt had begun to see that idea in terms of rights. From this initial campaign, his thinking on the subject showed a remarkable continuity over time.

Eleanor Roosevelt believed that her husband had been affected by a small incident that occurred when he was a young man. He arrived to take her home from her volunteer work at the Rivington Street settlement in New York City and came upon a very sick child, whom he carried up several flights of stairs to an ill-lit, unsanitary tenement. Stunned by what he saw, the future president declared, "If ever I get a chance to hit that thing, I'll hit it hard." Whatever the early influences, the line of development of the second bill of rights can be traced through six crucial points: the initial proposal of "an economic declaration of rights" in a campaign speech in 1932; the emphasis on the "right to work" and the "right to live" in his speech before the Democratic National Convention in 1936; the identification in 1941 of "freedom from want" as one of the four freedoms; the Atlantic Charter, signed by Great Britain and the United States in 1941; the specification of the second bill of rights through the efforts of an obscure institution, the National Public Resources Board, in the early 1940s; and the presentation of the fully conceived second bill in the 1944 State of the Union address.

Roosevelt was a public official, not a philosopher. He was far from a systematic thinker. The communist Leon Trotsky said contemptuously but astutely of Roosevelt: "Your President abhors 'systems' and 'generalities.'" Joseph Alsop put the same point more sympathetically: "Franklin D. Roosevelt was not an ideologist, or a theory-mongerer, or a man with a gospel to peddle. If he dismissed an argument on the ground that 'it's all very theoretical,' that was a final dismissal. He disliked and distrusted ideologists, whether of the right or the left. Results were his only tests where political action was under consideration." Frances Perkins wrote bluntly: "The notion that the New Deal had a preconceived theoretical position is ridiculous." Roosevelt responded to events and perceived needs; he did not seek to engraft a theory of government onto the American polity. But from his first campaign for the presidency, he did believe that a new conception of rights was required, one that would grow out of conspicuous injustices in the existing social order.

In building toward the second bill, Roosevelt emphasized that government was not an enemy of liberty or individualism. All rights, including the right to property, depend on government. It was necessary to define rights in a way that went well beyond the founding period and provided better protection of human liberty under modern conditions. Above all, the second bill emerged from a synthesis of New Deal reform with an appreciation of the need to develop an account of liberal democracy that would respond to the threats from fascism and communism. In the 1930s, Roosevelt spoke, with increasing firmness, of the need to develop a new conception of freedom with the same level of ambition as the Constitution's founding. In the 1940s, the specter of war shone a spotlight on human rights in general, prompting Roosevelt to emphasize "freedom from fear" and "freedom from want" and argue that the two were intertwined. The second bill grew out of the interaction between New Deal thinking and the perceived need to develop a novel synthesis of American ideals.

Let us now explore the major stages in the development of the second bill.

Reconceiving Rights:
"An Economic Constitutional Order"

Many of the themes of the second bill were first laid down in an extraordinary speech to the Commonwealth Club in San Francisco on September 23, 1932. The speech was largely written by Adolf Berle, a Columbia law professor who had been preoccupied, for most of his academic life, with the modern role of corporations.

For Berle, corporate power was a serious threat to both democracy and economic growth. He believed that corporations had increasingly obtained the status of monopolies and did violence to the old idea of free and open competition. Thus Berle, along with his coauthor Gardiner Means, feared that the "rise of the modern corporation has brought a concentration of economic power which can compete on equal terms with the modern state—economic power versus political power, each strong in its own field," but with the corporation steadily becoming more powerful. In fact the corporation threatened to supersede the state and become "the dominant form of social organization." Thus the law of corporations was emerging as a "potential constitutional law for the new economic state." Adam Smith had celebrated the system of competition by small units, and he was right to do so. But this position was growing increasingly anachronistic, as competition became dominated by a few great enterprises. Emphasizing this point, Berle argued in favor of new mechanisms of political control, designed to reduce the growing threat of private tyranny.

Roosevelt's speech was in many ways a summary of Berle's academic work. It also showed the influence of Herbert Croly's ambitious and widely read book, *The Promise of American Life*. Croly stressed what he saw as radical new developments in the American economy, stemming from the rise of industrialization; he argued for a new kind of democratic planning to combat corporate domination of economic and political life. But Roosevelt's Commonwealth Club speech had three elements not found in the work of either Berle or Croly. First, it showed a direct engagement with unemployment and its human meaning—an engagement that led to a novel emphasis on the centrality of security. Second, the speech reflected a high degree of optimism, entirely characteristic of Roosevelt himself; this optimism found expression in Roosevelt's words before and after the Depression. Third, the speech referred, as Berle and Croley had never done, to the need for a new understanding of rights. We should see the Commonwealth Club address as a synthesis of Berle's views of the economy with Roosevelt's confidence about America's potential and (most important) a fresh understanding of rights, growing out of the Depression.

Roosevelt called, first and foremost, for a "redefinition of rights in terms of a changing and growing social order." He explicitly proposed "the development of an economic declaration of rights, an economic constitutional order" that would recognize that "every man has a right to live," which also entailed "a right to make a comfortable living." A person "may by sloth or crime decline to exercise that right; but it may not be denied to him." Roosevelt complained that under modern conditions, equality of opportunity had become a myth. He argued that the economic declaration of rights was necessary to ensure a system that would be "more permanently safe" and contended that a new conception of government was necessary to promote the values of American individualism, properly understood.

Roosevelt began by offering a brief account of the origins of government, which he described as an effort "to impose peace upon ruling barons." This peace was in the interest of individuals, above all because it helped to promote security. Thus the "victory of the central government, the creation of a strong central government, was a haven of refuge to the individual," because that government ensured a "master far away" rather than "the exploitation and cruelty of the smaller master near at hand." In this way, Roosevelt linked the existence of a powerful government with security, seeing public force as an ally of individual safety rather than its enemy. But in the new system, there "came a growing feeling that government was conducted for the benefit of a few who thrived unduly at the expense of all." What was necessary was "a limiting force," one that came through the popular checks on government. "The American colonies were borne in this struggle," and the American Revolution "was a turning point in it."

But the process of constitution making had been a struggle. The great conflict was between Alexander Hamilton, who feared democratic self-rule, and Thomas Jefferson, who was hospitable to it. Among those who shared his views, Hamilton was the "most brilliant, honest, and able"—and in Roosevelt's rendition, something of an aristocrat, skeptical of the public and supportive of guidance by "a small group of able and public spirited citizens" who would oversee a strong and energetic central government. Hamilton's adversary, Thomas Jefferson, was an enthusiast for both freedom and rights of property. Jefferson insisted that because of America's unique circumstances, we "have no paupers." In our nation, workers were able to have property, cultivate land, and "feed abundantly, clothe above mere decency, to labor moderately and raise their families." Unlike Hamilton, Jefferson was skeptical of a powerful national government. But in Roosevelt's account, "even Jefferson realized that the exercise of the property rights might so interfere with the rights of the individual that the government, without whose assistance the property rights could not exist, must intervene, not to destroy individualism but to protect it." Here, then, is Roosevelt's initial emphasis on the myth of laissez-faire—on the need for government to ensure that property rights exist in the first place. Here too is a suggestion that if individualism is the goal, government interference with property rights might be necessary in order to achieve it—a suggestion that turned out to play a central role in the New Deal.

In Roosevelt's account, Hamilton was the foundation for the Republican party, and Jefferson the foundation of the Democratic party. In the election of 1800, Jefferson won. For a half century or so, individualism remained, under Jeffersonian principles, "the great watchword of American life." Everyone who wanted to work had the opportunity to do so; the right to work, and hence the right to live, was guaranteed in practice if not in theory. Because America had "no paupers," the nation consisted largely of laborers who were able to "possess property." Private property was hence widely distributed; most people had some. (Slavery is of course a glaring omission here.) In our largely agricultural economy, "starvation and dislocation were practically impossible." Liberty and equality were ensured by the rights "involved in acquiring and possessing property," alongside the ballot and the liberty to live by one's "own lights." And with abundant natural resources, the nation could provide relief to its own people and to many immigrants from all over the world. "The happiest of economic conditions made that day long and splendid," especially because "on the Western frontier, land was substantially free."

But in the middle of the nineteenth century, the situation changed radically. The industrial revolution created a new kind of economy, in which powerful private financiers—"financial Titans," in Roosevelt's phrase—moved to the fore. They did so not because of natural processes, but with active governmental assistance. "The railroads were subsidized, sometimes by grants of money, oftener by grants of land; some of the most valuable oil lands in the United States were granted to assist the financial growth of the railroad which pushed through the Southwest."

Roosevelt argued that all of these acts of assistance undermined the supposed commitment to noninterference by government. Objections to government as such had become merely strategic. "The same man who tells us that he does not want to see the government interfere in business . . . is the first to go to Washington." But there was a still more serious problem. By the turn of the twentieth century, a new danger emerged. The large corporations, no less than the old feudal barons, "might threaten the economic freedom of individuals to earn a living." Hence Theodore Roosevelt attempted to break up corporate power with antitrust laws. To Franklin Roosevelt, this step had become inadequate. Directly echoing Berle, Roosevelt said that it was not possible "to turn the clock back, to destroy the large combinations and to return to the time when every man owned his individual small business."

At this stage Roosevelt offered his affirmative argument. In the current period "equality of opportunity as we have known it no longer exists." The nation lacked "a safety valve." Rising tariffs had reduced production and created unemployment. The modern era "calls for a re-appraisal of values." What was necessary was "the development of an economic declaration of rights, an economic constitutional order." Private economic power would have to be seen as holding a public trust. Here Roosevelt emphasized two rights that would be central to the new system. The first was the "right to life," which means "also a right to make a comfortable living." It followed that the government "owes to everyone an avenue to possess himself of [its] plenty sufficient for his needs, through his own work." The second right was to property, "which means a right to be assured, to the fullest extent attainable," of the safety of savings. This safety was necessary to assure people that they could live through situations that "afford no chance of labor: childhood, sickness, old age." Roosevelt described these rights in a way that responded specifically to the financial problems of the Depression and pointed the way toward greater government involvement in increasing employment and regulating the banking and brokerage industries. It is a short step from his claims about work and property to the creation of public employment programs and federal deposit insurance.

Roosevelt's initial campaign offered a wide range of claims and arguments, and the Commonwealth Club speech captured only a part of them; it would be wrong to say that his campaign was organized or unified by the argument offered there. But similar themes, involving the need for a new conception of rights, echoed throughout Roosevelt's campaign speeches in the 1932. On May 22, he asserted that it "is well within the inventive capacity of man, who has built up this great social and economic machine capable of satisfying the wants of all, to insure that all who are willing and able to work received from it at least the necessities of life." In accepting the Democratic nomination on July 2 of the same year, he asked, "What do the people of America want more than anything else? To my mind, they want two things: work, with all the moral and spiritual values that go with it; and with work, a reasonable measure of security—security for themselves and for their wives and children. Work and security—

these are more than words. They are more than facts. They are the spiritual values, the true goal toward which our efforts of reconstruction should lead." The idea of security later defined the goals of his presidency.

In the same speech, Roosevelt attempted to dismiss the idea that poverty and distress were a product of "laws" rather than human choices. In his account, social deprivation resulted from human law rather than nature. "Our Republican leaders tell us economic laws—sacred, inviolable, unchangeable—cause panics which no one could prevent. But while they prate of economic laws, men and women are starving. We must lay hold of the fact that economic laws are not made by nature. They are made by human beings." On October 13, he went further: "I assert that modern society, acting through its Government, owes the definite obligation to prevent the starvation or dire want of any of its fellow men and women who try to maintain themselves but cannot."

Many of his programs in 1933 were an effort to fulfill that obligation. In 1934 he announced the creation of the Committee on Economic Security, which would be responsible for an initial draft of the Social Security Act of 1935. In this announcement, he referred to "the general welfare Constitution" and stressed that the new social rights should supplement the "old and sacred possessive rights" of property. In the modern era, Roosevelt contended that new governmental duties were necessary to ensure "a recovery" of the meaning of the old. Here the idea of security again came to the fore. "If, as our Constitution tells us, our Federal Government was established among other things, 'to promote the general welfare,' it is our plain duty to provide for that security upon which welfare depends. . . . The security of the home, the security of livelihood, and the security of social insurance—are, it seems to me, a minimum . . . of the promise that we can offer to the American people. They constitute a right which belongs to every individual and every family willing to work."

In 1935 and 1936, several members of Congress went further still, showing a keen interest in amending the Constitution to include social and economic guarantees. One congressman suggested that "the

time has come to extend the Bill of Rights to embrace such guarantees as 'the right to honest work,' an industry-wide 'minimum
standard of hours, wages, and fair competition,' and the like." Another suggested that an amendment was necessary so that the nation
would "unmistakably establish the right of the people to have both an
industrial democracy and a political democracy." Roosevelt never
took this approach; he showed no interest in explicit constitutional
amendments along these lines. But he continued to stress the theme
of security. Campaigning in 1936, Roosevelt asked, "What was our
hope in 1932? Above all other things the American people wanted
peace." By this he meant "peace of mind instead of gnawing fear."
Hence people "sought escape from the personal terror which had
stalked them for three years. They wanted the peace that comes from
security in their homes: safety for their savings, permanence in their
jobs, a fair profit from their enterprise." We can see a precursor of the
second bill even here.

"Right to Work" and "Right to Live"

A more ambitious statement about rights can be found in Roosevelt's
great speech before the Democratic National Convention on June 27,
1936, in Philadelphia—the most significant step toward the second
bill after the Commonwealth Club address, one that builds directly
on that earlier address. But where the 1932 speech showed Berle's
somewhat academic hand, its 1936 successor had Roosevelt's distinctive spirit and his characteristic clarity and simplicity.

In his papers, the speech's title comes from its conclusion: "We
Are Fighting to Save a Great and Precious Form of Government for
Ourselves and the World." This was a campaign speech, and Roosevelt relished the opportunity to deliver it. In the previous year, he
had been confident of victory, telling his cabinet, "We will win easily
next year, but we are going to make it into a crusade." Herbert
Hoover, Roosevelt's old nemesis, had by coincidence spoken in identical terms: "For a year and a half, I have been conducting a crusade

vital to the American people to regenerate real, individual freedom in the United States. The election of Governor Landon is the next step to the attainment of that purpose."

Amid the dueling crusades, the nation's economy had improved significantly. Under the New Deal, 6 million new jobs had been created and unemployment had fallen by 4 million, a decrease of almost half. Industrial production nearly doubled, with billions of dollars in increased income for farmers; stock prices and payrolls in manufacturing had also doubled. National income had increased dramatically, $64.7 billion in 1936, more than 50 percent higher than the $39.6 billion in 1933. Corporate profits rose to $5 million, after having fallen to minus $2 million in 1933. Stock prices had nearly doubled since 1933. Behind the numbers was a huge change in national mood, marking a movement in the direction that Roosevelt had charted in the 1932 campaign. "The old subserviency of worker to employer, of mortgagee to mortgage holder, of farmer to shipper and middleman, of tenant farmer to landlord, may have remained in its essential form," Arthur Schlesinger Jr. wrote, "but the laws and spirit of the New Deal had instilled in these relations some of the equality and dignity that marked the old American dream."

Notwithstanding these successes, Roosevelt was badly torn in early 1936 between two possible campaign strategies. One alternative was to be essentially defensive—run on his record, propose little that was new, and mend fences with his adversaries, particularly in the business community. This option held considerable appeal. Roosevelt was under intense criticism from the press and business groups, who contended that he was compromising national values and even freedom itself. A campaign of national unity was tempting. The second possibility was to mount a genuine crusade—to promise to continue, and expand on, the initiatives of the New Deal, arguing that something dramatic and genuinely new was afoot. In making his choice, Roosevelt faced some unanticipated political developments. He had hoped that Hoover would oppose him, in part because he believed Hoover to be the only Republican with "the massive convictions and intelligence to provide an alternative to the New Deal." In a contest with Hoover, the election would be an unambiguous referendum on Roosevelt's program of security and work. But the Republicans decided instead on Alf M. Landon, a businessman willing to run on a cautious and moderate program—a precursor, so to speak, of "compassionate conservatism." At the same time, anti–New Deal Democrats were rumored to be mounting their own attack from the right, perhaps as part of a third party. Left-wing forces were setting up their own party. In June, Roosevelt's popularity was dropping.

For whatever reason, Roosevelt opted for a crusade. He played a crucial role in an unusually bold party platform. Unhappy with the original draft, he said, "I would like to have as short a platform as possible this year and . . . I would like to have it based on the sentence of the Declaration of Independence, 'We hold these truths to be self-evident.'" Thus the platform began: "We hold this truth to be self-evident—that government in a modern civilization has certain inescapable obligations to its citizens, among which are: (1) Protection of the family and the home; (2) Establishment of a democracy of opportunity for all the people; (3) Aid to those overtaken by disaster." Roosevelt delivered his acceptance speech at Philadelphia's Franklin Field. Over 100,000 people were in attendance. It immediately became clear to all that this would not be a defensive campaign.

Roosevelt began by giving a clear sense of the momentous nature of the occasion, which he analogized to the American Revolution itself: "The rush of modern civilization itself has raised for us new difficulties, new problems which must be solved if we are to preserve to the United States the political and economic freedom for which Washington and Jefferson planned and fought." He continued that "Philadelphia is a good city in which to write American history" and pledged "to restore to the people a wider freedom; to give to 1936 as the founders gave to 1776—an American way of life." These were the remarks of someone seeking change of the most fundamental kind. Roosevelt offered an explicit comparison between the American Revolution and the response to the crisis of the Depression, suggesting that the two were of similar importance. In a way, he suggested, he was completing the revolution itself. Here he reiterated the theme of the Commonwealth Club speech—but in a way that emphasized the sense in which the New Deal counted as a kind of constitutional renovation.

The purpose of the Revolution of 1776 "was to win freedom from the tyranny of political autocracy—from the eighteenth century royalists who held special privileges from the crown." The goal was to put "the business of governing into the hands of the average man, who won the right with his neighbors to make and order his own destiny through his own government." Hence "it was to win freedom from the tyranny of political autocracy that the American Revolution was fought." The victory meant that "political tyranny was wiped out at Philadelphia on July 4, 1776." But a new challenge had arisen in the form of economic powers that "sought to regiment the people, their labor, and their property." With the industrial revolution, "economic royalists carved out new dynasties." (This had been Berle's theme in his academic writings.) A "new industrial dictatorship" had concentrated "into their own hands an almost complete control over other people's money, other people's labor—other people's lives." And here Roosevelt went far beyond Berle, urging that "as a result the average man once more confronts the problem that faced the Minute Man." Because of the new control, "the political equality we once had won was meaningless in the face of economic inequality." The new "royalists" and "despots" had "reached out for control over Government itself." They had even placed their authority "in the robes of legal sanction"—Roosevelt's clear reminder that the law, and not nature, was behind the economic order.

The result was an interference with freedom itself, for "necessitous men are not free men." Liberty requires not merely protection from government interference but also an "opportunity to make a living— a living decent according to the standard of the time, a living which gives man not only enough to live by, but something to live for." As a result of the drastic imbalance of economic power, many people found that "life was no longer free" and liberty was "no longer real." Those who defended that power, the "royalists of the economic order," had "granted that the government could protect the citizen in his right to vote, but they denied that the government could do anything to protect the citizen in his right to work and his right to live." Roosevelt's answer was simple: "Today we stand committed to the proposition that freedom is no half-and-half affair."

That commitment called for a "fight for freedom in a modern civilization." Thus the nation would be committed to lifting "from every recess of American life the dread fear of the unemployed that they are not needed in this world." That commitment called for government action: "Governments can err, Presidents do make mistakes, but the immortal Dante tells us that divine justice weighs the sins of the cold-blooded and the sins of the warm-hearted in different scales. Better the occasional faults of a Government that lives in a spirit of charity than the consistent omissions of a Government frozen in the ice of its own indifference."

Roosevelt's adviser Harold Ickes described this address as "the greatest political speech I have ever heard," a statement that captured the sentiment of most who were there. At this early stage, Roosevelt offered the essential foundation of the plea for a second bill of rights. Notice the self-conscious contrast of the original revolution to contemporary needs, and the suggestion that freedom from desperate conditions is a necessary supplement to political liberty. The 1936 speech refers explicitly to a "right to work" and a "right to live." Roosevelt had yet to suggest that these rights could be translated into a real bill, something that could stand alongside the original one.

I have emphasized that the New Deal was highly experimental and pragmatic, not organized by a clear theory of any kind. But on November 1, 1937, Roosevelt discussed his objectives, saying that they "were, have been, and still are":

- A chance for men and women to work in industry at decent wages and reasonable hours or to engage in farming at a decent return.
- A chance for adequate recreation, better housing and sounder health.
- A chance to make reasonable profit in business protected

against monopolies and unfair competition, but organized so as to provide fair prices for the consuming public.
- Planning and use of natural resources for the benefit of average men and women.
- Security against the hardships of old age.
- Security against unexpected or seasonal unemployment.
- Security against new as well as old types of criminals.
- Security against war.

This catalog of objectives was not cast in terms of rights. But with a little effort, it could easily be translated into those terms. It took an external threat to push Roosevelt to take that step.

FREEDOM FROM WANT

After 1937, Roosevelt's domestic agenda encountered difficulty in an increasingly conservative Congress. Efforts to build on the New Deal stalled, and Roosevelt's personal energies were redirected to the threat from abroad. While that threat deflected attention from the New Deal's reconception of rights, it eventually played a crucial role in the development of the second bill, forcing Roosevelt to make his general and somewhat vague statement more international, more ambitious, and more specific.

The initial developments came with two press conferences, on June 5 and July 5, 1940. Here Roosevelt's eye was directly on the war in Europe and the rise of fascism. On June 5, with war looming, he briefly referred to "four fears" and his goal of eliminating all of them. These included the fear that one could not worship God as one wished, the fear of not being able to speak out or engage in dissent, the fear of armed conflict, and the fear of being unable to have ordinary social and economic relationships with other nations.

On July 5, he spoke far more ambitiously. Asked about his "long-range peace objectives," Roosevelt launched into an extended and apparently extemporaneous set of remarks, in which he compared the American system with "certain new systems of Government," notably in Italy, Russia, and Germany. His preoccupation was with the idea of "efficiency" in government. He emphasized that "Americans were the first to seek and to establish" certain fundamental principles in government, rooted in a commitment to individual rights and three branches of government rather than one. Roosevelt contended that the new system, which he called "the corporate state," is "extremely efficient," partly because it abolished the legislative and judicial branches. This efficiency could not have been lost on Roosevelt, who was frequently blocked by the legislature. But he noted, with evident regret, that a large number of Americans seemed willing to consider the corporate state for America itself. Roosevelt was speaking against a background in which fascism appealed to a number of Americans, with one writer publishing a well-known book under the title *The Coming American Fascism.* That book was intended not as a warning but as a celebration of the better system to come, with the author asserting that his argument "is addressed to the thoughtful who are not frightened by new and unpopular terms and concepts."

Having stressed the efficiency of other forms of government, Roosevelt abruptly turned to a description of "certain freedoms." The first he called "freedom of information," meant to be broader than "freedom of the press." People all over the country should be able to "get news of what is going on in every part of the country and in every part of the world without censorship and through many forms of communication." This emphasis on "freedom of information" was eerily prescient. The same basic idea is the title of one of the most important American reforms of the 1970s: the Freedom of Information Act, which goes well beyond freedom of speech to allow access to information held by government. Of course no modern reader can consider Roosevelt's account without thinking of the Internet. Roosevelt contended that freedom of information is closely connected to peace because international stability depends on that freedom.

The second freedom was religious liberty—the right to worship as one chooses. The third was freedom of expression, understood as the right to say what one likes "as long as you don't advocate the overthrow of Government." And the fourth was "freedom from fear, so that people won't be afraid of being bombed from the air or attacked, one way or the other, by some other nation." This freedom required "a removal of the weapons that cause fear—in other words, disarmament." He contrasted a government that respected these freedoms to a government that "removed those four freedoms in the interest of a greater efficiency."

At this point there was a question from a reporter, Mr. Harkness: "I had a fifth in mind which you might describe as 'freedom from want'—free trade, opening up trade?" This question connected well with Roosevelt's own emphasis, for many years, on the importance of free trade to employment and an expanding economy. He responded with enthusiasm: "Yes, that is true. I had that in mind but forgot it." He then repeated the phrase "freedom from want" and defined it as "the removal of cultural barriers between nations, cultural in the first place and commercial in the second place." But he failed to explain the connection between that particular freedom and removal of those barriers. It was not at all clear what "freedom from want" was supposed to include.

With this press conference, the stage was set for Roosevelt's four freedoms speech, the next great step toward the second bill, delivered as his State of the Union address on January 6, 1941. Much of the speech was devoted to international relations, with a sustained attack on isolationism. The upshot of Roosevelt's argument was that "the future and the safety of our country and of our democracy are overwhelmingly involved in events far beyond our borders." Hence he urged a strong commitment to national defense. In particular, he sought authority to send aid to England and other countries fighting for survival against Germany, Italy, and Japan. "Let us say to the democracies: We Americans are vitally concerned in your defense of freedom." But even more than that, he added that America's commitment would have to be rooted in an understanding of the "things worth fighting for." Notably, he did not refer to rights at all. But he did identify "the foundations of a healthy and strong democracy," urging that they included the "basic things expected by our people of their political and economic systems." These were:

- Equality of opportunity for youth and others.
- Jobs for those who can work.
- Security for those who need it.
- The ending of special privilege for the few.
- The preservation of civil liberties for all.
- The enjoyment of the fruits of scientific progress in a wider and constantly rising standard of living.

To promote these ends, Roosevelt argued for a set of domestic policy initiatives building on the New Deal itself. He contended that the nation "should bring more citizens under the coverage of old-age pensions and unemployment insurance"; "should widen the opportunities for adequate medical care"; and "should plan a better system by which persons deserving or needing gainful employment may obtain it." All this was striking and important—an effort, amid the threat of war, to propose a bold new series of domestic reforms. But what made the speech memorable was Roosevelt's closing peroration. He pointed to the future, "which we seek to make secure" as "we look forward to a world founded upon four essential human freedoms."

The first is freedom of speech and expression—everywhere in the world.

The second is freedom of every person to worship God in his own way—everywhere in the world.

The third is freedom from want—which, translated into world terms, means economic understandings which will secure to every nation a healthy peacetime life for its inhabitants—everywhere in the world.

The fourth is freedom from fear—which, translated into world terms, means a world-wide reduction of armaments to such a point and in such a thorough fashion that no nation will be in a position to commit an act of physical aggression against any neighbor—anywhere in the world.

This, Roosevelt insisted, "is no vision of a distant millennium. It is a definite basis for a kind of world attainable in our own time and generation." He contrasted it to "the so-called new order of tyranny which the dictators seek to create with the crash of a bomb." He recognized that he was asking for something new, not merely attempting to recover the past. But he was unembarrassed about this and suggested, as in his speeches in 1932 and 1936, that a kind of revolution was afoot. "Since the beginning of our American history, we have been engaged in change—in a perpetual peaceful revolution—a revolution which goes on steadily, quietly adjusting itself to changing conditions—without the concentration camp or the quick-lime in the ditch."

The four freedoms speech owed everything to Eleanor Roosevelt and the president personally. She had been reading a new book, *And Beacons Burn Again*, which argued that England, at war with Germany, would be saved by workers, miners, and people from the slums, not by the wealthy. In her column on New Year's Day, Eleanor Roosevelt wrote, "Justice for all, security in certain living standards, a recognition of the dignity and the right of an individual human being without regard to his race, creed or color—these are the things for which vast numbers of our citizens will willingly sacrifice themselves." Her friend Trude Pratt Lash claimed that "Eleanor was forever discussing how the world would look after the war, and finally her ideas took hold in the president's call for four freedoms in his State of the Union."

Lash's claim is probably an overstatement, but the drafting history is not inconsistent with her account. The very idea of four freedoms was absent from initial version of the speech, which ended somewhat drearily. On several occasions, Roosevelt asked his speechwriters to come up with something sharper and more dramatic. Little emerged from their efforts. As White House discussions proceeded, Roosevelt announced to the little assembly that he had an idea for a peroration. In the words of Samuel Rosenman, one of Roosevelt's speechwriters, "We waited as he leaned back in his swivel chair with his gaze on the ceiling. It was a long pause—so long that it began to become uncomfortable." And then Roosevelt dictated the four freedoms passage in essentially final form. In Rosenman's account, the words, essentially identical to those he ultimately delivered, "seemed to roll off his tongue."

Those words were not uncontroversial among the president's own team members. At their conclusion, Harry Hopkins, Roosevelt's principal adviser, expressed grave doubts about the phrase "everywhere in the world." "That covers a lot of territory, Mr. President. I don't know how interested Americans are going to be in the people of Java." Roosevelt answered, "I'm afraid they'll have to be some day, Harry. The world is getting so small that even the people in Java are getting to be our neighbors now." In the ensuing discussion, Hopkins concurred with Roosevelt but wondered how the public would view the international focus. Nonetheless, the phrase "everywhere in the world" was retained, and later repeated for each of the freedoms.

It should be obvious that Roosevelt's objectives for a democracy are a precursor of the second bill of rights. The list itself had an intriguing origin that shows a great deal about Roosevelt's goals during the period. In Rosenman's account, Roosevelt wanted to emphasize "that what we were fighting for was economic as well as political democracy." What Rosenman called a "renewed summation of the New Deal" came from two items in Roosevelt's annual message file. One of them was an editorial in the *New York Post* from December 26, 1940, which quoted five proposals jointly made by the leaders of the Roman Catholics and Protestants in England. These proposals sought a long-term program to eliminate fear, mistrust, and hatred, including education for all and the abolition of extreme inequalities in wealth. The second item was a letter of September 27, 1940, from Roosevelt adviser Harold Ickes, referring to a book called *All Out* by Samuel Grafton. It quoted a specific passage: "In September of 1940, the better sections of the English press began to debate the need for an 'economic bill of rights,' to defeat Hitlerism in the world forever by establishing 'minimum standards of housing, food, education, and medical care,' along with free speech, free press, and free worship."

Here is an evident inspiration for the idea of freedom from want. The goal of defeating "Hitlerism in the world forever" was part and parcel of the insistence on that form of freedom. Thus Roosevelt linked the New Deal reformation to the fight against fascism.

THE ATLANTIC CHARTER

The "four freedoms" speech was followed in close order by the Atlantic Charter, issued on August 14, 1941. The charter was the outcome of a dramatic meeting between Roosevelt and Winston Churchill, whom Roosevelt met during World War I as assistant secretary of the navy. The 1941 meeting was suggested by Roosevelt, responding to the war's escalation. One of Roosevelt's central goals was to set out principles and aspirations to guide the policies of the Allies during and after the conflict. The meeting took place on August 9–12 on two ships—the British battleship *Prince of Wales* and the American cruiser *Augusta,* at sea near Argentia, Newfoundland. This first encounter between Roosevelt and Churchill as national leaders marked the beginning of an extraordinarily close relationship. Churchill boarded the *Augusta* on August 9 as the military band played "God Save the King." Roosevelt sat still briefly and then smiled radiantly. "I have never seen such a smile," one of Churchill's advisers later reported.

Roosevelt and Churchill agreed that the Atlantic Charter would capture the principles for which the European war was being fought. It began by noting "certain common principles in the national policies" of England and America "on which they base their hopes for a better future for the world." These principles included political liberty and self-determination, "the right of all peoples to choose the form of government under which they will live," including sovereign rights and self-government. The charter did not refer to individual rights, but it reveals the strong influence of the four freedoms speech. Clause 5 acknowledged the two nations' shared "desire to bring about the fullest collaboration between all nations in the economic field, with the object of securing, for all, improved labour standards, economic advancement and social security." This clause strongly indicated a commitment to social and economic rights. More specifically still, clause 6 noted the importance of producing a peace "which will afford to all nations the means of dwelling in safety within their own boundaries, and which will afford assurance that all the men in all the lands may live out their lives in freedom from fear and want." In a personal gloss, Roosevelt emphasized that "the declaration of principles at this time presents a goal which is worth while for our civilization to seek. . . . It is also unnecessary for me to point out that the declaration of principles includes of necessity the world need for freedom of religion and freedom of information." As Roosevelt had it, these freedoms "are a part of the whole freedom for which we strive."

THE NATIONAL PUBLIC RESOURCES BOARD

The four freedoms speech and the Atlantic Charter helped inspire the idea of a second bill and provided the indispensable background for it. In the early 1940s it was refined, as broad, somewhat vague principles were eventually concretized in the form of the second bill.

The particular idea came not from Roosevelt but from a distinctive and now forgotten institution, the National Resources Planning Board (NRPB), originally created as the National Planning Board in the Public Works Administration in 1933 and operating directly under Roosevelt. The board lasted for ten years. It coordinated national planning in general, but it was also charged with developing new ideas and experiments, with the goal of promoting employment and economic security. The NRPB turned out to be a central actor in the development of the second bill. Its specific components and indeed the general idea were a product of an agency that originated in plans during the New Deal. In its last years it focused on the novel conception of American government that grew out of World War II.

Much of the NRPB's work consisted of producing detailed, statistics-filled, dreary reports on the state of the economy and on what might be done about it. Taken as a whole, these reports ran to over 43,000 pages. Those who have spent some time with them (I confess that I am one) would have guessed that they are much longer than that. With the onset of the war in Europe, the NRPB became involved in what it called "post-defense planning." Frederic Delano, Roosevelt's uncle, ran the board from its inception. Luther Gulick, an exceptionally able adviser to Roosevelt, was hired as a consultant in 1941. Between 1941 and 1943, the NRPB produced and sent detailed reports to countless groups throughout the country.

The idea of adding to the bill of rights first emerged in a meeting in August 1939. With the New Deal on hold and the fascist threat looming, Delano "suggested to President Roosevelt the idea of expanding the Bill of Rights from the political to the social arena, to enumerate educational opportunity, health and medical care, decent shelter, the right to work, and economic security." Delano elaborated on that idea in a memorandum written for the president in the summer of 1940. Shortly after the four freedoms speech, the National Public Resources Board began serious work on producing a second bill of rights. Gulick was the director of the project. On June 29, 1941, an economic bill of rights was specifically proposed to Roosevelt by NRPB advisers in Hyde Park; Roosevelt approved of the idea and asked for a revision. Their list, released to Congress in March 1943, took the following form:

1. The right to work, usefully and creatively through the productive years;
2. The right to fair play, adequate to command the necessities and amenities of life in exchange for work, ideas, thrift, and other socially valuable service;
3. The right to adequate food, clothing, shelter, and medical care;
4. The right to security, with freedom from fear of old age, want, dependency, sickness, unemployment, and accident;
5. The right to live in a system of free enterprise, free from compulsory labor, irresponsible state power, arbitrary public authority, and unregulated monopolies;

6. The right to come and go, to speak or to be silent, free from the spyings of secret political police;
7. The right to equality before the law, with equal access to justice in fact;
8. The right to education, for work, for citizenship, and for personal growth and happiness; and
9. The right to rest, recreation, and adventure, the opportunity to enjoy life and take part in advancing civilization.

This was the beginning of an extraordinary, detailed report of more than 100,000 words. The NRPB proposed a number of steps to protect these rights, including a national health and education program, a broadened system of social security, strengthened protections against monopoly, and a permanent policy for large-scale public works. In the words of historian Patrick Reagan, this ambitious document was a direct challenge to "the belief system of fascist and communist ideologies in a way that no previous planning document had quite captured," producing "an expansive vision of a postwar America freed from the wreckage of the Great Depression, inspired by the possibilities of economic abundance, distrustful of centralized state power, and imbued with the American ideals of individualism."

The NRPB proposals were not popular with Congress, to put it mildly. A skeptical legislature, focused on the war rather than domestic planning, had lost all interest in the board's activities. The NRPB was killed by an appropriations bill just three months after issuing this report. Nonetheless, Roosevelt was greatly influenced by the first draft of this document, and it played a part in the Atlantic Charter.

The governing ideas played a role in later correspondence in 1943. On December 14, Louis Brownlow, an occasional adviser, wrote Roosevelt with a "plea," urging that "as soon as you can—perhaps in your annual message to the Congress—you sound the bugle call again for our domestic agenda." Brownlow suggested that it was time for Roosevelt to "say that when we have won the war we have won it for all the people of our home land . . . that the way back to peace and prosperity is to realize the four freedoms through the five fundamentals of the right to work, the duty of production, fairness of distribution, equal access to education and the enjoyment of personal security." What was "needed and needed now," wrote Brownlow, was something that would "rekindle the flame of hope in the common man." On December 29, Roosevelt wrote back, agreeing "that it is a good idea to sound a note such as you suggest," and that "even now we must look ahead and lay plans for the kind of America we want to see after the peace has been made."

In the same period, Chester Bowles, director of the Office of Price Administration, sent Samuel Rosenman a memorandum discussing a "second bill of rights" and urging that Roosevelt "reannounce his liberal program and his determination to push it as soon as the exigencies of war permitted." During discussions of the annual message for 1943, Rosenman showed the Bowles memorandum and the National Resources Planning Board's catalog of rights to Roosevelt himself, who insisted that the topic should be covered in his message. Hence the second bill of rights speech was born—and with it a set of ideas that have influenced constitutions and human rights documents throughout the world.

THE SECOND BILL IN CHICAGO

The second bill of rights made an additional public appearance on October 28, 1944. On a blustery day in Chicago, Roosevelt delivered the most spirited address of his last campaign. He began with characteristic Rooseveltian irony, announcing that though he was a veteran campaigner, "this is the strangest campaign I have ever seen":

> I have listened to the various Republican orators who are urging the people to throw the present Administration out and put them in. And what do they say?
>
> Well, they say in effect, just this:
>
> "Those incompetent blunderers and bunglers in Washington have passed a lot of excellent laws about social security and

labor and farm relief and soil conservation—and many others—and we promise that if elected we will not change any of
them."

And they go—on to say, "Those same quarrelsome, tired old
men—they have built the greatest military machine the world
has ever known, which is fighting its way to victory; and," they
say, "if you elect us, we promise not to change any of that,
either."

"Therefore," say these Republican orators, "it is time for a
change."

Tonight I want to talk simply to you about the future of
America—about this land of ours, this land of unlimited opportunity. I shall give the Republican campaign orators some more
opportunities to say—"me too."

To that end he stressed the need for an aggressive effort to address
the problems of peace, one no less bold than those addressing the
problems of war. Recalling his State of the Union address, he listed,
one by one, the items on the second bill of rights. He acknowledged
the presence of skepticism, noting that some "have sneered at these
ideals, characterizing them as the unattainable dreams of starry-eyed
New Dealers." But in his view, the American public "agrees with these
principles" and is "determined to get them." He urged a massive ex-
pansion of the nation's productive capacity that would result in tens
of millions of new jobs. He argued for tax incentives and an expan-
sion of foreign trade to help "assure the full realization of the right to
a useful and remunerative employment."

More than ever before, he stressed that the new bill of rights should
be "applied to all our citizens, irrespective or race, or creed, or color."
He urged that Congress should create a permanent Fair Employment
Practice Committee to prevent discrimination. He reiterated his commitment to free enterprise and the profit system—and contended that
they were capable of giving "full employment to our people." This
would be possible because "America has always been a land of action—
a land of adventurous pioneering—a land of growing and building."

With respect to the cause of security and providing decent standards of living for all, he urged that "we are going forward together."

Less than six months later, Roosevelt completed a draft of his final speech, the Jefferson Day address, which he wrote largely in his own hand. "The only limit to our realization of tomorrow," he concluded, "will be our doubts of today. Let us move forward with strong and active faith." He was dead the next day.

FREEDOM AND SECURITY

"Necessitous men are not free men," Roosevelt said. What does this mean? The answer depends on our conception of freedom. Consider the old understanding, rooted in the republican tradition and familiar to the framers of the American Constitution, that freedom requires self-government. If we accept this understanding of freedom, necessitous men are not free in the particular sense that they are incapable of self-governance. They lack the independence—the security—that self-governance requires. Citizens who do not have a decent minimum cannot participate in politics; those without security cannot easily be citizens at all. Hence the idea that only property owners can truly be citizens. It would not be difficult to defend some parts of the second bill in exactly these terms, seeing the right to a decent minimum as akin to, even as a part of, the right to private property itself. If liberty includes freedom from desperate conditions, it might be because that form of freedom is indispensable for citizenship. In the aftermath of the Civil War, many people argued that the newly freed slaves should be provided with "forty acres and a mule" precisely in the interest of ensuring the material preconditions of citizenship.

But citizenship is not what Roosevelt tended to emphasize; he stressed the need for security as such. Roosevelt meant to make a plea for social protection in the event that certain risks come to fruition—and to see that protection as a form of liberty. In an uncharacteristically sweeping suggestion, Roosevelt said that security "means a kind of feeling within our individual selves that we have lacked through all the course of history." For all of that history, human beings have had to take their chances in multiple domains. "I have believed for a great many years that the time has come in our civilization when a great many of these chances should be eliminated from our lives." The elimination of those chances, Roosevelt thought, amounted to a form of freedom. Of course his thinking on this count was a direct outgrowth of the nation's experience with the Depression. To Roosevelt, human distress could no longer be taken as an inevitable by-product of life, society, or "nature"; it was an artifact of social policies and choices. Much human misery is preventable. The only question is whether a government is determined to prevent it. Hence the words of his secretary of Labor, Frances Perkins: "Foremost was the idea that poverty is preventable, that poverty is destructive, wasteful, demoralizing, and that poverty is morally unacceptable in a Christian and democratic society." Roosevelt's emphasis on security, and security as a form of freedom, must be understood in this light.

Is it too speculative to connect Roosevelt's thoughts to his own biography? He was, after all, a child of great privilege, a high-spirited, active, dashing, perhaps superficial golden boy who encountered no obvious hardship until stricken with polio at the height of his powers. We can only guess about the personal devastation this event must have caused. At the age of thirty-nine, while on vacation, Roosevelt took a swim in a local lake with two of his sons. He jogged home and soon went to bed, having felt a chill. The next day he was sick with a fever and serious pain. A local doctor concluded that he had a cold, but after two weeks of confusion and uncertainty, polio was diagnosed. Roosevelt experienced paralysis in his back and arms and suffered agonizing pain. He also fell into an acute depression. After a month he was moved to a hospital in New York, where Dr. George Draper, his physician there, found a distressing and essentially hopeless situation: Roosevelt was unable to sit up, could not move his feet, and showed only slight movement in his toes. Dr. Draper wrote: "He has such courage, such ambition, and yet at the same time such an extraordinarily sensitive emotional mechanism that it will take all the skill that we can muster to lead him successfully to a recognition of what he really faces without crushing him."

Dr. Draper's reference to an "extraordinarily sensitive emotional mechanism," one in danger of being "crushed," is the anomaly and I believe the revelation here. Whatever those who knew Roosevelt said about him, they did not think he was extraordinarily sensitive, at least not about himself. They certainly did not consider him fragile—quite the reverse. Roosevelt continued to suffer severe pain for a long period. "The parts of his body that were mainly affected remained inflamed for months, and the inflammation and the inevitable muscular adjustments and distortions at first made even bedbound passivity near-torture for him." But after the short period of depression, Roosevelt regained his optimism, even to an unrealistic degree. He repeatedly stated that he would recover entirely—apparently believing that he would eventually walk again. For seven years, he searched unsuccessfully for a cure. For years after that, he refused to admit that he was permanently handicapped.

It is generally agreed that polio transformed and deepened Roosevelt. Having known him before and after his illness, Frances Perkins "was instantly struck by his growth. He was young, he was crippled, he was physically weak, but he had a firmer grip on life and on himself than ever before. He was serious, not playing now." Roosevelt's uncle Frederic Delano, so important to the second bill, wrote, "His severest test was the 'Polio,' and to my mind that is what really made him what he is—a twice-born man.'" His valet reported that "when he was sick, he didn't say a murmuring word. . . . He complained as little as any man I ever saw. . . . He could throw off anything." But the trauma and the lifelong handicap could not have left him unmarked. It must have alerted him, years before the Depression, to the omnipresence of human vulnerability—to the pervasive possibility of disaster that no one can control. For the rest of his life, Roosevelt "remained the physical prisoner of his still-paralyzed legs . . . needing assistance from others at every turn, . . . and in general immobilized by his disease once he had made the great effort to arrange himself in any new environment until the time came for another move, when he would need help again. . . ."

And yet Roosevelt achieved great mastery over his situation. His own fearlessness and his sense of security and serenity were clear to all; they were among his most defining characteristics. He himself linked his serenity to his illness: "If you had spent two years in bed trying to wiggle your big toe, after that anything else would seem easy!" He made a joke out of his plight: Amused by stories, he would exclaim, "Really, it's as funny as a crutch!" Nor was he embarrassed by his physical condition. According to Francis Biddle, his attorney general, Roosevelt "had more serenity than any man I have ever seen. One felt that nothing ultimately would upset him." Eleanor Roosevelt said, "In all the years of my husband's public life, I never once heard him make a remark which indicated that any crisis could not be solved." After the attack on Pearl Harbor, she said that "he was completely calm. His reaction to any event was always to be calm."

In a wonderful essay, the philosopher Isaiah Berlin laid principal emphasis on Roosevelt's contagious sense of optimism and hopefulness, describing him as the only statesman in the world on whom "no cloud rested," and "one of the few statesmen of the twentieth or any other century who seemed to have no fear at all of the future." In Berlin's account, "Roosevelt stands out principally by his astonishing appetite for life and by his apparently complete freedom from fear of the future; as a man who welcomes the future eagerly as such, and conveyed the feeling that whatever the times might bring, all would be grist to his mill, nothing would be too formidable or crushing to be subdued and used and moulded into the building of which he, Roosevelt, and his allies and devoted subordinates would throw themselves with unheard-of energy and gusto." In this respect, Roosevelt seems to me to have been the most characteristically American of American presidents—not only our most magnificent leader, but also the leader who most typified the nation's spirit. (Roosevelt's cloudlessness put him at the opposite pole from his greatest predecessor, the melancholy Abraham Lincoln.)

But this sense of mastery, this unheard-of energy and gusto, this apparently complete freedom from fear could not have been easily won. There must have been something beneath it. Roosevelt's sudden physical vulnerability must have produced a form of terror. There was surely a link between that vulnerability, his own repeated emphasis on freedom from fear, and Berlin's suggestion that what Roosevelt "could not abide was, before all, passivity, stillness, melancholy, fear of life or preoccupation with eternity or death, however great the insight or delicate the sensibility by which they were accompanied." What had happened to Roosevelt was almost certainly part of his intense sense of connection with people in the most difficult circumstances. Perkins wrote that after the onset of his illness, Roosevelt "had become conscious of other people, of weak people, of human frailty." Consider, as a case in point, his underpublicized but lifelong relationships with victims of paralysis at Warm Springs, Georgia, where many people, including Roosevelt himself, hoped to be strengthened by swimming in the local waters: "He was one of them— he was a big brother—he had been through it—he was smiling—he was courageous—he was feeling fine—he encouraged you to try—he said you could do it." During World War II, Roosevelt made special efforts to visit hospitals and attend to soldiers who were permanently handicapped: "Even in the last year of his life, when the strain was beginning to show, he continued to visit the hospital wards. There is no question that his hearty, 'You'll make it, brother' helped to keep up the morale of these men."

This sense of fraternity with those in the most difficult circumstances surfaced in many of his remarks. Here is a representative statement:

I am getting sick and tired of these people on the WPA and local relief rolls being called chiselers and cheats. . . . These people . . . are just like the rest of us. They don't drink any more than the rest of us, they don't lie any more, they're no lazier than the rest of us—they're pretty much a cross-section of the American people. . . . I have never believed that with our capitalistic system people have to be poor. I think it is an outrage that we should permit hundreds and hundreds of thousands of people to be ill clad, to live in miserable homes, not to have enough to eat; not be to able to send their children to school for the only reason that they are poor.

Note that Roosevelt was explicitly dismissing any claims about the essentially different nature of those who are poor and about the inevitability of economic distress. If people are poor, it is not because they "have" to be; it is because "we," the nation, are permitting it to happen. Here the states of poverty and deprivation are denaturalized; they are seen as a product of conscious social choices.

The second bill of rights was a direct outgrowth of this understanding. It attempted to provide security in the face of a wide range of social risks—and to see that security as a basic right, a condition of freedom.

PART II

AMERICA

5

A Puzzle and an Overview

IN CHAPTER 4 I distinguished between constitutional rights and constitutive commitments, and I emphasized that Roosevelt saw the second bill as the latter rather than the former. He did not argue for constitutional change, and the second bill did not become part of the American Constitution through amendment or interpretation. (I will qualify this too simple statement shortly; let us take it as mostly true for now.) It is more difficult to say whether the second bill has become part of the nation's constitutive commitments. Very plausibly, the right to a good education has attained that status. No public official at the federal, state, or local level could reject that right as a matter of principle. Still, many American children do not receive a good education, and so it is unclear whether the right exists in practice. A right that does not exist in practice might be said not to exist at all, but we should be cautious about this claim. The right to be free from unreasonable searches and seizures, though often violated in the real world, is guaranteed by the Constitution. It matters, a lot, that the right is recognized as such. It is fair to say that the right to a good education has achieved constitutive status in America today.

I have suggested that the right to social security, an important part of the second bill, has also attained that status. In the American culture, the social security system is far more than a mere policy, revocable with changing political winds. It would take a fundamental cultural change for social security to seem less than a basic right. So too, I believe, for the right to be free from monopoly. The basic legal prohibitions on monopoly and monopolistic practices are extremely well entrenched, and no one can seriously argue for their repeal. Of course this is more complicated terrain. Many reasonable people complain that certain companies have actual monopolies or near monopolies, and that the law is not being brought to bear against them. (Continuing debates in the area of communications, where some companies own numerous outlets, are a case in point.) In principle, however, the prohibition on monopoly falls in the category of constitutive commitments. But it is hard to say the same for all of the second bill. Does the American public believe in a right to a decent and remunerative job? This is far from clear.

I will return to the issue of constitutive commitments in Part III. My topic here is the Constitution itself—the meaning of America's founding document. I want to ask why, as a matter of fact, the second bill has no place in it.

RIGHTS AROUND THE WORLD: A BRIEF TOUR

The puzzle is heightened by the fact that the international community has reached a firm consensus in favor of the second bill of rights. Consider the Universal Declaration of Human Rights, which protects a wide range of such rights, adopted by the General Assembly of the United Nations on December 10, 1948. The Universal Declaration has been accepted by most nations in the world, including the United States. In fact the Universal Declaration was produced under the leadership of Eleanor Roosevelt, who was directly influenced by the American experience during the Great Depression and the New Deal. Her husband's four freedoms speech and his proposal for the second bill played a crucial role in determining the contents of the Universal Declaration. Indeed, President Roosevelt's speeches put the United States on record in favor of social and economic rights in a way that made American support for them almost inevitable. More than any other document, the Universal Declaration reflects an international agreement about the rights that people have. And it provides a dramatic contrast to the American Constitution.

The Universal Declaration proclaims that "everyone" has a "right to a standard of living adequate for the health and well-being of himself and his family, including food, clothing, housing and medical care and necessary social services, and the right to security in the event of unemployment, sickness, disability, widowhood, old age or other lack of livelihood in circumstances beyond his control." The declaration also provides a right to education and social security. It proclaims that everyone "has a right to work, to free choice of employment, to just and favourable conditions of work and to protection against unemployment." It recognizes a "right to equal pay for equal work," a right "to form and to join trade unions for protection," and a right to "just and favourable remuneration ensuring for himself and his family an existence worthy of human dignity, and supplemented, if necessary, by other means of social protection."

What is the relationship between these rights and the more familiar civil and political rights? The history is illuminating. The authors of the Universal Declaration insisted that political and economic rights were an integrated whole. In 1950 the General Assembly of the United Nations agreed, proclaiming all categories of human rights "interdependent." The General Assembly asked the United Nations Commission on Human Rights to adopt a single convention—a document that would go beyond the declaration to impose enforceable duties on the nations that chose to ratify it. But in the next year, the commission decided instead to split the Universal Declaration into two independent international covenants, one dealing with civil and political rights, the other with economic, social, and cultural rights.

The International Covenant on Civil and Political Rights has now been ratified by 147 nations, the overwhelming majority of countries in the world. The International Covenant on Economic, Social, and Cultural Rights has been ratified by all but five of those nations: Botswana, Haiti, Mozambique, South Africa, and the United States. The latter covenant essentially follows the Universal Declaration but goes beyond it by attempting to turn the recognition of social and economic rights into binding commitments. Notably, it recognizes the dependence of these rights on available resources. "Each State Party to the present Covenant undertakes to take steps . . . to the maximum of its available resources, with a view to achieving progressively the full realization of the rights recognized in the present Covenant by all appropriate means, including particularly the adoption of legislative measures." The covenant is to be enforced not by courts but through reports and public monitoring.

To the same general effect, consider the European Social Charter, a treaty now in force in the Council of Europe, signed by twenty-four member states, including such diverse nations as Austria, Cyprus, Denmark, Finland, France, Germany, Hungary, Iceland, Norway, Poland, Spain, Sweden, Turkey, and the United Kingdom. The charter protects the right to work, the right to fair remuneration, the right to protection of health, the right to social security, the right to social and medical assistance, and the right to benefit from social welfare services. As with the International Covenant on Economic, Social, and Cultural Rights, enforcement occurs through the submission of periodic reports. In the 1990s, a number of efforts were made to increase the likelihood of effective enforcement. According to the European Committee on Social Rights, which is entrusted with monitoring compliance, nations are obliged to provide domestic remedies for violations, at least for some of the guaranteed rights.

Recognition of the second bill goes well beyond declarations, covenants, and treaties. All over the globe, modern constitutions follow the Universal Declaration in creating social and economic rights, sometimes using its precise words. They guarantee citizens a wide range of social entitlements. Of course this was also true for the Soviet constitution. Socialist and communist nations often insisted on the importance of social and economic guarantees even while objecting to (and failing miserably on) political rights. But many noncommunist and postcommunist constitutions include economic rights as well. The current constitution of Finland says that "everyone shall be guaranteed by an Act the right to basic subsistence in the event of unemployment, illness, and disability and during old age as well as the birth of a child or the loss of a provider." The constitution of Norway imposes on the state the responsibility "to create conditions enabling every person capable of work to earn a living by his work." The constitution of Spain says, "To citizens in old age, the public authorities shall guarantee economic sufficiency through adequate and periodically updated pensions." Similarly, the constitutions of Ukraine, Romania, Syria, Bulgaria, Hungary, Russia, and Peru (to name a few) recognize some or all of the economic rights cataloged by Franklin Roosevelt.

Other nations take a different approach. They recognize social and economic guarantees as goals but not legally enforceable rights. India offers a range of civil and political rights and separately offers "directive principles of state policy," saying that the state shall "direct its policy towards securing" an adequate means of livelihood, equal pay for equal work for both men and women, and other rights. The constitution of Switzerland says that "the Confederation and the cantons seek to ensure" certain rights involving social security, necessary health care, and more. This strategy is taken as well in Ireland, Nigeria, and Papua New Guinea. This approach promises to do some good and little harm. It helps create a cultural expectation about what government ought to do—which can have real effects on human lives. If a constitution recognizes a right to a good education or a right to health care, then the government comes under serious pressure to legislate in a way that respects those rights. To be sure, the absence of judicial enforcement creates some risks. It increases the possibility that the second bill will be mere words without any meaning in the real world.

For this reason it might be preferable to adopt the distinctive South African approach. Following the International Covenant on Economic, Social, and Cultural Rights, the South African constitution recognizes a wide range of social and economic rights but also acknowledges that the government has limited resources and cannot respond to all problems at once. Hence the South African constitution obliges the state, in most of the relevant provisions, to "take reasonable legislative and other measures, within its available resources, to achieve the progressive realisation of" the relevant right. Most of the provisions of the second bill must be protected within the limits of available resources, but not absolutely. Though ambiguous, provisions of this kind have sometimes been held to be enforceable by national courts, obliging governments to fulfill certain obligations. This approach allows for a degree of judicial enforcement in a way that respects the fact that nations, particularly poor ones, cannot do all that should be done.

How should a nation choose between the two approaches? There is no simple answer. The advantage of the Indian approach is that it minimizes the difficulties produced by judicial entanglement with questions of priority setting. The disadvantage is that it decreases the likelihood that the second bill will have real-world effects. Note in this regard that communist constitutions were filled with strong guarantees of individual rights—political, civil, social, and economic. These guarantees meant nothing in the real world, partly because of the absence of judicial enforcement. Advocates for the "directive principles" approach might hope that such principles will ensure that social and economic rights are taken seriously; when those rights have constitutional status, elected officials might see them as real obligations. But there is a pervasive risk that societies, even democratic ones, will be inattentive to the needs of their most vulnerable members. One study finds, for example, that in Australia, indirect forms of protection, relying solely on political processes, are quite inadequate to ensure compliance with the International Covenant on Economic, Social, and Cultural Rights, which is technically binding on the Australian government. When courts are involved, it is more likely that the relevant rights will receive respect. The disadvantage is that judicial involvement might displace reasonable legislative judgments about sensible priority setting. I will return to these issues in Part III.

Is there a pattern to the world's constitutions? Are social and economic rights connected to socialism? To a left-wing influence? The answers are not clear. A careful study of sixty-four constitutions finds that forty-seven offer a right to social security. Fifty-one provide the right to education. Nearly half provide a right to housing and health care. The strongest commitments to economic rights are found in Portugal, Brazil, Poland, Finland, Uruguay, and Paraguay. The weakest commitments belong to Austria, New Zealand, Singapore, Trinidad—and the United States. Nations with an English common law background are far less likely to contain social and economic rights than those with a French civil law background. Notably, the commitment to such rights tends to be higher in democratic nations. Newer constitutions are only slightly more likely to contain social and economic rights, and the difference is not statistically significant.

A Puzzle

Now let us turn to the particular puzzle. The constitutions of many nations, with diverse backgrounds, create social and economic rights, whether or not they are enforceable. But the American Constitution does nothing of the kind. Why? What makes it so distinctive in this regard? I am not asking whether the American Constitution *should* include any or all of the second bill; I am asking why it actually doesn't. In exploring that question and considering four possible answers, I hope to cast some light on rights in general, the effects of constitutions, American culture, and the second bill in particular.

The first and most obvious explanation is chronological. The American Constitution is the oldest in force in the world. The very oldest constitutions lack social and economic guarantees, which are largely a creation of the twentieth century. We shall see that this explanation is helpful, but that it does not nearly tell us all that we need to know. For those who emphasize chronology, the most serious problem is that the American Constitution is not frozen in time. It explicitly provides for its own amendment. But more fundamentally, the Constitution is not frozen because its meaning changes through interpretation. In one sense it is old, but its meaning is a product of contemporary understandings of its terms. The key question—unanswered by the chronological explanation—is why the existing document has not been interpreted to include social and economic guarantees.

The second explanation is the most ambitious. It proposes that something in American culture is especially hostile to social and economic rights. Perhaps America has a distinctly libertarian or individualist culture that prizes the right to be free from government intrusion. The citizens of such a culture might well provide private charity, perhaps a great deal of it. But their government will not provide food, housing, and clothing as a matter of right. The cultural explanation is closely associated with what is sometimes called *American exceptionalism:* the absence of a significant socialist or even a social democratic movement in the United States.

American culture is indeed distinctive, and in some ways it purports to be hostile to government intervention, at least of a certain sort. The distinctiveness of American culture does help to explain the absence of the second bill from current constitutional understandings. But it is far too simple to explain the absence of social and economic rights on this ground. For one thing, the cultural explanation fails to mention an important variable: race. When Roosevelt spoke, the second bill did not raise racial issues even implicitly. In past decades, any effort to give special attention to those in economic distress has been seen in racial terms, which greatly complicates matters. My central point is that the cultural explanation is inadequate even if it emphasizes racial questions. The reason is that *an essentially individualistic culture, one that is firmly committed to capitalist institutions, can also accept the second bill of rights, and do so in the name of individualism itself.* This, in fact, was one of Roosevelt's principal claims. The very idea of a second bill arose from the American experience in the early decades of the twentieth century. For this very reason, it is hard to argue that the second bill is fatally inconsistent with American culture. As we shall see, in the 1960s the Supreme Court came close to interpreting the Constitution to recognize social and economic rights—a development that complicates the view that American culture repudiates such rights.

The third explanation begins with the fact that the American Constitution is enforced by courts. Some nations regard constitutions as a place for setting out general goals and aspirations—symbols not meant for real-world implementation. But in America, rights are not mere aspirations. Citizens are entitled to expect that independent judges will ensure that the government respects those rights in practice. If we emphasize this point, we might conclude that the American Constitution does not recognize social and economic rights for one simple (as well as good) reason: Judges cannot enforce those rights. Inevitably the second bill would become a set of goals rather than rights. When other nations place all or part of the second bill in their constitutions, it is because they believe that their founding document need not be limited to provisions with real meaning in the world.

This point reveals something true and important about the nature of American constitutionalism, but it does not adequately explain the absence of social and economic rights. For one thing, it is much too complicated, even subtle. It might *justify* a decision not to include social and economic rights in a constitution; reasonable people might conclude that because such rights are difficult for courts to enforce, they should not be included. But this argument does not *explain* why the American Constitution does not contain such rights. For another thing, courts can in fact enforce social and economic rights, at least to a degree. As we shall see, some nations that protect the second bill of rights also have judicial review—and in some cases, courts have acted aggressively to protect people from the worst kinds of deprivation.

This very possibility underlies the fourth explanation, which emphasizes some remarkable twists and turns in American constitutional law in the 1960s and 1970s. For a short period, the Supreme Court was increasingly receptive to the idea that the existing Constitution protects at least part of the second bill of rights. Interpreting the Constitution's equal protection and due process clauses, the Court ruled that government could not discriminate against the poor. In some pathbreaking decisions, the Court went much further. It held that the government was under an affirmative duty to give resources to poor people so as to enable them both to vote and to litigate. In a key decision, sometimes called the *Finnegan's Wake* of constitutional law, the Court invalidated California's effort to impose a six-month residency requirement on people seeking welfare payments. Building on the Court's decisions, prominent academic commentators insisted that the Court should find a constitutional right to minimum welfare guarantees. In the late 1960s, it would not have been foolish to predict that the Court would eventually do just that.

What stopped this development? The answer lies in the 1968 election, as Richard M. Nixon narrowly defeated Hubert Humphrey. Nixon won with 43.6 percent of the popular vote to Humphrey's 42.6 percent. President Nixon appointed four justices who promptly reversed the emerging trend, insisting that the Constitution does not include social and economic guarantees. Hence the Court's small steps toward recognizing such guarantees have become a historical footnote. The irony is that with a relatively small shift in the presidential vote, the American Constitution might well have been understood to create a wide range of social and economic rights.

The fourth explanation accounts for a great deal of the current situation. As a practical matter, the Constitution means what the Supreme Court says that it means. With a modest shift in personnel, the Constitution would have been understood to create social and economic rights of the sort recognized in many modern constitutions. This conclusion suggests that there is nothing inevitable in the current situation. With modest shifts in the future, parts of the second bill of rights could well be included in our constitutional understandings, and certainly in the nation's constitutive commitments, which is where they belong.

6

The Oldest
Constitution on Earth

Whenever there is in any country, uncultivated lands and
unemployed poor, it is clear that the laws of property have
been so far extended as to violate natural right. The earth is
given as a common stock for man to labor and live on.

Thomas Jefferson

I F WE ARE TRYING to explain the absence of social and
economic guarantees from the American Constitution, the most
tempting answer is chronological. The United States has the oldest constitution in the world still in force. It was ratified during the late
eighteenth century, a time when constitutions were not thought to
include such guarantees. The framers built on rights as they were
understood in the British tradition. In addition, they were responding
to the particular problems that they experienced under British rule
and the Articles of Confederation. No one suggested that the bill of
rights should contain social guarantees of this kind. There is a weak
relationship, worldwide, between the age of a constitution and the
inclusion of social and economic rights. But constitutions written before 1900 are highly unlikely to contain anything like the second bill.

The absence of social and economic rights from the American
Constitution might thus be simply a matter of timing. When modern

constitutions were drawn up, the international understanding was altogether different, and thus social and economic rights are found in the constitutions of, for example, Bulgaria, South Africa, Norway, and Russia. The American Constitution lacks the second bill of rights because the concept of economic rights did not exist at the time of its framing, at least not as a constitutional possibility.

JAMES MADISON'S CONVERSION

At its inception, the Constitution did not include a bill of rights. The Constitution's structure—its system of checks and balances—was supposed to be sufficient. When the Constitution was first proposed, Alexander Hamilton argued that there was no need for a separate bill: "The truth is, after all the declamations we have heard, that the Constitution itself is, in every rational sense, and to every useful purpose, A BILL OF RIGHTS." Hamilton firmly believed in rights, but he insisted that they would be adequately guaranteed by the structure of government itself. The system of separation of powers—between branches of the federal government and between the federal government and the states—would ensure that excesses would be firmly controlled. Liberty would be guaranteed by the ability of each part to restrain the rest.

The idea of a bill of rights was not pressed by the founders but by their anti-Federalist adversaries, who opposed the proposed Constitution and feared the national government that it created. The anti-Federalists thought that this remote government needed to be limited through an explicit system of rights. For a time, James Madison, one of the most influential of the founders, agreed with Hamilton that a separate bill of rights would be unnecessary and even counterproductive. After extended deliberation, however, the original advocates of the Constitution, above all Madison, came to believe that the anti-Federalists were correct. Madison's arguments are worth close attention because they help illuminate constitutions both old and new.

In an important letter to Thomas Jefferson on October 17, 1788, Madison wrote, "What use, then, . . . can a bill of rights serve in popular Governments?" He offered two answers. The first was that the "political truths declared in that solemn manner acquire by degrees the character of fundamental maxims of free Government, and as they become incorporated with the National sentiment, counteract the impulses of interest and passion." A bill of rights, in other words, would become a part of a nation's culture—its own self-understanding—in a way that would provide protection against the harms caused by Madison's two great fears, "interest" and "passion." If self-interested or passionate majorities sought to intrude on rights, a culture that valued its bill of rights would be able to rely on these "fundamental maxims" as a safeguard. Madison was astonishingly prescient in this regard. The bill of rights has indeed become part of America's "National sentiment," in a way that provides exactly the protection he sought—not all, but much of the time. (Roosevelt's plea for a second bill should be understood in similar terms.)

Madison's second answer involved the risk of oppression from government itself. In the face of this risk, "a bill of rights will be a good ground for an appeal to the sense of the community." Thus Madison argued that "the community" would be emboldened by a bill of rights to attempt to counteract governmental oppression. The American Revolution, after all, reflected a shift in the understanding of sovereignty, which no longer reposed in a monarch but now resided in We the People. Madison argued that with a bill of rights, the public would be better equipped to resist government tyranny. In this way, the bill would have an educational function. Three years later Madison wrote in exactly the same vein: "In proportion as Government is influenced by opinion, must it be so by whatever influences opinion. This decides the question concerning a bill of rights, which acquires efficacy as time sanctifies and incorporates it with public sentiment." Madison spoke not in terms of judicial protection but of protection through "public sentiment" influenced by a bill of rights. In emphasizing public sentiment, Madison offered a distinctive position, separate, for example, from that of Thomas Jefferson, who emphasized the protection that would come from courts. Thus Stanford historian Jack Rakove writes that "Madison placed his greatest hopes for the Bill of Rights in its educative value."

CITIZENS AND THE ORIGINAL BILL: AN OVERVIEW

What is the original bill of rights about? Does it have a unifying theme? The framers were concerned above all to guarantee the preconditions for genuine self-government. They were attempting to ensure popular sovereignty. We will fail to understand the first bill of rights if we see it as based on opposition to government or as a kind of laissez-faire individualism. We do better to see the first bill as an effort to protect *citizenship*. If we are looking for a unifying theme for the first bill, this is it.

For example, the First Amendment guarantees several rights that are indispensable to self-governance: freedom of speech and freedom of the press, the right of peaceful assembly, the right to petition the government for the redress of grievances. These are the quintessential political rights, ensuring that the citizens control the government rather than the other way around. In fact they have an important majoritarian feature. The right of the people, as a collectivity, is expressly recognized in the assembly and petition clauses. The First Amendment also bans Congress from enacting any "law respecting an establishment of religion, or prohibiting the free exercise thereof." Thus it creates the two components of the American right to freedom of religion: protection against an official church (the establishment clause) and protection against government interference in religious practices (the free exercise clause). These are individual rights, to be sure, but they also protect self-government itself. A democracy that becomes entangled with religion and religious disputes is unlikely to be able to maintain itself—a point to which the framers were closely attuned. In a diverse society, the separation of church and state protects government as much as it protects religion.

The Second Amendment, safeguarding the right to keep and bear arms, can be understood in similar terms. This too is a political right, understood as pivotal to republican government. Its central goal is to protect against an overbearing national government. Consider the opening words: "A well-regulated Militia, being necessary to the security of a free State . . " At a minimum, the Second Amendment prevents the federal government from outlawing state militias, and clearly the framers understood state militias as performing an important democratic function. Militias provided a kind of training ground for the cultivation of republican virtue; they also placed a constraint on a potentially tyrannical federal government. Thus there has long been a connection between the right to bear arms and popular sovereignty, a connection that the American Revolution served to underline. In the twentieth century, many people have argued that the Second Amendment creates an individual right to bear arms for self-defense. This view is probably incorrect, and the Supreme Court has not accepted it. But even if it is ultimately convincing, the central goal of the Second Amendment was to create a kind of political right ensuring that people would be citizens rather than subjects.

The right to a jury trial, protected by the Sixth and Seventh Amendments, is another example. This right is usually thought of as an effort to safeguard those accused of crime against the government, and indeed it does provide a large measure of individual protection. But its goal is also to ensure citizenship. One of the functions of the jury trial right is to ensure an active role for citizens in the administration of both civil and criminal justice. Jury trials give a continuing place to ordinary people in designing the content of law—especially when the stakes are very high. Thus a system with juries allows people to serve, in a limited but important sense, as lawmakers. Many early enthusiasts for the jury system spoke in these terms, treating the jury as a kind of democratic branch of judicial power. If government has enacted an unfair or oppressive law, jurors might well refuse to punish people for violating it. At least they can moderate its harsh edges, by finding people innocent in close cases. Service as a juror also serves an important educative function. It gives people a sense of what their government is all about. This form of education might well have continuing effects in a democratic culture.

Understanding the original bill of rights in terms of citizenship gives us a new perspective on what seems to be the quintessential protection of individual rights: the constitutional protection of private property. Under the Fifth Amendment, private property cannot "be taken for public use, without just compensation." By protecting people's holdings against government, the Fifth Amendment does indeed create a sphere of individual control. But we can also see the Fifth Amendment as way to protect the independence that citizens require. The republican tradition posits a close connection between citizenship and the right to property. If government cannot take your property without paying you its fair value, you are to some extent free from its control, and you can do and say as you wish with less fear of reprisal. Because of this effect, property rights can be seen as a necessary precondition for the status of citizenship. Personal security and personal independence from the government are guaranteed in a system in which rights of ownership are protected through public institutions.

When private property does not exist, citizens are dependent on the goodwill of government officials, on an almost daily basis. Whatever citizens have is a privilege and not a right. They come to the state as supplicants or beggars rather than as right holders. Anyone who challenges the state may be stifled or driven underground if the goods that give people basic security can be withdrawn. A right to private property, free from government interference, is in this sense a necessary or at least helpful foundation for a democracy.

Many provisions of the bill of rights are designed to protect citizens from abuse of the system of criminal justice. It is entirely right to see these provisions as an effort to guard against an overreaching government. People are entitled to be secure in their "persons, houses, papers, and effects," through protection against unreasonable searches and seizures. Government is not permitted to issue general warrants for the invasion of homes; if it wants a warrant, it is required to give specifics. People cannot be compelled to testify against themselves. They have a right to the assistance of counsel. They must be given a trial that is both speedy and public. The government is forbidden to impose excessive bail, excessive fines, and cruel and unusual punishments. These provisions do indeed protect individual rights. But like the right to private property, they also safeguard the preconditions of citizenship. People cannot exercise the independence that citizenship requires if they are entirely vulnerable to the power of the state, and these safeguards are indispensable to that independence.

The general point is straightforward. We are used to thinking of the original bill of rights solely as a way of protecting the individual against the government—by creating a sphere of private liberty, immune from collective control. But this is a thoroughly modern position. The original bill is largely an effort to create the conditions for citizenship. To be sure, citizenship is inextricably intertwined with the control of government. But that control was to be guaranteed through mechanisms for participation, security, and independence, not simple barriers against public officials.

We can find here a degree of continuity between the original constitutional project and the second bill. "Necessitous men," Roosevelt said, "are not free men." Citizenship might well require education and freedom from desperate insecurity. In these respects, Roosevelt was attempting to complete the American Revolution. "Freedom is no half-and-half affair."

The Second Generation in the First?

For better or worse, the Constitution's framers gave no thought to including social and economic guarantees in the bill of rights. Before we evaluate the claim I am investigating—the failure to include such guarantees is simply a matter of timing—we should note that the framers were not indifferent to poverty. On the contrary, some of their writing suggested a strong commitment to social and economic guarantees, though not at the constitutional level.

Consider the words of Madison himself, probably the most influential voice in the founding period. Madison offered the following means of combating "the evil of parties":

> 1. By establishing a political equality among all. 2. By withholding unnecessary opportunities from a few, to increase the inequality of property, by an immoderate, and especially an unmerited, accumulation of riches. 3. By the silent operation of laws, which, without violating the rights of property, reduce extreme wealth to a state of mediocrity, and *raise extreme indigence toward a state of comfort.* (emphasis added)

What is most striking about this passage is Madison's emphasis on the importance of "a state of comfort" for the poor and, in particular, his suggestion that "comfort" would provide protection against "the evil of parties," or self-interested factions, in government. He seems to be suggesting that gross inequality will likely lead to a kind of interest group competition within the process of governance. Here is a clear link between the elimination of poverty and the preconditions for democracy. For Madison, a well-functioning political process is endangered by both "extreme wealth" and "extreme indigence." Madison believed in the possibility of reducing extreme wealth and raising extreme indigence "without violating the rights of property," although he did not spell out what this would entail. But he clearly thought it possible. (Was Roosevelt a Madisonian in this regard?)

Thomas Jefferson was not a framer of the Constitution (he was in France at the time), but he exerted a strong influence during the founding period. Jefferson wrote in terms that were strikingly similar to Madison's:

> I am conscious that an equal division of property is impracticable. But the consequences of this enormous inequality producing so much misery to the bulk of mankind, legislatures cannot invest too many devices for subdividing property, only taking care to let their subdivisions go hand in hand with the natural affections of

the human mind. . . . Another means of silently lessening the inequality of property is to exempt all from taxation below a certain point, and to tax the higher portions of property in geometrical progression as they rise. Whenever there is in any country, uncultivated lands and unemployed poor, it is clear that the laws of property have been so far extended as to violate natural right. The earth is given as a common stock for man to labor and live on.

The idea of exempting those below a certain point, as well as imposing higher taxes on those who earn more, is often thought to be a product of the twentieth century. But it has a clear antecedent in Jefferson's thought.

Many of the classical liberal thinkers, far from rejecting social and economic rights, explicitly embraced them. The French social theorist Montesquieu, a great influence on the American framers, claimed, "The alms given to a naked man in the street do not fulfill the obligations of the state, which owes to every citizen a certain subsistence, a proper nourishment, convenient clothing, and a kind of life not incompatible with health." John Locke, who greatly influenced American political thought, wrote in similar terms: "As Justice gives every Man a Title to the product of his honest Industry, and the fair Acquisitions of his Ancestors descended to him, so Charity gives every man a Title to so much of another's plenty, as will keep him from extream want, where he has no means to subsist otherwise."

In early America, Thomas Paine was the most explicit advocate of social and economic guarantees. Paine emigrated to the United States in 1774. In 1776 he published his extraordinarily influential book, *Common Sense*. Fifteen years later, he published his first volume of *The Rights of Man*, a response to the conservative Edmund Burke, who had written with great skepticism about the French Revolution and the use of the idea of "rights" to justify popular rebellion. Paine strongly endorsed both civil and political rights, including freedom of speech and freedom from arbitrary deprivations of liberty. But in his second volume, published in 1792, Paine went much further. He urged something like a welfare state, including many of the ingredients of twentieth-century reforms.

Paine argued for public employment to assist those needing work; for social security for employees, allowing them to retire at the age of sixty; for state-supported money for poor families sufficient to permit them to educate and raise their children; and for benefits for recently married couples and mothers. Part II of Paine's *The Rights of Man* was widely read; 200,000 copies of the book were sold in Scotland, Wales, and England. Nor did Paine believe that the idea of rights was unsuitable for proposals of this kind. He urged that his suggestions about pensions were envisioned "not of the nature of a charity, but of a right," and he emphasized two years later that he was proposing "not charity but a right, not bounty but justice."

In the framing period, there was widespread support for legislation that would provide poor people with the basic necessities of life. Greatly influenced by English practice, the American colonies offered a number of strategies to ensure help for the destitute. The details will not detain us here. But public funds were widely used for this purpose, and it was generally agreed that assistance for the poor was a public responsibility. In the colonial period, welfare was called "relief" and was provided in many different forms. "Outdoor relief," the direct ancestor of modern welfare, took the form of jobs, apprenticeships, and much more. While England tried to forbid outdoor relief to able-bodied poor people, America was far more permissive; nearly all of the states allowed that form of assistance. An elected local official, the overseer of the poor, accepted applications from those who needed help and used tax money to provide clothing, fuel, food, and even assistance for medical treatment. Many cities in the young colonies also provided "indoor relief," providing assistance through poorhouses, which could be found in Boston, Salem, Philadelphia, New York City, Charleston, Providence, and Baltimore. The extent of the relief was highly variable. Many critics at the time feared that poor relief would encourage "idleness" and "improvidence"; they stressed the danger that poor people were "not left to feel the just consequences of their idleness." The themes of contemporary debates about welfare programs can be found in the earliest days of American history. But assistance for those in need was widely accepted.

In this light, no one can plausibly claim that the framers were opposed to social and economic protections. Nonetheless, no framer suggested that such protections should take the form of constitutional rights. It is natural to think that in the eighteenth century, the idea was simply not on people's viewscreens. And if this chronological explanation is right, it would remain necessary to explain the reason for the rise of the second bill—why rights recognized there were absent when they were absent, and why they arose when they did. This would not be a question about American practices in particular. It would be a question about changing conceptions of constitutional rights.

Undoubtedly the chronological explanation contains considerable truth. It correctly accounts for the drafting of the original bill. But as a complete explanation, it faces a serious problem: The meaning of the Constitution changes over time. In countless ways, the American Constitution has gone far beyond the original understanding of those who wrote and ratified it. Because it is not static, the absence of social and economic rights cannot be explained by reference to the age of the document.

CONSTITUTIONAL CHANGE 1: FORTY-ACRES AND A MULE

Sometimes constitutional change comes from explicit constitutional amendments, and this is the place to begin. After the Civil War, the Constitution was significantly altered. Originally the bill of rights applied only to the federal government. As far as the national Constitution was concerned, the states were free to suppress dissent, punish religious beliefs, or take property without just compensation. The framers sought to discipline the national government rather than the states—believing that political controls at the state level, alongside state constitutions, would protect against abuse by state governments. With the experience of slavery, this understanding shifted dramatically.

The states seemed a potential source of oppression and tyranny, and the national government a source of protection against state power. The principal result was the Civil War amendments, which are now understood to apply the bill of rights to state governments. The Civil War amendments also prohibit slavery or "involuntary servitude." They ban states from depriving any person of life, liberty, or property "without due process of law." And they prohibit states from denying any person "the equal protection of the laws" and thus forbid discrimination on the basis of race, sex, and other illicit grounds.

The Civil War amendments do not explicitly contain social and economic rights of the kind that Roosevelt sought. In a way this presents its own puzzle, for the question of economic rights was hotly debated at the time. The South had more than 4 million newly freed slaves who lacked land and shelter. It was frequently argued, Roosevelt-style, that without economic freedom, the political freedom of the newly freed slaves would be meaningless. The Radical Republicans in Congress sought to confiscate parts of Southern plantations and give them to the freedmen. Thaddeus Stevens, a Republican leader, urged that the freedman be given a small percentage of white-owned lands. Speaking before the Republican convention in September 1865, he contended that the government should seize 400 million acres belonging to the wealthiest 10 percent of Southerners, and transfer forty acres to each adult freedman, with the remaining (about 90 percent of the total) being sold "to the highest bidder" in plots no larger than 500 acres.

Some of the confiscated land had already been donated to newly freed slaves under the general rubric of "forty acres and a mule"—an unmistakable precursor of modern thinking about economic rights. In 1865 General William T. Sherman and Secretary of War Edwin M. Stanton met with twenty African American community leaders of Savannah, Georgia. According to Garrison Frazier, a Baptist preacher and former slave, "freedom required" that the former slaves "have land, and turn and till it by our labor . . . and we can soon maintain ourselves." As a result of the discussion, Sherman issued a special field order, under which freedmen would have the forty-acre homesteads "where by faithful industry they can readily achieve an independence." In South Carolina and Georgia, forty-acre plots were given to more than 40,000 freedmen; in Davis Bend, Mississippi, large tracts of confiscated land were given to 1,800 former slaves. On a national level, jurisdiction over this and other land was given to the Freedmen's Bureau, which sought to provide land and schools to the newly freed slaves, not simply legal protection. Shortly thereafter, however, President Johnson issued special pardons, returning the property to the ex-Confederates.

In the Reconstruction Congress, there was a great deal of discussion of land reform in the South but insufficient support for any specific proposals. The idea of "forty acres and a mule" was challenged as a violation of property rights and as unnecessary in light of the political liberties granted by the new amendments: the right to vote, hold office, own property, and the like. African Americans were divided, with many arguing that education, the vote, and equal civil rights would be adequate to ensure freedom and citizenship. Others disagreed, saying "we want Homesteads; we were promised Homesteads by the government."

In short, the Civil War era saw much discussion of the relationship between freedom and a social minimum; many people insisted that citizenship and liberty required a certain level of material goods. But there was no serious interest, after the Civil War, in amending the Constitution to include social and economic rights. No one suggested that any such rights should be included in the Civil War amendments. A chronological point is relevant here as well: In the Anglo-American world of the late nineteenth century, social and economic rights were generally unfamiliar. Perhaps this fact supports the chronological explanation. But there are other problems.

Constitutional Change 2: The New Deal and Beyond

What about the New Deal? Was the Constitution changed in that period? In an obvious sense, the answer is no. The New Deal did not alter one word of the founding document. But we have seen that by 1940, the *meaning* of the Constitution was fundamentally different from what it was in 1930. At the state level, constitutional amendments endorsing aspects of the second bill of rights were indeed ratified. Several states now offer social and economic rights. The New York constitution, for example, provides that "the aid, care, and support of the needy are public concerns and shall be provided by the state and by such of its subdivisions, and in such manner, and by such means, as the legislature may from time to time determine." As we shall see, the claim that America is exceptional as a *cultural* matter is complicated not only by Roosevelt's plea for a second bill of rights but also by considerable constitutional innovation at the state level—activity that has not made much difference in the actual lives of poor people.

Crucially, the New Dealers did not pursue constitutional reform. Their approach was fully consistent with their general strategy, which was to avoid official amendments entirely and use political processes and constitutional interpretation to move law and politics in the directions they sought. The New Deal was not the only twentieth-century effort to ensure freedom from desperate conditions. President Johnson's Great Society included the War on Poverty, featuring a range of steps to provide opportunities and resources to those without them. During the 1960s and 1970s, various social groups showed a great deal of interest in aspects of the second bill, such as housing rights and welfare rights. Their interest notwithstanding, there was no significant discussion of adding social and economic rights to the American Constitution. Here is my central objection: The chronological explanation, emphasizing that such rights were foreign to the founders, cannot explain constitutional inaction in the twentieth century.

CONSTITUTIONAL CHANGE 3: INTERPRETATION

The chronological explanation faces an even more serious problem. Constitutional change is often a product not of textual amendment but of judicial interpretation, leading to new understandings of old provisions. Throughout American history, the meaning of the Constitution is often very different from what it was even two decades before. Even if the eighteenth-century constitution did not contain social and economic rights, the American Constitution might have been interpreted to do so. In fact this could still happen. There is nothing in widely accepted methods of interpretation that rules out this possibility.

Does it seem impossible to imagine a Supreme Court ruling that some or all of the second bill is protected by the Constitution that America now has? I will return to the question in Chapter 9. But consider some analogies.

- In 1900, it was clear that the Constitution permitted racial segregation. By 1970, it was universally agreed that racial segregation was forbidden.
- In 1960, the Constitution permitted sex discrimination. By 1990, it was clear that sex discrimination was almost always forbidden.
- In 1930, the Constitution allowed government to suppress political dissent if it had a bad or dangerous tendency. By 1970, it was clear that the government could almost never suppress political dissent.
- In 1910, the Constitution prohibited maximum hour and minimum wage laws. By 1940, it was clear that the Constitution permitted maximum hour and minimum wage laws.
- In 1960, it was clear that the Constitution allowed government to regulate commercial speech, which was not protected by the free speech principle. By 2000, it was clear that the Constitution generally did not allow government to regulate commercial speech unless it was false or misleading.
- In 1970, it would have been preposterous to argue that the Constitution protected the right to engage in homosexual sodomy. In 1987, it was well settled that the Constitution did not protect that right. By 2004, it was clear that the Constitution did protect the right to engage in homosexual sodomy.

All of these changes occurred without the slightest change in the text of the Constitution. And this is just the tip of the iceberg; there are countless other examples.

Does this mean that America lacks a stable Constitution? That the Constitution is meaningless? That it means whatever the judges say that it means? These would be silly conclusions. The Constitution is meaningful and relatively stable, and it doesn't mean whatever judges say that it means. But constitutional law does not consist of staring at constitutional text and history and announcing the document's meaning. Many of the key provisions of the Constitution are general and ambiguous. What counts as "the freedom of speech"? What does "due process" require? What does it mean to deny someone "equal protection of the laws"? We might want to answer these questions by asking how these terms were understood by the people who originally ratified them. Some Supreme Court justices, notably Justices Antonin Scalia and Clarence Thomas, have argued that the "original understanding" is the only legitimate basis for constitutional law. But the Court has not accepted their view, and the original understanding leaves many gaps and uncertainties (as Justices Scalia and Thomas acknowledge). Hence the meaning of the document changes over time, and these changes usually arise from alterations in social values.

The Supreme Court is often portrayed as a "countermajoritarian" or undemocratic force in American government—as setting itself against the will of democratically elected branches of government. This portrayal is grossly exaggerated. Shifts in the Court's understandings typically follow, and do not lead, public opinion. We might linger over Mr. Dooley's century-old comment that "no matter whether th' constitution follows th' flag or not, th' supreme court follows th 'ilection returns." Does the Court really follow the election returns? The suggestion makes a lot of sense if we understand it to mean that the Court is unlikely to depart from a firm national consensus. Many of the Court's most celebrated decisions, even those striking down legislation, reflected the views of current political majorities. For example, the origins of the modern right to privacy lie in *Griswold v. Connecticut*, in which the Court invalidated a law forbidding married people to use contraceptives. This was an aggressive decision. But Connecticut was one of only two states with such a ban, and the Court was vindicating, not opposing, widely held commitments within the nation as a whole. *Brown v. Board of Education*, invalidating school segregation and creating a large-scale controversy about the role of the Court, actually reflected the view of the nation's majority. Most Americans opposed school segregation. Decided in 1954, *Brown* received regional criticism but widespread national support, which would not have been the case in 1900, 1910, or 1920. It is most revealing that the Court was unwilling to oppose segregation until the citizenry did.

When the Court began to invalidate sex discrimination in the 1970s and 1980s, it was not making a revolution on its own. On the contrary, it was following a mounting social consensus to the effect that sex discrimination was illegitimate. Perhaps *Roe v. Wade*, protecting the right to choose abortion, is difficult to fit into this framework. Many Americans reject the notion of a right to choose abortion. But even here, the Court's decision almost certainly fit with the convictions of the nation's majority. It would be a mistake to portray the Court as imposing moral judgments that lack strong support from the nation's citizens. Note that I am not attempting to defend the Court's decisions. I am simply remarking the fact that they are far less countermajoritarian than is often claimed.

In our constitutional tradition, the Constitution's meaning is settled through case-by-case judgments, building from precedents in a way that allows evolution over time. Theoretically it would have been possible for this process to have produced something like a second bill of rights. The absence of social and economic rights from our constitutional understandings therefore cannot possibly be explained by pointing to the fact that the Constitution was ratified in the eighteenth century.

If this seems fanciful, return to the question of sex discrimination. Most modern constitutions explicitly ban sex discrimination. The American Constitution doesn't. Why is the American constitution so different? A chronological account offers part of an answer: When the bill of rights was ratified, sex discrimination was not thought to be a problem. But this explanation is ludicrously incomplete. The Equal Rights Amendment, expressly forbidding sex discrimination and heavily debated in the 1970s and 1980s, might have been ratified but wasn't. Why not? Here is part of the answer: Sex discrimination is a problem all over the world, but there is nothing in American culture that is particularly opposed to sex equality. In fact America is more committed to equality on the basis of sex than are many countries that guarantee it in their constitutions. The Equal Rights Amendment failed partly *because it was widely seen as unnecessary*. As a result of dramatic post–1970s changes in judicial interpretation of the equal protection clause, the American constitution now has something very much like a constitutional ban on sex discrimination—not because of the original understanding of its text but because of new judicial interpretations. If this has happened in the context of sex equality, why hasn't it happened for social and economic rights as well?

The chronological explanation offers no answer. We have to look elsewhere.

7

American Culture and American Exceptionalism

The fervent New Deal bureaucrats dreamed of a much greater level of social justice, of a truer community, than the United States had as yet achieved. They, of course, wanted more production and more jobs, but they also wanted everyone to have a sense of meaningful involvement and worth.

Paul Conkin

INOW TURN TO what may well be the most tempting explanation for why the second bill did not become part of the American Constitution, which points to some distinctive facts about American history and culture. Begin with the fact that socialism has never been a powerful force in the United States, as it has been in otherwise quite similar nations such as England, Canada, Germany, and France. In academic circles, the absence of a strong socialist movement is often described as "American exceptionalism." On this view, what makes America exceptional is that "it didn't happen here": There was never a strong effort to move the United States in the direction of socialism or even social democracy. The New Deal created a range of protections for those who did not fare well in a capitalist economy. But its architects had absolutely no enthusiasm or even sympathy for socialism. The New Deal might be described as an effort not to incorporate socialist thinking but to preserve capitalism by removing its harshest edges. Roosevelt himself was puzzled by the hostility of business: "One of my principal tasks is to prevent bankers and businessmen from committing suicide."

American exceptionalism, and America's special culture, might explain why our founding document lacks a second bill of rights. No group that might have been interested in such rights was ever powerful enough to obtain them. Compare the debate over the Universal Declaration of Human Rights; the socialist and communist nations, most notably the Soviet Union, were particularly eager to press social and economic guarantees. Whatever Roosevelt might have said, and whatever the nature of the four freedoms, capitalist nations were somewhat uneasy about them. During the Cold War, the debate over such guarantees took the form of a pervasive disagreement between the United States and its communist adversaries. Americans emphasized the importance of civil and political liberties, above all free speech and freedom of religion, while communist nations stressed the right to a job, health care, and a social minimum. I think this debate was unhelpful; it is most plausible to see the two sets of rights as mutually reinforcing, not antagonistic. As we shall see, political liberties help reduce the risk of massive deprivation, and those who live under desperate conditions are most unlikely to be able to enjoy their political and civil rights. But the perception of an opposition between the two has played a large role in international debates.

The content of a constitution reflects the nation's political culture, and the American political culture is distinctive. We have seen that key terms of the second bill attract widespread support in the United States. But compared to Europeans, Americans are less likely to believe that government should provide a minimum income guarantee, a job for everyone, or a decent standard of living for the unemployed. Perhaps this, in a nutshell, is the best explanation for the American Constitution's failure to include the second bill. This point is closely linked with the previous discussion of constitutional interpretation. I have suggested that when interpretation changes, it is often because the culture has changed. With respect to social and economic rights, American culture has not changed. If Americans were committed in principle to the second bill, the existing Constitution would move toward such a commitment too.

What's Exceptional?

There is an extensive literature on American exceptionalism, with many competing views, and the key terms need to be clarified. How should we define socialism? What, precisely, makes America "exceptional" in its hostility to socialism? What is the "it" that didn't happen here? A valuable analysis offers a summary: "Parties calling themselves Socialist, Social Democratic, Labor, or Communist have been major forces in every democratic country in the world with the exception of the United States." But labels might not be helpful. Some critics of the New Deal, from the 1930s to the present, complain that Roosevelt produced a kind of American-grown socialism—suggesting it really did happen here but without the label.

If socialism is understood as the abolition of private property and the public ownership of the means of production, then Americans have shown no real interest in socialism. Roosevelt had no serious desire to nationalize industries. If a socialist movement is understood as one that rejects free enterprise, Roosevelt, an emphatic advocate of capitalism, was no socialist. His goal was to rescue the free enterprise system, not to replace it. But in France, England, Germany, and elsewhere, self-styled socialist movements have often not been radical. Their goals have been in line with those of the political left: some redistribution of resources from rich to poor, unemployment insurance, ceilings on economic wealth, greater authority for labor unions, controls on corporate power, health care, and social security for all. While no major American political movement has embraced socialism as such, powerful American officials have nonetheless sought, within the framework of the capitalist system, to promote all of these goals. Roosevelt's programs included social security, greater authority for labor unions, ceilings on economic wealth, and redistribution of resources from rich to poor. To a greater or lesser extent, the same is true of many other American political figures, including President Lyndon Baines Johnson and Senator Ted Kennedy. Left-wing political programs are hardly foreign to American debate. Is American exceptionalism simply a matter of labels?

I do not believe so. Perhaps the difference between America and Europe is mostly one of degree, but it is no less real for that. For many decades, what is centrist in Europe falls on the far left in the United States. On many issues, Margaret Thatcher, a highly conservative leader in Europe, would have been left of center in America. Socialism is largely beside the point; few of the relevant positions really qualify as socialist. But compared to people in many other nations, Americans have been unwilling to moderate central features of the free enterprise system. Americans have been less enthusiastic about a welfare system that provides extensive protection to the disadvantaged. Different polls find different numbers, but the difference between Americans and Europeans is robust. One poll finds that only 23 percent of Americans accept the view that government has a duty to "take care of very poor people who can't take care of themselves." In 1990 strong majorities of citizens, both rich and poor, in Italy, the Netherlands, and West Germany agreed with the proposition that the "government should provide a job for everyone" and that the "government should provide a decent standard of living for the unemployed." By contrast, only 32 percent of wealthier Americans agreed with the former statement, and only 23 percent accepted the latter. Less wealthy Americans accepted these statements by 61 percent and 52 percent majorities respectively, but even these numbers were significantly lower than the corresponding European figures.

Asked whether "government should provide everyone with a guaranteed basic income," only 12 percent of wealthier Americans agreed, and only 33 percent of less wealthy Americans did so. By contrast, this proposition commanded majority support among less wealthy citizens of Great Britain, West Germany, the Netherlands, and Italy, and near majority support among wealthier citizens. We have seen that in the early 1990s, some polls found majority support in the United States for an adequate standard of living for all and government provision of a job for all those willing to work. But clearly Europeans support these rights more strongly than Americans do.

Social attitudes have real effects on policy. An extensive study shows that U.S. tax and welfare laws do comparatively little to assist poor people or reduce inequality. Other nations are far more aggressive on these counts. Perhaps "American exceptionalism" amounts not to the absence of a self-styled socialist movement but to a smaller and weaker political left or a lack of enthusiasm for redistributive programs.

But I think that more is involved. Socialism in any form has had little appeal in America, and a large part of the reason lies in the fact that the notion of "class conflict" has usually fallen on deaf ears. It is fully acceptable for American officials to argue for "opportunities for all," defend "compassionate conservatism," and even urge a "war on poverty." But it is not acceptable for American politicians to claim that economic classes are engaged in a battle with one another and that voters have to take one side or another. Even mild suggestions along these lines raise American hackles. Consider George W. Bush's contention in 2000, responding to Al Gore's suggestion that he favored "the people" over "the powerful," that Gore was engaging in "class warfare." Perhaps America is exceptional in its hostility to thinking of political life in terms of class. If this is so, the absence of a second bill of rights from American constitutional understandings might be an outgrowth of the absence of class-based thinking in the United States.

Why Exceptional?

Let us assume that American exceptionalism exists and that it can be understood as an unwillingness to embrace large-scale programs of redistribution and as hostility to anything that sounds like an appeal to class antagonism. A further question remains: Why is America exceptional on these counts?

Many explanations have been offered. Some people suggest that American workers have had, or have believed that they have, a high degree of upward mobility, muting dissatisfaction with their present situation. Strong majorities of Americans believe that they will, in the future, have an above-average income. And if some of us are poor, at least it is possible that our children or grandchildren will do far better. A sense of open possibility dampens any feeling of class conflict. Unfortunately, the evidence does not provide much support for the view that Americans have unusually high levels of mobility. Evidence suggests that people in the United States have less mobility than those in many other nations, including Sweden and Peru; one study of a large number of countries found American mobility ranking toward the bottom, alongside South Africa and England. What is important here is perception rather than reality. If Americans believe that they are likely to be doing well in the future, they are less likely to favor steps to help those who will do poorly. And if redistributive or socialist-type reforms appeal to people who think that they are at economic risk, then such reforms will gain little ground in the United States.

Others have suggested that feudalism is a necessary precursor for socialism. In a feudal system, people define themselves in terms of their ascribed social position, and hence a society with a feudal past is especially ripe for efforts to understand advantage and disadvantage in terms of class. Americans, lacking a feudal past, have never thought of themselves as masters and serfs; hence political appeals to entrenched social positions would likely fall on deaf ears. Still others suggest that powerful private groups were quick to suppress socialist movements whenever they threatened to be effective. In their view, McCarthyism is simply the tip of the iceberg. In a variety of ways, subtle and less subtle, public and private actions have made it most difficult for socialism to have any traction in the United States. Many of those actions have involved cooptation rather than suppression. They accepted the reformers' most plausible proposals and goals without moving in a radical direction.

Roosevelt himself was an important case in point. Of all the periods in American history, the Great Depression provided the most promising conditions for the emergence of socialism in the United States.

Roosevelt's response was to engage in "conscious efforts to undercut left-wing radicals, to preserve capitalism." Some of those efforts involved meeting with radicals and suggesting that he would address their central concerns. A potentially inflamed labor movement was brought on board in this way. In the late 1920s, there was no federal right to organize; those who sought to establish a union, or even join one, could lose their jobs. One of the simplest proposals in the early New Deal was to provide, at the national level, that employers could not punish employees for the mere fact of organization. Consider the words of a union leader in the mid–1930s: "Early in 1933 I visited the White House. . . . At that time our union did not have enough members to pay the officers and during the course of that interview with the President he said this, 'Boys, go home and have a good night's sleep because if I don't do anything else during my administration as President of the United States I am going to give the miners an opportunity to organize in the United Mine Workers of America.' . . . certainly after that I was for the President, and nothing he has done since would cause me to be against him." By supporting the Wagner Act, which ensured the right to organize, Roosevelt delivered on his commitment.

A more subtle explanation involves the American electoral system, which is distinctly unpromising for third party movements. It has only two dominant parties and an elaborate set of checks and balances. As a result, it has successfully dampened socialist efforts that succeeded elsewhere. Because the American system lacks proportional representation, candidates who draw less than half the vote will usually not appear in government at all. (Let's put the 2000 presidential election to one side.) For that reason, a vote for a third party seems "wasted." This fact tends to moderate political divisions, weakening extreme groups on both right and left. Even if an extreme group gained access to power, it would be checked and constrained by other groups, making it most unlikely that government as a whole would move dramatically in one or another direction.

We need not choose among these competing explanations. What matters is the underlying weakness of any kind of socialist movement in the United States.

CULTURE BEYOND SOCIALISM—AND RACE

But all of these points seem to be missing something. Perhaps the best version of the cultural account points not to the absence of a socialist movement in the United States but to broader features of the nation's culture: America's underlying individualism, its belief that poverty can be escaped through sheer effort, and its caution about strong efforts to redistribute resources from the wealthy to the poor. Again there are large differences between Americans and Europeans on these counts. In one poll, for example, 70 percent of Americans said that people are poor because of laziness, not because of society, whereas 70 percent of West Germans said that people are poor because of society rather than laziness. Asked whether poor people are able to work their way out of poverty, 71 percent of Americans agreed, whereas only 40 percent of Europeans did. There is good evidence of a link between a nation's public beliefs and its patterns of spending. Where people tend to think that economic success is a product of sheer luck, their government is more likely to provide social spending. On this count, the beliefs of Americans are distinctly unpromising.

These features of American culture must be explained. Some of the same factors brought forward to account for American exceptionalism might be invoked here as well. The absence of a feudal background, for example, might contribute to the widely held belief that poverty is not immutable. Powerful private groups mount intense lobbying efforts against redistributive proposals, while well-funded think tanks, nominally independent, provide empirical support for political opposition to these proposals.

The evidence suggests an additional point. In the United States, racial issues have played a large role in determining the shape and nature of redistributive programs. A careful study shows that southern Democrats hostile to African Americans played a crucial role in defeating the Full Employment Act, President Truman's most ambitious effort to implement aspects of the second bill of rights. Compared to Europeans, Americans are especially likely to think of poor people as coming from a different racial group. Since Roosevelt's death, social responses to redistributive programs have been inextricably intertwined with racial issues. "Racial fragmentation in the US and the disproportionate representation of minorities among the poor has clearly played a major role in stopping rich-poor redistribution within the US. . . . This history of American redistribution makes it quite clear that hostility to welfare comes in part from the fact that welfare spending in the US goes disproportionately to minorities." This is very different from Roosevelt's time, when programs for redistribution were thought to help a heterogeneous group of citizens, coming from numerous racial, ethnic, and religious groups. Against the backdrop of the Depression, Roosevelt's proposals were hardly seen as targeted at any particular ethnic or racial group.

The absence of a European-style social welfare state is certainly connected with the widespread perception among the white majority that the relevant programs would disproportionately benefit African Americans (and more recently Hispanics). The details need not detain us here. Whether for racial or for other reasons, there can be little doubt that American culture is uneasy with large-scale programs for redistribution, and that uneasiness helps explain the absence of social and economic rights from the American Constitution.

New Deal Constitutionalism and Cultural Change

There is some truth in the cultural explanation. Let us begin with a simple empirical fact: The existence of social and economic rights in a nation's constitution is correlated with the strength of left-wing elements in that nation's polity. Nations that have powerful socialist or left-wing groups are more likely to embrace social or economic rights in their constitution. In America, a strong socialist movement might have sought a constitutional amendment or fostered political changes that would have produced novel interpretations. As we shall see, a different political leadership would have produced a different Supreme Court, one that would likely have interpreted the Constitution to recognize parts of the second bill. For this reason it is correct to insist that the absence of such rights from American constitutional law owes something to the absence of a significant socialist movement in the United States.

As a full account of the situation, however, the cultural explanation is plainly inadequate. Nations that have socialist movements or insist on obligations to those who need help do not always put such rights in their founding documents. Consider Canada and Israel, nations that have strong socialist movements but lack social and economic rights. Such nations might believe that constitutions are not the proper place to protect such rights, even though legislatures have a duty to recognize them in principle. They might fear that judicial enforcement of social and economic rights would create serious problems or do little good. Or they might believe that the purpose of a constitution is to protect nations against the particular problems to which their own political culture gives rise. If a nation's political culture is firmly committed to something like the second bill, then the absence of social and economic rights from the constitution might come from a belief that placing them in the founding document is unnecessary.

On the other hand, a nation that lacks a strong socialist movement and has a highly individualist culture may have considerable enthusiasm for social and economic rights and even include them in its founding document. Social and economic rights can exist without a strong socialist movement or anything like it. New York, for example, makes a constitutional commitment to a decent minimum, and socialism never had much influence in that state. To argue for the second bill, it is not necessary to believe in public ownership of the means of production, to reject free enterprise, or to argue for low ceilings for those at the top and high floors for those at the bottom. The economist Milton Friedman, no socialist, supports the negative income tax designed to provide a social safety net for all; it is easy to think of that very net in terms of rights. A number of other American states contain aspects of the second bill in their constitution. These states did not have significant socialist movements, and they are not less individualist than states whose constitutions lack such provisions.

Franklin Roosevelt was no socialist; indeed, he strongly believed in capitalist institutions. But he was committed to "freedom from want." He invoked that form of freedom not in spite of his commitment to individualism but because of it.

A somewhat different Roosevelt, with the same set of beliefs about freedom, might have believed that constitutional change enshrining the second bill was the correct course. Why did America's Roosevelt take a different course? The reason does not lie in American culture or in the absence of a strong socialist movement in the United States. The reason lies in the simple fact that Roosevelt believed that constitutional change was difficult, that courts could not be trusted, and that a change in the text of the founding document was far less important than political will—less important, that is, than an affirmation by the public of its deepest commitments.

A different culture might have produced constitutional change. A nation more inclined to large-scale redistribution would be more inclined to treat the second bill as part of its constitution. And no one should deny that racial issues have played a significant role in debates over how to think about some of the rights of that Roosevelt urged. But nothing in American culture is fatally inconsistent with the second bill. With a little nudge or a slight change in emphasis, our culture could have gone, and could still go, in many different directions.

One of the most serious problems with cultural explanations is that they treat cultures as if they were static or homogeneous, when they are typically dynamic and full of disparate elements. In 1925, for example, the United States seemed averse to any kind of welfare state; its policies and even its constitution appeared to be set firmly against them. It would have been plausible to maintain that American-style individualism was fatally inconsistent with the emergence of a national welfare state. But by 1937, an American welfare state was firmly in place at the national level. In 1965 the United States did not embrace a principle of sex equality. It would have been easy to argue that any such principle would be fatally inconsistent with our cultural commitments. But in 1990 the commitment to sex equality was a defining part of our constitutional ideals. In the late 1980s, discrimination against homosexuals was perfectly legal, and the Supreme Court had made it plain that laws forbidding homosexual relations were consistent with the Constitution. The Court said it would be "facetious" to contend that our cultural history raised the slightest doubts about those laws. In 2003 the Court invalidated laws forbidding homosexual relations in a broad decision that seems to respond to and energize a component of our culture that seeks equal rights for gays and lesbians.

With respect to the second bill, it is utterly implausible to suggest that something in the nature's culture foreordains our practices, present and future.

8

America's
Pragmatic Constitution

What excited Roosevelt was not grand economic or political
theory but concrete achievements that people could touch
and see and use.

James MacGregor Burns

IN THE 1980s, I was one of four Westerners asked to meet in
Prague with a small group of people entrusted with the task of
producing a new constitution for Ukraine. The discussion proceeded straightforwardly and well, until we came to the subject of
freedom of speech. Two of the Ukrainian drafters asked, "Shouldn't
we put in a provision requiring the press to be objective?" The out-
siders were flabbergasted by the question. I responded, "Isn't the
point of freedom of speech to allow people not to be objective—to
say whatever they want?" My answer was met with an awkward silence,
as if I had spoken nonsense.

At the time, it was not easy for me to understand what the skepticism was about. How could the Ukrainian constitution require the
press to be "objective"? How could its drafters seek to impose that requirement through their founding document? The Ukrainians were
not tyrants. On the contrary, they were clearly committed to democracy and freedom of the press. Some of them had played pivotal roles

in breaking up the Soviet Union—not through violence but through sustained arguments against communist rule. True, the drafters did want the constitution to require the press to be "objective." But this was not because they sought to authorize the government to punish anyone for a lack of objectivity. Their goal was to express an *aspiration*—to the effect that their journalists should try, as best they could, to be objective and truthful. In meeting my question with silence, they were saying, in essence, that I had entirely missed the point. And indeed I had, if the constitution was understood to express national aspirations rather than specify enforceable commitments.

PRAGMATIC AND EXPRESSIVE CONSTITUTIONS

It is crucial to distinguish between two conceptions of constitutionalism: the *pragmatic* and the *expressive*. When presented with a proposed constitutional provision, Americans tend to ask, "What will this provision *do*? How will courts apply it when faced with real cases?" Such questions played a major role in debates over the proposed Equal Rights Amendment, which would have guaranteed equality on the basis of sex. What would be the effect of an Equal Rights Amendment? Would it mean that bathrooms could not be segregated? That women and men would have to participate on equal terms in military combat? Whether or not these were good questions, they were pivotal to American debates, simply because Americans understand that constitutional provisions have real-world consequences. Such provisions are taken seriously; they are enforced by courts treating the Constitution as real law. Indeed, the very idea of the rule of law requires constitutions to mean in reality something close to what they seem to mean on paper.

But other people, and not just Eastern Europeans, think of constitutions as containing not only law but also expressions of their nation's deepest hopes and highest aspirations. They like to ask, What values does this provision affirm in principle? They see a constitution as including principles that amount to declarations, perhaps not meant to be enforced by courts and perhaps not even destined for full compliance—something like the American Declaration of Independence, which states a number of principles but has no legal effect: "We hold these truths to be self-evident, that all men are created equal, that they are endowed by their Creator with certain unalienable Rights, that among these are Life, Liberty and the pursuit of Happiness." These words express basic values, no less but also no more. In courts, the Declaration of Independence has no legal status. Throughout the world, some constitutional provisions, and even some constitutions, have the same character.

Consider, for example, the fact that some constitutions describe duties as well as rights; they outline what citizens are expected to do. Article 52 of the constitution of Haiti, for example, lists the duties of citizens, who are to respect the property of others, provide assistance to persons in danger, respect "scrupulously" the revenues and property of the State, and vote in elections. Many of the world's constitutions simply borrowed their provisions on social and economic rights from the Universal Declaration of Human Rights. And of course the Universal Declaration is just that—a declaration setting out aspirations that are not enforceable by anyone. There is some doubt about whether the social and economic rights listed in many constitutions have been, or could ever be, enforced by the citizens. For some nations that include such rights, the question of enforcement is really beside the point.

Why would anyone take an expressive approach to a constitution? Perhaps people think that a statement of basic commitments has value in itself. Perhaps it is intrinsically valuable for citizens to say that they believe, in principle, in certain rights and duties. Or perhaps a statement of commitments will have educative and cultural effects, inclining both ordinary citizens and officials in the proper direction. If a nation's legislature is deciding how to set priorities, it might be important that the constitution creates (for example) a right to housing. But those who favor a pragmatic approach would ask whether social and economic rights truly belong in an enforceable constitution containing the important institution of judicial review. Should a constitution really create a "right to just and favourable remuneration"? To "a standard of living adequate for the health and leisure of" one's family, "including food, clothing, housing and medical care and necessary social services"? To "rest and leisure"? What would these provisions mean, concretely? What would they mean in a poor nation with high unemployment and inadequate medical care and housing? What would they mean, concretely, in a wealthy nation like the United States or France? If a nation failed to protect the relevant rights, would courts be authorized to intervene—as they usually are when rights are violated?

It is interesting to ask here whether there is a connection between social and economic rights and government policy. An extensive study gives some partial answers, indicating that such rights can have real effects. Many constitutions promise help for those who are unemployed, disabled, unemployed, or simply poor, and a constitutional right of this kind is strongly connected with larger transfer payments for such people, even if we control for other variables that might confound the analysis. On the other hand, a constitutional right to education is associated with *lower* expenditures for public education. The right to health services has a positive association with public health expenditures, but the association is weak and not statistically significant.

No Aspirations Here?

In light of the ambiguity of this evidence and the American emphasis on judicial enforcement of constitutional guarantees, we might explain the absence of social and economic rights from the American Constitution on the ground that Americans see constitutional rights as pragmatic instruments. The second bill of rights is missing from our Constitution because we do not include mere aspirations. We want our rights to be enforceable by courts. We might explain the inclusion of such rights elsewhere in the world as a sign that they are goals that need not mean much, if anything, in practice. Such rights are meant as *signals*, domestically and internationally, but they are not legally enforceable instruments. The Ukrainian constitution makers were willing to consider a requirement that the press be "objective," a requirement that would be unthinkable in the American context.

On this view, Americans need not be thought skeptical of social and economic guarantees in principle; Ronald Reagan, no fan of the welfare state, was committed to a social safety net. The real source of American skepticism is an understanding of what kind of document a constitution really is, and what kinds of rights belong in it. Americans are suspicious of the idea that courts can oversee rights to education, recreation, or employment. Would courts create bureaucracies? Oversee them? Would they order taxes to be raised? If the second bill put judges in an impossible managerial position, then it might be rejected as part of an effective constitution for that very reason. Perhaps social and economic rights are absent from the American Constitution simply because Americans want their founding document to be subject to real enforcement.

There is some important truth in this explanation. As I have emphasized, Roosevelt did not suggest that the Constitution should be amended to include the second bill, perhaps because he thought that judicial enforcement made little sense. Instead he argued that protection of the relevant rights was a congressional responsibility. Since Roosevelt's time, political officials, even those greatly interested in helping poor people, have not sought constitutional change. President Lyndon Johnson launched the War on Poverty, but he did not enlist constitutional amendments in the cause. Apparently public officials, and citizens too, have been skeptical about constitutional provisions that might be ignored in practice. We shall see that American courts have been reluctant to recognize social and economic rights in part because of their belief that enforcement and protection of such rights would strain judicial capacities. Several other nations, such as India, have recognized the difficulty of judicial enforcement of social and economic rights. And as I have noted, such rights have served as aspirations, without evident real-world effects, in some nations. Importantly, nations whose constitutions protect people at the bottom seem to do a better job of protecting people at the bottom. But it is not easy to show that when nations are relatively likely to help poor people, it is *because* they have constitutional provisions calling for such help.

PROBLEMS AND PROSPECTS

But these points do not give a full explanation of American practice. There are three problems. The first is that even if the difficulties with judicial enforcement *justify* American practice, they do not *explain* it. Can it be seriously argued that the United States Constitution lacks social and economic rights *because* it would be difficult for courts to protect those rights? It might well be difficult for courts to protect those rights. But the point is too lawyerly, too academic, too bookish to provide a convincing account of why social and economic rights are actually missing. Undoubtedly some people, otherwise inclined to accept such rights, oppose their inclusion in the Constitution because of the enforcement problems. But it is reasonable to think that most of those who oppose their inclusion do so for other reasons.

The second problem is that the American Constitution is not only pragmatic. It is expressive too. Parts of the document are widely understood to state aspirations that are not subject to judicial enforcement. For example, it requires states to have a "republican form of government." The requirement is historically important; the framers sought to ensure that states would be republican rather than monarchical. But federal courts do not investigate or monitor state governments or their practices to ensure that they really deserve the name "republican." In fact the Supreme Court has ruled that the requirement of a republican form of government is "nonjusticiable," meaning that it cannot be enforced by courts. The provision is expressive in the same sense that social and economic guarantees threaten to be.

But the problem goes deeper than that. Some provisions of the bill of rights, for instance the prohibition on unreasonable searches and seizures, are violated every day. It would be foolish to contend that all of our constitutional rights are protected all of the time. A few years ago my car was stolen in Chicago. A police officer helped recover the car. As we walked toward it, he asked me what I do for a living. I told him that I teach constitutional law, and he gave me an odd look. I asked him the natural question: "Does the Constitution give you any trouble?" His answer: "I never violated the Constitution unless I *say* that I violated the Constitution, and I never *say* that I violated the Constitution." The officer was indicating that in his frequently dangerous work, he does not always do what the Constitution requires. But he doesn't get in trouble because he doesn't advertise his departures from the rules. Thus the bill of rights states aspirations to which our practice, particularly in the criminal justice system, does not always conform. The bill of rights is partly expressive.

The final problem is that courts could in fact take steps to protect social and economic rights. With respect to the possibility of judicial enforcement, we should not overstate the differences between the original bill of rights and the second bill. In the abstract, many existing constitutional provisions might seem hard for courts to enforce. Is it a problem, for those who want constitutions to be pragmatic instruments, if such provisions are quite vague? Many constitutional provisions are vague: Does "freedom of speech" include commercial advertising, hate speech, libel, and violations of copyright law? Such questions are hardly easy to answer, but courts have done so, and few people argue that the difficulty of that task is an argument against including freedom of speech as part of the bill of rights. Vagueness is also a problem for the constitutional ban on cruel and unusual punishment, for the requirement that states provide "equal protection of the law," for the requirement of "due process," and indeed for most of the bill of rights. If courts cannot enforce the second bill, this is not because its provisions are vague.

If there is a distinctive problem with judicial enforcement of the second bill it is that courts are not in a good position to insist that resources should be spent on one problem rather than another. Courts cannot create bureaucracies, and it is worse than awkward for judges to ask the elected branches to raise funds. Suppose, for example, that many people lack decent housing, and courts are asked to order government to respond to that problem in the name of the "right to housing." Perhaps the resources needed for housing would have to be diverted from other programs, some of which protect parts of the second bill too, such as those providing for education, employment training, and medical care. Resources devoted to the second bill might have to be diverted from other important problems, such as national defense and police and fire protection. The legislative branch, not the judiciary, oversees the tax system. Moreover, judicial enforcement of a right to decent housing would seem to place courts in a managerial role for which they lack the tools.

These are serious problems, to which I shall return. I believe that difficulties with judicial enforcement suggest the enduring wisdom of Roosevelt's suggestion that the second bill was the responsibility of legislatures, not courts. But the problems should not be overstated. In the United States itself, state constitutions protect social and economic rights, and some courts are willing to enforce them to some degree. Some of the rights on the second bill create more serious problems than others. The basic right to education, for example, could be protected by building on existing institutions and without requiring additional expenditures. For all of the rights on the second bill, bureaucracies already exist at the state and national levels. To protect those rights, courts could do a great deal without requiring increased appropriations. We shall see that American courts have already moved in this direction. For example, they require states to give hearings to people before cutting off their welfare benefits and to provide free public education to the children of illegal aliens. In South Africa, courts have taken steps toward ensuring that the government at least creates "programs" that ensure minimal attention to basic needs—not toward careful judicial oversight of the welfare system and not toward requiring that every individual has decent shelter and food.

Of course social and economic rights would strain judicial capacities. No court, in poor or rich nations, can ensure that every single person has decent food, clothing, medical care, and housing. Following Roosevelt, reasonable people might conclude that the second bill should be seen as a set of constitutive commitments, not as a formal part of the Constitution. But other reasonable people might argue that courts could take steps to ensure that basic needs receive a degree of legislative priority and that the most conspicuous forms of neglect are corrected.

In the end, it is implausible to account for the absence of the second bill by referring to problems with judicial enforcement. We can obtain a better understanding of my claim here by attending to some remarkable developments in American constitutional law, in which the Supreme Court moved some distance toward recognizing important parts of the second bill.

9

How the Supreme Court
(Almost) Quietly Adopted
the Second Bill

Property can have no more dangerous, even if unwitting, enemy than one who would make its possession a pretext for unequal or exclusive civil rights.

Robert Jackson

O NE OF THE PEOPLE killed during the terrorist attacks of 9/11 was Barbara Olson, a well-known lawyer, writer, and television commentator, and also the wife of Theodore Olson, the solicitor general of the United States under President George W. Bush. A few months after the attacks, the solicitor general delivered the first annual Barbara K. Olson Memorial Lecture at the meeting of the Federalist Society in Washington, D.C. Much of his speech consisted of a comparison between the commitments of free nations and the commitments of terrorists and despots.

In his extraordinary and moving remarks, Olson did not say that America itself was perfect; this was no simple celebration of our history. "We do not claim that America has been or is today without imperfections or shortcomings." On the contrary, our "Constitution was undeniably flawed at its origin." Efforts to implement our ideals have "never been without error, and some of our mistakes have been shameful." At the same time, Olson said, there "has been constant, if occasionally erratic, progress from the articulation of those lofty ideals to the extension of their reality to all our people." As a key example, Olson contrasted "despots who will not permit children to go to school" with America, "whose Supreme Court has said that free public education cannot even be withheld from those who are in this country illegally." Thus Olson, a conservative appointee of a conservative president speaking before a conservative audience, spoke with approval of the idea that under our founding document, there is something like a right to a "free public education."

Does the Constitution really protect the right to education? Has this part of the second bill been adopted? In a way, it has. In the early 1980s, Texas enacted a law that allowed school districts to deny free public education to children who had not been legally admitted into the United States. Acting under that law, one Texas school district decided that "undocumented" children could attend public schools—but only if they paid a tuition fee. In the extraordinary case of *Plyler v. Doe*, a group of school-age children from Mexico complained that the district's decision violated their constitutional rights. This was an adventurous argument. Nowhere does the Constitution explicitly say that people have a right to a free public education.

Nonetheless, a majority of the Supreme Court agreed that Texas had violated the Constitution. The Court emphasized that education has a special status in a democratic society. "Education," Justice William Brennan wrote for the majority, "provides the basic tools by which individuals might lead economically productive lives to the benefit of us all." Illiteracy "is an enduring disability," handicapping "the individual deprived of a basic education each and every day of his life." One reason lies in the close connection between education and citizenship. "Both the importance of education in maintaining our basic institutions, and the lasting impact of its deprivation on the life of the child" make education distinctive. The Court did not conclude that public education is a constitutionally protected right. It did not say that the Constitution would be offended if a state decided to get out of the education business entirely and rely solely on private institutions. But the Court made it clear that any *selective* deprivation of public education, harming some children but not others, would run into serious constitutional difficulties. This is the clear implication of the Court's remarkable ruling that Texas must provide free public education to children who are unlawfully in the United States. And because any deprivation of public education will inevitably be selective—no state is going to stop providing public education—the decision comes very close to saying that under the Constitution, every child has a right to be educated.

How did the Court reach this conclusion? How did it come to rule that the children of illegal immigrants must be educated for free—in a decision celebrated by a high-level government official in a conservative administration in the immediate aftermath of the attacks of September 11?

AMERICA'S CHANGING CONSTITUTION

I have emphasized that the meaning of the American Constitution changes because of new interpretations. If the Constitution meant what it originally meant, American constitutional rights would be far less robust than they are. The authors of the Constitution believed in freedom of speech and put a right to free speech in the Constitution. But their own understanding of it would allow a great deal of censorship. Judicial interpretation, especially in the late twentieth century, has led to a free speech principle far stronger than anything envisaged by the First Amendment's authors and ratifiers. Nothing in that amendment's original meaning forbids government from requiring school prayer. The current separation of church and state owes every thing to judicial interpretations in the twentieth century. Most Americans would be startled to learn that no provision of the Constitution explicitly forbids the national government from discriminating on the basis of race. If Congress wanted to segregate the armed forces or ban African Americans from working for the national government, nothing in the Constitution expressly stands in the way. (The Fourteenth Amendment forbids states, not the nation, from denying any person the "equal protection" of the laws.) When the bill of rights was first ratified, racial discrimination was perfectly acceptable. Nonetheless, the Supreme Court has reinterpreted the original document to prohibit race discrimination at the national level. I have mentioned that the Fourteenth Amendment, when originally ratified, did not prohibit sex discrimination at all. But the American Constitution is now understood to ban most forms of sex discrimination—and indeed to contain a far stronger ban than can be found under many of the world's constitutions that contain *explicit* prohibitions on sex discrimination.

If the American Constitution meant what it originally meant, it would mean far less than it now does—and the constitutional protection of individual rights, far from being a source of pride, would be something of an embarrassment. Here is my hypothesis: A judicial interpretation of the Fourteenth Amendment that called for much of the second bill would not, in fact, stretch the document any further than many interpretations that are now taken for granted in American constitutional law. What the Court has done, in short, is to treat constitutional rights not as rigid rules laid down once for all time, but as general principles capable of growth and change over time. If the Constitution now prohibits sex discrimination, and if it provides broad protection to sexually explicit speech and commercial advertising, it would not be at all implausible for the Constitution to be construed to protect some or all of the second bill of rights. I will not fully defend the hypothesis here; to do so, it would be necessary to say a great deal about what constitutional interpretation entails. But I am building on actual practice and conventional understandings. I am not suggesting that the Constitution *should* be interpreted to include all or most of the second bill. I am only describing a possible path.

All this is relatively abstract. What I am calling the judicial explanation for American practice is more concrete. It emphasizes that American constitutional law is, to a considerable degree, a form of common law based on analogical reasoning. The Court's understanding of constitutional rights develops through comparing the case at hand to the cases that came before. The judicial explanation suggests that American constitutional law could easily have come to recognize social and economic rights. The crucial historical development was the election of President Nixon in 1968. Nixon made four Supreme Court appointments, which created a critical mass of justices willing to reject the claim that social and economic rights were part of the Constitution. Of course it remains necessary to explain the election of President Nixon, and cultural factors obviously contributed to his victory. But the election was very close and hardly inevitable.

In the 1960s, the Supreme Court of the United States came very close to ruling that the Constitution protects important parts of the second bill of rights. More precisely, the Court held that some aspects of the second bill are protected by the existing Constitution, and it was moving toward ruling that the Constitution requires government to provide a decent minimum for all. In a number of decisions, the Court held that the government must allow poor people to protect their interests, and that the government must provide them resources in order to enable them to do so. Harvard law professor Frank Michelman wrote in 1969 that "the Court has directly shielded poor persons from the most elemental consequences of poverty: lack of funds to exchange for needed goods, services, or privileges of access." Michelman's analysis was extremely influential; his essay was cited by dozens of courts and hundreds of law review authors. But by 1974, the Court had backed off; there was no further shielding. In American law, this is the revolution that wasn't.

What prevented the revolution? The answer is simple: In one of the closest elections in American history, Richard Nixon defeated Hubert Humphrey. If the election had been held two weeks later, Humphrey, whose candidacy was surging, might well have won. If third-party candidate Eugene McCarthy had dropped out of the race, Humphrey would almost certainly have won. And if Humphrey had won, he would in all likelihood have appointed justices who understood the Constitution to protect social and economic rights.

President Nixon's four appointments were Chief Justice Warren Burger and Justices Harry Blackmun, Lewis Powell, and William Rehnquist. To the surprise of many and the enduring disappointment of some, these justices did not dramatically shift the Court to the right. The Burger Court's path did not dramatically diverge from that the Warren Court. But the area of social and economic rights is the one crucial exception. The Warren Court laid the groundwork for some dramatic developments, requiring government to provide financial and other assistance to those who need it. The Burger Court nipped these developments in the bud, and by 1975 the whole idea of minimum welfare guarantees had become implausible.

The developments I mean to trace constitute an extraordinary and overlooked episode in American history; they also contain many lessons. Above all, they suggest that it would have been quite possible for the United States to have a very different set of constitutional understandings. They also dramatize the extent to which constitutional meaning depends on the particular personnel on the Court. Writing from the vantage point of the twenty-first century, it seems absurd to think that the Constitution protects any significant part of the second bill. But in the late 1960s, the Court seemed well on its way to ruling that freedom from desperate conditions was a constitutional right.

BEGINNINGS

The idea that the Constitution might protect social and economic rights can be traced to an obscure Supreme Court decision in 1941— revealingly, the same year Roosevelt gave his four freedoms speech. California had enacted a law banning people from bringing indigents into the state. The Court ruled that the ban violated the commerce clause. States are not entitled to regulate interstate commerce, and if a state prohibited people from transporting the poor from one state to another, it was effectively regulating such commerce. But the Court also went further, suggesting that states would not be permitted to discriminate against poor people. "Whatever may have been the [previously prevailing] notion, we do not think that it will not be seriously contended that because a person is without employment and without funds he constitutes a 'moral pestilence.' Poverty and immorality are not synonymous." In this way, the Court showed the clear influence of the New Deal.

Justice Robert Jackson, a close adviser to Roosevelt and his former attorney general, went much further, with an emphasis on the idea of citizenship:

> We should say now, and in no uncertain terms, that a man's mere property status, without more, cannot be used by a state to test, qualify, or limit his rights as a citizen of the United States. "Indigence" in itself is neither a source of rights nor a basis for denying them. The mere state of being without funds is a neutral fact—constitutionally an irrelevance, like race, creed, or color. . . . Any measure which would divide our citizenry on the basis of property into one class free to move from state to state and another class that is poverty-bound to the place where it has suffered misfortune is not only at war with the habit and custom by which our country has expanded, but is also a short-sighted blow at the security of property itself. Property can have no more dangerous, even if unwitting, enemy than one who would make its possession a pretext for unequal or exclusive civil rights.

This passage, and especially Jackson's last sentence, could be understood to have far-reaching implications. In fact Jackson was speaking Roosevelt's language here. But the Court's ruling was quite narrow. All the Court did was forbid governments from discriminating against poor people—for example, through laws saying that people with low earnings or little savings cannot use public parks or streets. Such laws are exceedingly rare. Harder problems, not resolved by the Court's decision, arise when states say that everyone, poor as well as rich, must pay for some social benefit. Suppose, for example, that the government requires all people to pay for education and for lawyers; is that constitutional? If not, then the Constitution already moves in the direction of the second bill of rights. Still harder cases arise when people claim an affirmative right to employment, medical care, welfare, or social security. In a short period from 1957 through 1969, the Court explored several of these issues, and it reacted sympathetically to people's complaints. In some of them, the Court went so far as to hold that the government must subsidize poor people in certain domains.

The Right to Protect Your Rights: Litigating and Voting

Start with the right to litigate—the right to protect your rights. Litigation is expensive. You can't litigate if you lack the funds to do it. An early harbinger came in 1956 in *Griffin v. Illinois*. There the Supreme Court held that the equal protection clause requires states to provide trial transcripts (or their equivalent) at no cost to poor people appealing their criminal convictions. In defending its practice of charging for these documents, Illinois claimed that there was no problem of discrimination. Poor people and rich people alike were asked to pay for transcripts. Those without funds were not treated worse than anyone else. The Court responded that a "law nondiscriminatory on its face may be grossly discriminatory in its operation. . . . In criminal trials a State can no more discriminate on account of poverty than on account of religion, race, or color." The Court also spoke in more general terms: "Providing equal justice for poor and rich, weak and powerful alike is an age-old problem. People have never ceased to hope and strive to move closer to that goal."

The Court built on *Griffin* in its crucial decision in *Gideon v. Wainwright*, decided in 1963. This decision, one of the most famous in American law, is often celebrated as an effort to make good on the constitutional commitment to give everyone the assistance of counsel in criminal cases. It was also a small but unmistakable step toward recognizing social and economic rights. The central ruling in *Gideon* is that the Constitution requires the state to pay for defense counsel in criminal cases. The Court emphasized that money is central to the operation of the criminal justice system: "Governments, both state and federal, quite properly spend vast sums of money to establish machinery to try defendants accused of crime." The Court added that impartial justice cannot be provided unless the state funds legal assistance to those without resources: "From the very beginning, our state and national constitutions and laws have laid great emphasis on procedural and substantive safeguards designed to assure fair trials before impartial tribunals in which every defendant stands equal before the law. This noble ideal cannot be realized if the poor man charged with crime has to face his accusers without a lawyer to assist him." The *Gideon* decision conspicuously emphasized problems of liberty, not simply equality. If the state could incarcerate people without affording them a proper defense, individual freedom would be at obvious risk. (Recall Roosevelt's suggestion: "Necessitous men are not free men.")

In *Douglas v. California,* also decided in 1963, the Court went further. Building on *Griffin,* the Court ruled that poor people must be provided with counsel on their first appeal of a criminal conviction. Denial of counsel, it said, would be an "invidious" form of "discrimination." A more dramatic development came eight years later. In *Boddie v. Connecticut,* the Court was asked to extend its decisions beyond the criminal context, to say that even in the civil context of divorce, the state would have to pay for an indigent person's court fees and costs. The Court accepted the invitation. It acknowledged that previous cases had involved criminal defendants, rather than those "seeking access to the judicial process in the first instance." But it emphasized that in some cases, resort to the courts is "the only available, legitimate means of resolving private disputes." Because of the importance of marriage, and because the state monopolized "the means for legally dissolving this relationship," the Constitution did not permit government to deny poor people access to the courts. In other words, the state was under an affirmative obligation to subsidize divorces sought by the poor.

The Court's decision in *Boddie* aroused heated debates. Did the decision mean that poor people have a right to state support whenever they were defendants in civil cases? Whenever they brought suit to object to a denial of welfare benefits? Whenever they attempted to file for bankruptcy? Whenever they sued someone? Academic commentators at the time suggested that in principle, it would be exceedingly hard to limit the *Boddie* decision to the context of marriage. The state has a monopoly over both marriage and divorce, and perhaps this point makes those settings unique. But as a practical matter, the legal system also has a monopoly on the lawful use of force. Did *Boddie* suggest that the state had to subsidize people who sought to protect their rights in court? If so, the Court would not be going as far as the second bill, but it would be well on its way toward requiring the state to assist poor people in many domains. Perhaps poor people would have to be given the resources to protect their rights through lawful means. For the right to litigate, radical developments seemed in the offing.

People protect their rights through politics, not simply through the courts, and it is expensive to operate a system of voting. A state might decide to defray the expense by imposing a poll tax, requiring voters to pay to cast their ballot (a bit like a highway toll). Historically poll taxes have played a large role in democracies, including England and America. But are state poll taxes unconstitutional under the Fourteenth Amendment? For decades, no one even raised the question. The validity of the poll tax was entirely secure. In 1964 the federal Constitution was amended to forbid poll taxes in federal elections, but the fact that such taxes were not prohibited in state elections seemed to suggest that the national Constitution permitted them.

In 1966 the Supreme Court took a further step in the direction of social and economic rights by striking down a state poll tax (of $1.50, imposed by Virginia). In so doing, it effectively ruled that states must provide the vote free of charge. Reviving Justice Jackson's concurring opinion from 1941, the Court said that "wealth, like race, creed, and color, is not germane to one's ability to participate intelligently in the electoral process." It added that lines "drawn on the basis of wealth or property, like those of race," are "disfavored." As if to underline the novelty of what it was doing, the Court stressed that the Constitution and its equal protection clause are "not shackled to the political theory of a particular era." Notions of equality under the Constitution, the Court asserted, "do change."

The Court's reasoning contains two especially noteworthy features. The first is the suggestion that a fee requirement can count as an impermissible form of discrimination. If so, then many different kinds of fee requirements are unconstitutional. What about fees for education, medical care, housing, or food? If these are objectionable, then the state might be under a duty to provide financial assistance to poor people in many domains. The idea that seemingly neutral fees are "discrimination" could have extremely broad implications. The second noteworthy feature is the Court's emphasis on the changing nature of constitutional requirements. If the meaning of the Constitution is not "shackled" to any particular era, then it might be possible, in the fullness of time, to recognize a broad array of social and economic rights. In the poll tax case, the Court planted a seed that could have turned into a large oak.

FREEDOM FROM DESPERATE CONDITIONS

In other cases, the Court went further still. In *Shapiro v. Thompson*, the Court seemed to come close to saying that the Constitution conferred to a right to welfare benefits. The case involved a California law imposing a one-year waiting period before new arrivals to the state could receive welfare benefits. Obviously the state was trying to avoid becoming a magnet for poor people. Was this constitutional? California argued that states should have the right to create waiting periods to prevent fraud and protect the state's taxpayers from a flood of out-of-staters hoping to get benefits. In response, those attacking the law argued that the waiting period discriminated against them by depriving them of the basic necessities of life.

The Court agreed. In striking down the waiting period, the Court relied on the constitutional right to travel. The waiting period would "penalize" impoverished travelers and thus violate their constitutional right to go from one state to another. By itself, this conclusion seemed to raise the possibility that states might have an obligation to provide welfare benefits, and perhaps moderately generous levels at that. If a state had no welfare programs at all, wouldn't it "penalize" travelers in just the same way? If a state provided welfare benefits significantly below those of their neighbors, might it be "penalizing" travelers too? The Court spoke explicitly of the special needs of poor people, suggesting that those needs were relevant as a constitutional matter. In the Court's words, California denied "welfare aid upon which may depend the ability of the families to obtain the very means to subsist—food, shelter, and other necessities of life." If the decision turned only on the right to travel, this suggestion would seem purposeless. Thus the Court's emphasis on "food, shelter, and other necessities of life" seemed to recognize the special status of at least parts of the second bill. The *Shapiro* opinion embodied some of Roosevelt's most dramatic claims about individual rights.

The Court went even further a few years later, in *Memorial Hospital v. Maricopa County*. Arizona required a year's residence in the county as a condition for receiving nonemergency medical care at county expense. The state argued that nonemergency medical care was quite different from "the very means to subsist" and that the right to travel was not involved. The Supreme Court disagreed. It read *Shapiro* as holding the "denial of the basic 'necessities of life' to be a penalty." In an echo of Roosevelt, the Court added that it is "clear that medical care is as much 'a basic necessity of life' to an indigent as welfare assistance." Thus a majority of the Court said that it would be "odd" to conclude that a state must afford a poor person "welfare assistance to keep him from the discomfort of inadequate housing or the pangs of hunger but could deny him the medical care necessary to relieve him from the wheezing and gasping for breath that attend his illness." On the basis of this language, it would not be implausible to see the Court as suggesting that the Constitution requires the state to provide a degree of medical care.

Of course these decisions did not go so far. In *Shapiro* and *Maricopa County*, the Court dealt with a form of discrimination. It did not say that the Constitution requires government to provide all citizens with a basic minimum. In its 1970 decision in *Goldberg v. Kelly*, the Court issued an especially dramatic ruling. There it concluded that welfare benefits count as a kind of "new property," entitled to the protection of the Constitution's due process clause. The problem stemmed from the fact that New York refused to provide a full hearing before removing people from the welfare rolls. Was this constitutionally permissible? Under the due process clause, people are entitled to a hearing only if they can show that their "life, liberty, or property" is at stake. But since the nation's beginning, welfare benefits had been seen as a mere privilege, not a right. Such benefits certainly were not "liberty" or "property" within the meaning of the Constitution. The Court restricted the category of rights to the old kind of "property," such as land, cash, bank accounts, and investments. Government benefits were in a different category. Of course Roosevelt believed that a fair minimum should be seen as a matter of right, not charity. But the Constitution was not understood in Rooseveltian terms. To succeed, welfare recipients had to convince the Court to reconsider its long-standing view about the meaning of the Constitution.

Their arguments had considerable force. After the New Deal, the distinction between rights and privileges was increasingly difficult to maintain. Old-style property rights do not come from the sky. They come from law. As we enjoy them, they exist only because government is willing to create and protect them. How are welfare benefits any different? After the New Deal, this question was very hard to answer. It seemed entirely implausible to treat welfare benefits as fundamentally different from conventional property.

In *Goldberg*, the Court abandoned the right–privilege distinction and ruled that welfare was indeed a form of constitutional "property." Under the due process clause, the government must provide a hearing before it removes people from the rolls. In *Goldberg*, the Court emphasized the "brutal need" of those who depend on welfare benefits. In its most extraordinary passage, it noted, "From its founding the Nation's basic commitment has been to foster the dignity and well-being of all person within its borders. We have come to recognize that forces not within the control of the poor contribute to their poverty." Here is a clear reminder of a central lesson of the Great Depression. The Court continued: "Welfare, by meeting the basic demands of subsistence, can help bring within the reach of the poor the same opportunities that are available to others to participate meaningfully in the life of the community. [Public] assistance, then, is not mere charity, but a means to 'promote the general Welfare, and secure the Blessings of Liberty to ourselves and our Posterity.'" In a key footnote, the Court said, "It may be realistic today to regard welfare entitlements as more like 'property' than a 'gratuity.' Much of the existing wealth of this country takes the form of rights that do not fall within traditional common-law concepts of property."

Goldberg did not say that the government had to provide welfare benefits in the first place. It held only that if the government wanted to remove people from the rolls, it had to provide a hearing. But with its striking reference to the Constitution itself, the Court seemed to signal a willingness to consider the possibility that the Constitution grants a right to subsistence for those in need. Indeed, the Court's reference to the "blessings of liberty," a phrase from the preamble of the Constitution, suggested in Rooseveltian fashion that welfare benefits were central to both freedom and citizenship. Hence public assistance helps people not only to live decent lives but also to "participate meaningfully in the life of the community." The Court, no less than Roosevelt, seemed to think that "necessitous men are not free men."

THE COUNTERREVOLUTION

By the late 1960s, the Court seemed to be moving toward recognition of a robust set of social and economic rights. Prominent academic writing suggested that the Court was moving rapidly in exactly that direction. All the pieces were securely in place. In *Griffin, Gideon, Douglas, Boddie,* and *Harper,* the Court held that the government had to allow poor people access to both courts and to ballots, even at taxpayer expense. In *Shapiro,* it ruled that government could not impose waiting periods on new arrivals to the state and strongly suggested that it would look askance at government efforts to eliminate "food, shelter, and other necessities of life." In *Goldberg*, the Court said that welfare benefits went far beyond "mere charity" and were necessary to "secure the Blessings of Liberty."

If there are parallel universes, surely the Supreme Court has, in one of them, built on these decisions to hold that government has an affirmative obligation to ensure that its citizens have "food, shelter, and other necessities of life." In that universe, most of Roosevelt's second bill is a well-established part of the American Constitution.

Why isn't this our universe? What happened? The crucial event was the election of President Nixon in 1968 and his four appointments to the Court: Warren Burger in 1969, Harry Blackmun in 1970, and Lewis Powell and William Rehnquist in 1972. These appointees produced a stunning series of decisions, issued in amazingly rapid succession, which limited the reach of the decisions just described and eventually made it clear that for the most part, social and economic rights have no constitutional status.

The Burger Court's initial signal came in *Dandridge v. Williams*, decided in 1970. The plaintiffs attempted to persuade the Court to take a further step toward recognition of a constitutional right to welfare. The case involved a challenge to a Maryland law that set a maximum of $250 per month on welfare grants to poor families. The plaintiffs complained that this ceiling discriminated against poor children in large families. The per capita benefits to a child in a family of, say, eight would be so much smaller than the per capita benefits to a child in a family of three.

Building on the precedents I have described, a federal court of appeals enthusiastically accepted this argument. It concluded that the Maryland law amounted to a form of unconstitutional discrimination. In the court's view, the state would have to give a strong defense of any discrimination against members of the group of people receiving welfare benefits. The court did not rule that every American had a right to welfare benefits, but its decision was almost as far-reaching. Welfare programs must draw lines, and the lower court insisted that any lines would be carefully evaluated to ensure that they did not compromise anyone's access to the necessities of life. Obviously Maryland was seeking to control costs; it was also attempting to avoid giving poor women an incentive to produce more children. But the lower court found these justifications insufficient.

Under the new leadership of Chief Justice Warren Burger, the Supreme Court reversed the lower court. Its reasoning was more important than its conclusion. The Court announced that it would not concern itself with the details of welfare programs, even if they appeared to be discriminatory, and even if the programs made distinctions that seemed unjustified and harsh. The Court knew exactly what it was doing. It was aware that some of its precedents seemed to point in another direction and suggest that the Court would be especially protective of the interests of poor people. The Burger Court acknowledged that the "administration of public assistance . . . involves the most basic needs of impoverished human beings." It agreed that the *Dandridge* case was different from other cases in which it had upheld "state regulation of business or industry." But this "dramatically real factual difference" created "no basis for applying a different constitutional standard." Hence Maryland would be required only to show that its decision was minimally rational—meaning, in practice, that any distinctions at all would be permissible.

Writing in dissent, Justice Marshall, joined by Justice Brennan, was incredulous. He objected to "the Court's emasculation of the Equal Protection Clause as a constitutional principle applicable to the area of social welfare administration." For Marshall, the Maryland law produced a basic denial of equal treatment. While some needy families received full subsistence payments, others got far less than they needed. In a remarkable footnote, Marshall referred with approval to academic claims on behalf of a right to welfare assistance. He also cited article 25 of the Universal Declaration of Human Rights, which confers exactly that right. Thus Justice Marshall signaled his willingness to understand the Constitution as conferring something like a right to freedom from desperate conditions.

Dandridge was just one decision and did not necessarily mean a great deal. After all, Maryland provided welfare benefits to everyone.

Perhaps the family ceiling could be understood as an effort to ensure against discrimination in favor of large families. A major development involving a possible right to housing came two years later in *Lindsay v. Normet*. Donald and Edna Lindsey paid $100 a month for the use of a single-family residence in Portland, Oregon, until the City Bureau of Buildings declared the residence unfit for human habitation. Inspectors found broken windows, improper sanitation, missing rear steps, rusted gutters, and broken plaster, all in violation of the Portland housing code. In response, the Lindseys refused to pay rent until improvements were made. At that point their landlord threatened to obtain a court order to evict the Lindseys unless the rents were paid. Under Oregon law, tenants could be expelled from property whenever they failed to pay rent within ten days of its due date.

The Lindseys filed suit, contending that the Oregon eviction law was unconstitutional. They argued that the right to housing had a special status under the Constitution. The "need for decent shelter" and the "right to retain peaceful possession of one's home," they contended, are constitutionally fundamental interests, in large part because of their special importance to the poor. The government could interfere with those interests only if it could show an extremely good reason for doing so. Clearly the Lindsays were attempting to read the Constitution to create an important part of the second bill: the right to a decent home. Building on *Dandridge*, the Supreme Court rejected their argument. While denying any intention to "denigrate the importance of decent, safe, and sanitary housing," it added that the "Constitution does not provide judicial remedies for every social and economic ill. We are unable to perceive in that document any constitutional guarantee of access to dwellings of a particular quality."

Lindsay was an important decision. But the decisive step came in 1973, with the Court's decision in *San Antonio School District v. Rodriguez*. By this time, all four Nixon nominees were on the bench. Joined by Justice Stewart, they provided the 5–4 majority. All of the pre-Nixon justices dissented. *Rodriguez* was the death knell for the idea that the Constitution protects social and economic rights.

At issue was a constitutional challenge to the Texas system for financing public schools, which appeared to discriminate against poor people. Funds for public schools were based partly on the level of taxable wealth in the local area, so that per-pupil expenditures were much higher in wealthy areas than in poor ones. In the poorest areas, where there was usually a high percentage of minority pupils, per-pupil expenditures were just 37 percent of what they were in the wealthiest areas. For every $1,000 spent per child in the wealthy areas, only $370 was spent per child in the poorest areas. Building on the Supreme Court's wealth discrimination decisions, the lower court ruled that this system was constitutionally unacceptable. For two different reasons, the Supreme Court might have agreed. First, the Texas system could be seen as a form of discrimination against the poor. Second, the right to education might be seen as a fundamental right. In either case, the Texas funding system would probably have to be struck down. But the Court concluded otherwise.

The Court ruled that there was no discrimination against the poor. *Griffin* and *Douglas*, it reasoned, involved people who were completely unable to pay for an important benefit and as a result faced an "absolute deprivation" of the chance to enjoy that benefit. The Texas system had neither feature. Poor people could be found in wealthy as well as poor districts. Everyone in Texas received some kind of education, and hence there was no absolute deprivation. In a footnote, the Court noted that if education was made available only to those able to pay a tuition assessed against each pupil, there would indeed be an absolute deprivation. Such a case would present "a far more compelling set of circumstances for judicial intervention." Thus the Court left open the possibility that a minimal right to education could be found under the Constitution. As long as everyone was above the minimum, differences in per-pupil expenditures would not be taken to raise serious constitutional problems.

The Court also rejected the claim that education was "fundamental" for constitutional purposes. To be sure, education is exceedingly important. But in the Court's view, the real question is whether the right to education is protected implicitly or explicitly by the Constitution. Here the Court was skeptical. It acknowledged that education "is essential to the effective exercise of First Amendment freedoms and to intelligent utilization of the right to vote." But as long as educational opportunities were not absolutely denied, it was insufficient to point to a mere connection between education and constitutionally guaranteed rights. "How, for instance, is education to be distinguished from the significant personal interests in . . . decent food and shelter? Empirical examination might well buttress an assumption that the ill-fed, ill-clothed, and ill-housed are among the most ineffective participants in the political process."

This remarkable passage offers an eerie echo of both *Goldberg v. Kelly* and Roosevelt himself. It was Roosevelt who introduced the terms "ill-fed, ill-clothed, and ill-housed," and it was he who suggested that these forms of distress amounted to a lack of freedom. In addition, the idea that those who are ill-fed, ill-clothed, and ill-housed are "ineffective participants" is close to the Court's suggestion in *Goldberg* that welfare helps people become participants in the community. The oddity is that a different Supreme Court might well have concluded that *because* poor people are ineffective participants, the Constitution requires government to produce a very good reason for any program that discriminates against them. But under Chief Justice Burger, the Supreme Court went in the opposite direction. It treated this very conclusion as absurd; it sought to resist the potentially radical implications of any effort to take seriously, for constitutional purposes, the plight of the poor. *Rodriguez* ended the emergence of social and economic rights in the United States.

We can see the contours of the parallel universe in Justice Marshall's dissenting opinion. Marshall agreed that to decide whether interests were "fundamental," it was necessary to look at the text of the Constitution. In his view, the key task was "to determine the extent to which constitutionally guaranteed rights are dependent on interests not mentioned in the Constitution." When the connection between the constitutional guarantee and the nonconstitutional interest "draws closer," courts must look more carefully at the state's reason for infringing on the interest, especially if the infringement appeared to be discriminatory. In *Rodriguez*, the interest was very close to those the Constitution expressly protects, because education "directly affects the ability of a child to exercise his First Amendment rights, both as a source and as a receiver of information and ideas." Exercise of the franchise itself is connected with education. Marshall urged that education was genuinely unique, calling it "an essential step in providing the disadvantaged with the tools necessary to achieve economic self-sufficiency."

While conceding that the Texas system did not absolutely deprive anyone of education, Marshall argued that people were being discriminated against "on the basis of group wealth," a discrimination that "bears no relationship whatsoever to the interest of Texas schoolchildren in the educational opportunity afforded them." For this reason, the state would have to provide a convincing justification for its system of funding, and in his view, it had not done so. The idea of "local control" was by itself too abstract, especially because Texas already compromised local control in countless ways. Hence Justice Marshall would have invalidated the Texas financing system.

Justice Marshall's approach would have had significant implications. Any claimed right would be evaluated by asking whether an explicit constitutional right depended on it. If people were deprived of education, Marshall urged, then the constitutional rights to speak and to vote were implicated. Perhaps the connection between education and specifically acknowledged constitutional rights is especially clear. But we have every reason to believe that Marshall would also have found a connection between desperate poverty and acknowledged rights. A different Court would have shown considerable interest in moving in his direction. A number of state courts, invoking their state constitutions, have done exactly that.

THE PATH OF THE LAW

The brief period from 1970 through 1973 played a crucial and underappreciated role in American jurisprudence. Nixon's appointees stopped an unmistakable trend in the direction of recognizing social and economic rights. There can be no serious doubt that appointees by Hubert Humphrey would have seen things very differently. It is not too speculative to suggest that if Humphrey had been elected, aspects of the second bill would have been a solid part of the constitutional landscape.

It would be possible to respond that Nixon's election was a product of America's distinctive culture, which is hostile to social and economic rights. To be sure, Nixon won partly because of cultural forces; his victory had everything to do with the events of the time. The Civil Rights Act of 1964 helped convince southern voters to support Republican candidates. The social unrest of the period—including riots in the cities, protests over the Vietnam War, and the assassination of John Kennedy, Robert Kennedy, and Martin Luther King Jr.—led numerous citizens to vote for Nixon, with his strong "law and order" platform. Nixon's election might well be seen as signaling the end of a period of liberal ascendancy in American politics, beginning with Roosevelt and reaching its peak in the domestic policies of President Lyndon Baines Johnson. Nixon's victory was contingent, but it was hardly an accident; it reflected large-scale social forces. Perhaps those forces included antipathy to social and economic guarantees; perhaps Nixon won precisely because he could be expected to support an understanding of rights that did not include them. Perhaps Nixon was the anti-Roosevelt and was elected partly for that reason.

On the other hand, the 1968 election was exceptionally close, one of the closest in the nation's history, and it would be fantastic to suggest that the outcome was foreordained by a kind of national antipathy to social and economic rights. It is far more plausible to think that such rights were a casualty of an election that was fought out on other grounds. It is undoubtedly true that America's political culture has helped produce a federal judiciary that does not attempt to promote social and economic rights. Of course America's constitutional understandings have a great deal to do with its cultural understandings. What I am emphasizing here is that, if not for a close and contingent electoral outcome—one that was far from inevitable—the American

Constitution would almost certainly recognize some kinds of social and economic rights.

Are these rights entirely dead? They have shown some small but interesting signs of life. In its remarkable 1973 decision in *US Department of Ag. v. Moreno,* the Burger Court showed continuing interest in the protection of minimal economic security. The case involved a challenge to Congress' exclusion from the food stamp program of any household containing any individual who was unrelated to any other member of the household. Thus the statute required that any household receiving food stamps must consist solely of "related" individuals. The Court invalidated the statute. The Court noted that the legislative history suggested a congressional desire to exclude "hippies" and "hippie communes." To this the Court said: "[I]f the constitutional conception of 'equal protection of the laws' means anything, it must at the very least mean that a bare congressional desire to harm a politically unpopular group cannot constitute a legitimate governmental interest. . . ." The Court's decision can only be understood in light of the fact that food stamps were at stake. Without explicitly saying so, the Court was showing its willingness to require a substantial reason for any selective exclusion from that program. *Moreno* has not been overruled; it remains good law.

In *Papasan v. Allain,* decided in 1986, the Court struck down an educational funding disparity with similarities to that upheld in *Rodriguez.* The *Papasan* case involved an unusual and apparently discriminatory funding system in Mississippi. Schools attended by certain Native Americans received annual appropriations from a state educational fund amounting to only $0.63 per pupil—a tiny fraction of the state's average per-pupil expenditure of $73.34 for other pupils. In striking down the Mississippi system, the Court stressed that in *Rodriguez,* it was dealing with a system attempting to ensure local control, whereas in *Papasan,* the disparity resulted from an explicit and intentional decision, by the state itself, "to divide state resources unequally."

More interesting still is the Court's decision in *Plyler v. Doe,* mentioned above, which prohibited Texas from requiring undocumented aliens to pay a tuition fee in order to enroll in the public schools. The opinion itself is a bit of a mess. A fractured majority brought together a smorgasbord of ideas from the era in which social and economic rights seemed on the way, and tried to do so while recognizing that the Court had since refused to take those ideas seriously. Thus the Court emphasized three points: the children were not responsible for their undocumented status; the absolute deprivation of education was constitutionally troublesome; and the children at risk in the case were politically powerless. Justice Powell, the author of *Rodriguez*, provided the crucial fifth vote. He emphasized that the Texas law "threatens the creation of an underclass of future citizens and residents." But *Plyler*, like *Papasan*, has been a sharply limited decision. It has produced no further developments.

As the law now stands, it would be much too simple to say that the American Constitution does not recognize social and economic rights. The early cases still stand. Bits and pieces of the second bill are now part of the Constitution. Criminal defendants, if they are indigent, must be provided lawyers at government expense. The poll tax remains unconstitutional for elections at all levels of government. If a state thinks that people are no longer eligible for welfare benefits, it must provide them with a hearing in the event of a dispute about the facts. There may be a right to some minimal level of education. But the Court could have gone much further. With a modest shift of votes in 1968, it almost certainly would have done so.

PART III

CONSTITUTIONS AND COMMITMENTS

10

Citizenship, Opportunity, Security

Are we going to compel [people] to live under slum conditions? . . . Has society as a whole no obligation to these people? Or is society as a whole going to say we are licked by this problem? . . . I wish that you would give me a solution.

Franklin Delano Roosevelt

S O FAR WE HAVE SEEN that Roosevelt introduced a new set of rights into American understandings; that his plea for a second bill had an enormous international influence; that some aspects of the second bill have a home in American constitutional law; and that our constitutional order, largely because of a single closely contested election, does not truly recognize such rights. But the biggest questions remain. Should America have a second bill? In what sense?

I believe that Roosevelt was right. The second bill should count among our constitutive commitments; it should be similar to the Declaration of Independence in status. But the Constitution should not be amended to include the second bill. A major reason is that it would be difficult for courts to enforce the rights Roosevelt cataloged. Other nations, writing constitutions from scratch or without our distinctive traditions, would do well to take either the "directive principles" approach followed by India or the intriguing alternative followed by South Africa (explored in Chapter 12). But even in America, there is an argument for constitutional change, and one of my goals is to suggest that this argument is far more plausible than it might seem at first glance. And even in America, there is an argument, not for judicial interpretation of the existing constitution to incorporate the second bill, but for more narrow rulings, akin to those in *Goldberg, Shapiro,* and *Moreno,* that take seriously the most serious forms of human deprivation.

THEORY AND PRACTICE

In philosophical circles, the foundations and nature of human rights are the subject of intense debate. The utilitarian tradition, for example, sees rights as an outgrowth of ideas about what will promote human welfare, understood as "utility." Jeremy Bentham, the founder of utilitarianism, proposed that the goal of legal rights should be to maximize pleasure and minimize pain. Other utilitarian philosophers have argued that the ingredients of human welfare extend well beyond pain and pleasure. On any utilitarian account, rights should be assessed in terms of whether they are likely to make human lives, taken in the aggregate, to go better. The right to freedom of speech can be easily justified in the utilitarian framework. A society with free speech is likely to be more capable of avoiding blunders and governing itself well. In addition, such a society will be able to enjoy more in the way of material and scientific progress.

Many people reject the utilitarian account of rights. Some insist that human beings should be treated as ends rather than means, and that government must treat its citizens with respect. On this view, government cannot act in ways that use people as mere instruments. For those who reject utilitarianism, the right to free speech is not best justified as a way of ensuring against blunders or producing progress. That right has intrinsic rather than merely instrumental value:

Human beings have the right to speak freely simply because they are entitled to be treated respectfully. An alternative view, emphasized by Amartya Sen and Martha Nussbaum, holds that accounts of rights have everything to do with an understanding of *human capabilities*—of what human beings are able to do and to be. For example, human beings have the capability to reason and engage in self-governance, and free speech is indispensable to both of these. Under the "capabilities approach," the right to free speech is protected because of its connection to central human capabilities.

I do not intend to take a stand here on the foundations of rights. I believe that the rights listed in the second bill, like the right to free speech, can command support from people with diverse and even incompatible views about how rights are best justified. The broader point is that for many purposes, it is unnecessary to resolve the deepest disputes in order to make a great deal of progress in political and social life. People often agree on *practices* even when they disagree on *theories*. They concur about what to do even amid disagreement or uncertainty about why they ought to do it. In the domain of constitutional provisions and social commitments, it is often possible to set aside questions about philosophical foundations and agree on such provisions and commitments despite disagreements or uncertainty about the foundational issues. In America, for example, the right to religious liberty is firmly entrenched, and diverse people accept it. We lack consensus on the grounds for the right; we have a consensus on its existence. What is true of religious liberty is true for most of the rights enshrined in the Constitution and cherished today. The right to protection of freedom of speech might be justified as a way of protecting personal autonomy in matters of conscience, or a way of ensuring correction of social errors, or a way of safeguarding democracy itself, by putting some of the most contentious issues off-limits to politics. A nation's constitutional rights are often respected without anything like agreement about what best justifies them.

Consider the experience of those who designed the Universal Declaration of Human Rights, which was written and adopted by the United Nations in the aftermath of World War II. The philosopher

Jacques Maritain played a significant role in the deliberations that led to the declaration. Astonishingly, people of radically opposed views had been able to agree on fundamental human rights. Maritain liked to say, "Yes, we agree about the rights but on condition that no one asks us why." According to Maritain, the only feasible goal was to reach agreement "not on the basis of common speculative ideas, but on common practical ideas, not on the affirmation of one and the same conception of the world, of man, and of knowledge, but upon the affirmation of a single body of beliefs for guidance on action."

Maritain was speaking in practical terms—the same terms used by Roosevelt himself. Roosevelt described his own philosophical position in a comically unhelpful way: "social-mindedness." But it is often possible to do what Roosevelt sought, which is to obtain *incompletely theorized agreements* on both rights and practices—agreements on what to do amid disagreements or uncertainty about why to do it.

The framers of the United States Constitution followed exactly this path. They themselves did not share a clear account of its foundations. Today most people who accept the original bill of rights do not share any such account, with some stressing democratic goals, others referring to liberty, others emphasizing utilitarian considerations, and still others stressing theology. Roosevelt thought that the second bill could be accepted by people with diverse views about the basis of rights, and without any clear view about how rights are best justified. I believe that he was right to do so. If there is a good argument for a second bill, it does not rest on contentious theoretical claims. Instead the bill can receive support from many disparate positions.

To put the argument in its simplest form: The most fundamental legal rights should be seen as pragmatic instruments designed to protect important human interests, however they are defined. The second bill protects two such interests: basic opportunity and minimal security, which on any account are exceedingly important. A decent society is committed to safeguarding them. The second bill attempts to specify the rights that are necessary to ensure basic opportunity and minimal security. We can certainly quibble about the details, and our second bill need not exactly track Roosevelt's. But a decent nation is committed, at the most fundamental level, to protecting the kinds of rights Roosevelt cataloged.

PRINCIPLES AND AMENDMENTS

Let us now return to the earlier distinction among constitutional rights, constitutive commitments, and mere policies. Roosevelt emphatically did not seek a constitutional amendment. But he also believed that the second bill went far beyond a statement of current policies. He wanted Americans to understand the second bill as part of their defining principles and their heritage—as setting out the basic principles to which the nation is committed. Roosevelt was walking directly in the path set out by James Madison. Madison urged the original bill of rights as a set of commitments that would define the citizenry's own values, not as a lawyer's document or a code for judicial enforcement. We have seen that Madison supported the original bill with the suggestion that it would become a central part of the nation's culture and operate for that reason as a safeguard of liberty. In this regard he was remarkably prescient. I have emphasized that the very meaning of the bill of rights often derives from widely held cultural commitments. The protection now accorded to free speech, for example, owes everything to the fact that Americans prize that freedom in a way that has led to a far more robust free speech principle than anything favored by the founding generation.

At a minimum, the second bill should be seen as part and parcel of America's constitutive commitments. Roosevelt's speech proposing the second bill deserves a place among the great documents in the nation's history. Indeed, it can be seen as occupying a place akin to the Declaration of Independence, or perhaps somewhere between the Declaration and the Constitution. While it lacks the legal status of the latter, it has more specificity and concreteness, as a catalog of existing rights, than the former. As we shall see, parts of the second bill already have the status of constitutive commitments. But what has happened is far short of what Roosevelt sought. We have yet to recognize the second bill as an account of some of the nation's deepest aspirations and its understanding of rights themselves.

Does it make sense to go further? This is a hard question without a simple answer. Consider the explosion of constitution making all over the world following the fall of communism. As a general rule, modern efforts at constitutional design include parts of the second bill. It is a strong candidate for inclusion for nations writing their constitutions from scratch. But what about America, where the courts' power to interpret and enforce the Constitution is taken for granted? Should our founding document be amended or understood to contain some version of the second bill? Might Roosevelt have been too unambitious in this regard?

Roosevelt did not argue for constitutional change as such because he believed the second bill would and should be implemented through democratic processes, not the courts. In Roosevelt's view, the nation had already accepted the second bill, at least as a general commitment. What remained was the task of implementation. This required action by Congress, which would occur if the public demanded it. Roosevelt wanted to spur that demand. From Roosevelt's point of view, the idea of constitutional change must have seemed quite unattractive. The first problem is the sheer difficulty of obtaining it. Any effort at altering the nation's founding document takes years of sustained effort, with no hope of ultimate success. By contrast, the nation obtained the Social Security Act and the National Labor Relations Act—both now constitutive commitments—without any change in the Constitution itself. Evidently Roosevelt believed that the second bill could be approved and implemented in the absence of a formal amendment, which would therefore be a waste of time. From his perspective, judicial enforcement of the second bill might do little or no good. In his era, as so often in American history, the courts were the enemy and not the agent of desirable social change. In these circumstances, the benefits of constitutional amendment were small and the costs high.

I agree with Roosevelt. But from a modern point of view the matter is not entirely clear. For those concerned about the rights recognized in the second bill, it might well be hazardous to rely on ordinary political processes. Consider the mixed and in some ways disgraceful record of the United States, permitting violations of those rights to persist amid great plenty. For example, tens of millions of children receive inadequate education; tens of millions of citizens lack decent health care. This record attests to the hazard of depending on political processes alone. It is reasonable to argue that a constitution should be understood, not as a place to set out aspirations or goals, or even the rights to which human beings are entitled in principle, but as a safeguard against the concrete problems that are likely to arise in the particular nation for which a constitution is being designed. Good constitutions are, in a sense, *countercultural*; they work to reduce the distinctive problems that will predictably arise in any particular nation. If this is a useful way to think about constitutional provisions, the argument for adopting the second bill in the United States is far from implausible.

In nations escaping from communist rule there was a strong argument for aggressive constitutional protection of private property and freedom of contract, precisely to ensure the preconditions for a market economy. In the aftermath of communism, it was (and remains) exceedingly important to create a social and legal culture that respects free markets. But the argument for the second bill was relatively weak because a cultural commitment to protect to those in economic need already existed. In other words, some nations have less need for a second bill because the rights it recognizes are already constitutive commitments.

The United States is different. Notwithstanding our astonishingly high per capita income—by far the highest in the world—the country does far less than it might to protect those at the bottom of the economic ladder. A second bill, of the sort recognized in either India or South Africa, might do a great deal of good for citizens of the United States. If constitutional change were not so difficult to obtain, and if a second bill could be ratified relatively easily, there would be a legitimate argument on its behalf. Engage in the following thought experiment: Suppose that after extended social deliberation, the citizens of the United States have used the ordinary legal forms to ratify something like the second bill and make it part of our Constitution. The amendment has been ratified after extended debate about its contents and about the issue of judicial enforcement. We could imagine a provision that would either eliminate a judicial role (as in India's directive principles) or reduce it, so as to allow courts to respond only to large-scale violations (as in South Africa, discussed below).

Would the Constitution be better, or worse, after this amendment? Beware of an easy negative answer. True, an India-style change would be in tension with our traditions of judicial enforcement, and it might be regarded as less than meaningful. And the South African approach would certainly strain judicial capacities. But if the result of the change ensured more in the way of basic opportunity and security for those who lack it, there would be a real argument in its favor.

VERSIONS, REAL AND HYPOTHETICAL

Does this seem purely hypothetical? In fact a proposed constitutional amendment, H. J. Res. 35, was referred to the House Committee on the Judiciary in 2003:

> SECTION 1. Every citizen has the right to work, to free choice of employment, to just and favorable conditions of work, and to protection against unemployment.
>
> SECTION 2. Every citizen, without any discrimination, has the right to equal pay for equal work.
>
> SECTION 3. Every citizen who works has the right to just and favorable remuneration ensuring for themselves and their family an existence worthy of human dignity, and supplemented, if necessary, by other means of social protection.
>
> SECTION 4. Every citizen who works has the right to form and join trade unions for the protection of their interests.
>
> SECTION 5. The Congress shall have power to implement this article by appropriate legislation.

This proposal contains more and less than Roosevelt's second bill. Roosevelt did not envision equal pay for equal work—a right that would create an array of interpretive difficulties. But would something in this general vein be desirable? As capturing constitutive commitments? As real constitutional change?

Consider what seems to me a better version, one that amends Roosevelt's catalog in several ways:

Section 1. Every citizen has the right to a good education.

Section 2. Every citizen has the right to adequate protection in the event of extreme need stemming from illness, accident, old age, or unemployment.

Section 3. Every citizen has the right of access to adequate food, shelter, clothing, and health care.

Section 4. Every citizen has the right to a chance at remunerative employment.

Section 5. Every citizen has the right to freedom from unfair competition and domination by monopolies at home or abroad.

Section 6. Congress and state governments must take reasonable legislative and other measures, within available resources, to achieve the realization of these rights.

This version expressly states that the obligation to secure these rights is legislative, and that limitations in available resources are relevant to the legislature's duty. This version also deletes the right of every farmer to raise and sell his products at a return that will give him and his family a decent living—a right that might have made some sense in the 1930s, when the economy depended on agriculture, but is hard to defend today. In fact some farmers should go out of business. There is no more reason to guarantee "every" farmer a reasonable profit than to make this guarantee for computer companies, airlines, or real estate agents. Other changes are designed to eliminate redundancy and promote clarity. I think that any such catalog is better seen as a statement of constitutive commitments than as a formal change to the Constitution, but sensible people can differ on that question.

Let us now explore the grounds of a second bill in more specific terms.

RELATIONSHIPS

The most obvious question involves the relationship between the first bill of rights and Roosevelt's second. Are they in some sense antagonists? Are there issues of mutual interdependence?

Some people write as if there were real tension between civil and political rights on the one hand and social and economic rights on the other—as if societies had to choose between them. This is a large error. For one thing, political rights can be a strong ally of social and economic well-being. When a democracy works well, it is more likely that the second bill will be respected. As evidence, consider Amartya Sen's remarkable finding that in the history of the world, no famine has ever occurred in a nation with a free press and democratic elections, where political safeguards provide a strong check on neglect of the risk of mass starvation. In a way that is highly reminiscent of Roosevelt, Sen argues that famines are not an inevitable product of food scarcity but have everything to do with social policy. A government that is determined to avoid famines can do so—and a democratic government, responsive to voters, has every incentive to ensure that famines do not occur. Sen argues that "a free press and an active political opposition constitute the best 'early warning system' that a country threatened by famine can possess." (We can see an analogy here in China's ineffective handling of the SARS epidemic in 2003. A democratic society, checked by a free press, would have learned more at an early stage and would have been under great pressure to respond more rapidly and provide more accurate information about the threat.)

Famine is an extreme example of the countless ways in which freedom of speech and the right to vote provide a degree of protection against economic deprivation. In this respect, political liberty is a great ally of the second bill. But the point should not be overstated. To see why, return to James Madison's plea for political equality and his concern about the effects of great disparities in wealth. Economic inequalities, if they are large, can be translated into political inequalities that deprive the government of an appropriate incentive to respond to human distress. It may even have an incentive not to respond. Democratic pressure can insulate wealth and forestall efforts to reduce deprivation.

This point suggests a further one, signaled by both Roosevelt and Supreme Court Justice Thurgood Marshall. In some ways, the second bill can be seen as a precondition for the first. The most obvious example, as the Supreme Court itself has suggested, is education. A certain level of education is indispensable for effective citizenship, including the right to free speech and the right to vote. Recall John Adams's early suggestion: "Liberty cannot be preserved without a general knowledge among the people who have a right from the frame of their nature to knowledge." Of course people with little or no education may speak out and vote. But the role of citizen requires an ability to evaluate issues and options, and education is indispensable for that. The connection between citizenship and freedom from desperate conditions is even more straightforward. Those who lack adequate food or shelter are unlikely to be able to participate well in political processes and thus will be unable to protect their own interests. This is an important sense in which political rights and a degree of economic security are interdependent.

Roosevelt's own emphasis was on security. Here too we can see a link between the original bill and Roosevelt's proposal. Political rights provide a degree of security against an overreaching government—the problem of what the framers saw as self-interested representation. At the same time, those rights reduced the risk from factions (self-interested private groups) intent on using government power for parochial purposes. Citizenship is itself a form of security. Civil rights, protecting largely against abuse of governmental authority, serve a similar function. They are indispensable in protecting citizens against fear—the kind of fear that is a daily presence in tyran-nical societies. Roosevelt believed that an understanding of economic forces showed that fear could come from many kinds of threats, and the second bill would increase the domains in which citizens might be secure. To understand the argument for the second bill, we need to return to Roosevelt's goal, which was (1) to provide opportunities for all and (2) to provide a decent minimum for those who could not take advantage of those opportunities.

OPPORTUNITY

In principle, Americans on both right and left are committed to "equal opportunity." This goal is widely taken to be uncontroversial. But a moment's reflection should be enough to show that in a free so-ciety, equal opportunity is an extremely difficult and demanding goal. In fact it is impossible to achieve. Because some people have more wealth than others, some children will have more and better opportu-nities. I live in Chicago, where it is a fact that children who are born to parents who live around 58th Street and Dorchester Avenue have far better prospects than children who are born thirty blocks south. In the United States, as in other liberal democracies, equal opportu-nity does not exist. To provide it, the nation would have to engage in massive forms of redistribution. Those who think they are committed to equal opportunity are actually in favor of a more modest and prac-tical goal—decent opportunity for all, which was one of Roosevelt's central commitments.

The right to good education is the most obvious example. That right was presaged by some of Roosevelt's earliest speeches, in which he deplored the fact that many parents were unable to provide a real education for their children. By elevating good education to the sta-tus of a right, Roosevelt emphasized three points. The first is that in many domains, education is indispensable to decent prospects in life. The second is that education is a basic safeguard of security. The third is that education is necessary for citizenship itself. We have seen that the Supreme Court has made exactly this point, seeing a close link between decent education and the status of citizen. In this respect, the right to education belongs in the same category as the right to property. Of all the rights listed in the second bill, the right to education is by far the most frequently included in the constitutions of the states. Forty-nine of the fifty give it some kind of constitutional recognition. (Iowa is the only holdout.) As a matter of state constitutional law, education is firmly entrenched.

Other rights included in the second bill are centrally concerned with opportunity. Consider, for example, an item that is easy to overlook but should be understood as central: "The right of every businessman, large and small, to trade in an atmosphere of freedom from unfair competition and domination by monopolies at home or abroad." For real opportunity to exist, governments must take steps to ensure against private or public monopolies. Because they squelch competition, they deprive people of a fair chance at wealth. Genuinely free markets are indispensable to opportunity. Of course Roosevelt's stress here is on the rights of entrepreneurs, "large and small," and these rights are extremely important in themselves. In a free society, those who seek to start businesses are permitted to do so. They should not be hampered by anticompetitive practices.

But there is another point. When entrepreneurs are free to trade in an atmosphere of open competition, workers and consumers are large beneficiaries as well. Free trade greatly expands the pool of jobs. Hence a government that commits itself to preventing monopoly is simultaneously helping promote employment. According to the Small Business Administration, small firms employ over 50 percent of all private sector employees and pay 44.5 percent of the total U.S. payroll. They create 60–80 percent of net new jobs each year and more than 50 percent of nonfarm private gross domestic product. Over 500,000 new businesses are created each year. These numbers are highly relevant to actual policy. A right to freedom from unfair competition and domination by monopolies entails an extensive role for government, now largely performed by the Federal Trade Commission and the Department of Justice's Antitrust Division. The appropriate nature of that activity is subject to debate, but if freedom from monopoly is a right, government is obliged to act in the service of that freedom. Recall that Austrian economist Friedrich Hayek, socialism's greatest critic, insisted on exactly this point. This component of the second bill is intimately bound up with freedom of opportunity. For nations that are emerging from communist rule or other forms of state dictatorship, this part of the second bill is an excellent place to start.

What about the right to a "useful and remunerative job"? This right certainly can be connected with security. But does it have anything to do with opportunity? It is important to understand what Roosevelt meant by this. Against the backdrop of the Great Depression, Roosevelt was referring, first and foremost, to government's effort to manage the economy so as to provide basic opportunities for those who were able to work. Hence the best way to protect the right to a "useful and remunerative job" is not through publicly guaranteed employment or government jobs but through a flourishing economy that is constantly creating more positions. When Roosevelt insisted that he believed in a system of free enterprise, he was suggesting that such a system was entirely compatible with high levels of employment. But he also believed that government can play a constructive role. As the Depression demonstrated, and as many subsequent periods in American history have made clear, a system of free enterprise, improperly managed, can lead to devastatingly high unemployment. In recent years, for example, over 9 million Americans have lacked jobs, with an unemployment rate of over 6 percent—not extremely high by international or historical standards but nonetheless a disgrace. Roosevelt sought a set of policy initiatives that would increase the availability of decent positions for people who could work.

By itself, this goal is no longer controversial. Since Roosevelt's time, all presidents have made serious efforts to increase the employment rate. Voters hold them accountable if they fail. What Roosevelt was urging was that government policies promoting employment should be regarded as furthering human rights. This does not mean the unemployment rate must be zero or close to it. But it does mean

that government must make substantial efforts to promote employment for people who are able to work.

Roosevelt was not simply insisting on a right to a job. He urged as
well that the job should be "remunerative." Here we can see a
response to a situation in which, for example, wages fell to $0.05
cents an hour in sawmills and $0.08 cents an hour in general con-
tracting, and young girls were hired for less than $1 for a fifty-five-
hour week. At the federal level, minimum wage laws were an
important part of the New Deal. In the past decades, there has been
a vigorous debate over whether such laws decrease employment levels by increasing the cost of hiring and thus discouraging employers
from taking on new people. And in fact minimum wage requirements have many problems; there are far better ways to help low-
income workers. Policy analysts have learned a great deal about the
best way to make sure that work is genuinely "remunerative." I will
return to this issue shortly. For now, the key point is that in the
interest of ensuring opportunity, Roosevelt aspired to make work
both available and worthwhile.

SECURITY

Opportunity is the best way to provide economic security. But some
aspects of the second bill cannot be understood as guaranteeing opportunity. They aim at security directly by creating a floor below
which human lives are not supposed to fall. In Roosevelt's words,
"Government has a final responsibility for the well-being of its citizenship. If private co-operative endeavor fails to provide work for willing
hands and relief for the unfortunate, those suffering hardship from
no fault of their own have a right to call upon the Government for
aid; and a government worthy of its name must make fitting response." Certain aspects of the second bill protect *freedom from desperate conditions*—a form of liberty, not equality. It is indeed possible to
imagine a society that has little interest in egalitarianism and places
no ceiling on the accumulation of wealth but insists on a decent

minimum for all. Roosevelt attempted to move in this direction. He took the idea of a social safety net quite seriously.

We might even see freedom from desperate conditions as calling for a large-scale social insurance policy. What Roosevelt sought to provide was a kind of national insurance program that would help people suffering from the inevitable accidents and catastrophes of life. Of course the Depression made this program especially appealing. But citizens in any society are at risk from a wide range of sources. They might well be excessively optimistic about the hazards they actually face. (Unrealistic optimism seems to be part of the human condition; consider the fact that 90 percent of drivers think that they are safer than the average driver and less likely to be involved in a serious accident.) Roosevelt believed that, our confidence notwithstanding, each of us is vulnerable to dangers that cannot be wholly prevented "in this man-made world of ours." By ensuring food, clothing, shelter, and health care for all, the second bill would protect against the worst of those dangers.

A society that is seriously committed to freedom from desperate conditions faces many conceptual and practical problems. We can reasonably speak of a decent minimum—of enough food for basic nutrition and shelter from the elements. But human deprivation often involves relative rather than absolute poverty. As Amartya Sen explains, "In a generally opulent country, more income is needed to buy enough commodities to achieve the *same social functioning*." For people to "lead a life without shame, to be able to visit and entertain one's friends, to keep track of what is going on and what others are talking about, and so on, requires a more expensive bundle of goods and services in a society that is generally richer, and in which most people have, say, means of transport, affluent clothing, radios or television sets, etc." To participate in a community, you need the commodities that most people have, "and this imposes a strain on a relatively poor person in a rich country even when that person is at a much higher level of income compared with people in less opulent countries."

In wealthy countries, hunger itself can be produced in this way. This is one reason the poverty level is sometimes defined in relative terms—as in the suggestion that those in the bottom 10 percent are, by definition, impoverished. In any case our personal experience with goods and services depends heavily on comparisons with others. In a poor nation, minimal shelter and clothing will seem quite adequate simply because they are no less than what most others have. In a wealthy nation, the same shelter and clothing count as extreme poverty. What qualifies as enough, or a decent minimum, is affected by what other people possess. We can legitimately insist that a society with large disparities in income and wealth try to ensure a decent minimum for all—enough food, decent shelter, decent clothing, and access to a doctor for medical conditions that really need attention.

Why might a society attempt to do this? Why might it see minimal security as a central goal? Roosevelt's answer was pragmatic rather than philosophical. Arthur Schlesinger Jr. captured a part of it: Roosevelt "had no philosophy save experiment, which was a technique; constitutionalism, which was a procedure; and humanity, which was a faith." But by itself, the idea of experiment is unanchored. Without knowing why we are experimenting—without some criteria for success or failure—we have no reason to experiment at all. Roosevelt's brand of pragmatism had a conception of human ends, not merely a faith. Roosevelt best summarized it in 1936, when asked to state his objectives:

> To do what any honest Government of any country would do; try to increase the security and the happiness of a larger number of people in all occupations of life and in all parts of the country; to give them more of the good things of life, to give them a greater distribution not only of wealth in the narrow terms, but of wealth in the wider terms; to give them places to go in the summer time—recreation; to give them assurance that they are not going to starve in their old age; to give honest business a chance to go ahead and make a reasonable profit, and to give everyone a chance to earn a living.

Evidently Roosevelt believed that rights are instruments, or tools, designed to protect human interests. The more fundamental the interests, the more important the instruments. During his presidency his rhetoric progressed directly from terms like "chance" and "opportunity," the language of governmental policy, to "rights," the language of governmental duty. Nor should it seem unfamiliar or odd to think of rights as tools. We have seen that freedom of speech may be understood in these terms as an effort to protect a wide range of human values. Of course free speech is desirable and important in itself. If so, the (legal) right to free speech is a way to safeguard that important interest. The second bill can be analyzed similarly. It identifies a range of fundamental human interests and promises to protect them.

11

Objections:
Against the Second Bill?

A second-class intellect. But a first-class temperament!
Oliver Wendell Holmes

He knew he had been taking some kind of middle road;
more important, the hostility he felt toward Marxist
doctrines, whether socialist or communist, . . . was not
merely ideological. It was psychological in the sense that
Roosevelt distrusted the kind of doctrinaire and systematic
thinking that was implicit in intellectual radicalism.

James MacGregor Burns

I T WOULD BE FOOLISH to suppose that the second bill of
rights could easily command a national consensus. Roosevelt's
speech is widely neglected, even unknown; its very obscurity
might be evidence of doubts about the second bill. So far I have
sketched some arguments on its behalf but no counterarguments.
Why might the second bill be rejected or opposed?

Since the second bill contains a number of rights, it would be possible to embrace some while rejecting others. As we have seen, the
right to education is enshrined in the constitutions of almost all
American states. An amendment creating a federal constitutional

right to education would probably receive considerable support. The right to social security, at least in some form, is broadly accepted. The right to be free from monopoly is embraced by all committed to free markets, although there is disagreement about what that right specifically entails. In the context of television and radio, for example, some people believe that vibrant competition exists, whereas others contend that problems of monopoly are created if one or two companies dominate a local market. But the antimonopoly principle itself is widely accepted in American culture.

The most controversial aspects of the second bill fall under the general rubric of freedom from desperate conditions. Is there really a right to a "decent and remunerative job"? Over 6 million Americans were unemployed in 2003, and few people argued that their rights were violated. Should Americans have a right to "adequate medical care and the opportunity to achieve and enjoy good health"? Over 40 million Americans lack health insurance, and the Clinton administration's efforts to create something like a right to health insurance were generally rejected as "socialized medicine." Perhaps Americans are committed to some version of "the right to adequate protection from the economic fears of old age, sickness, accident, and unemployment." But this commitment seems weaker than the commitment to freedom of speech or religion, or to education. In coming to terms with objections to the second bill, I put to one side education, social security, and freedom from monopoly and instead emphasize its most controversial goals.

On Incentives and Sloth

The most obvious complaint about the second bill is pragmatic in spirit. It is that the second bill would destroy people's incentive. It would give citizens an unhealthy and even destructive sense of entitlement—a belief that whatever they do, the state owes them the material preconditions of a decent life. On this view, anything like the second bill is a terrible idea, not because it does not include important human interests but because a recognition of those interests as "rights" is actually destructive to social and individual welfare. In fact the second bill might be thought to harm the very people that it is supposed to benefit. For people whose economic welfare is at risk, the best kind of help is self-help—a willingness and ability to do what must be done to earn a decent living. In the face of government guarantees, self-help is likely to be corroded. The principle that "no one owes anyone a living" must be preserved to ensure that people develop the independence that allows them to make their own way. A sense of economic entitlement might have deleterious effects on the American character by producing the kind of enervated, docile, timid, security-obsessed citizenry that would spell an end to the American character.

This objection points to an important consideration. Any second bill, and any effort to implement it, could have unintended harmful consequences, above all because of incentive effects. If recognition of the relevant rights would actually injure human interests, then those rights should not be recognized. Roosevelt himself was entirely alert to the problem. Of the eight rights enumerated in the bill, the first four refer to employment, not welfare rights: jobs; earnings that provide food, clothing, and recreation; decent economic returns; freedom from domination by monopolies. The eighth right, education, involves opportunity, not welfare. The seventh involves circumstances of special vulnerability: old age, sickness, accident, and unemployment. The fifth, to a decent home, and the sixth, to adequate medical care, are the closest to conventional welfare rights. But even these are carefully circumscribed. Roosevelt hoped that protection of these rights would come through a mixture of private and public action, based fundamentally on free enterprise.

Throughout his presidency, Roosevelt's emphasis was not on government guarantees or welfare payments. He despised the dole. Recall his suggestion that he had "no intention or desire to force either upon the country or the unemployed themselves a system of relief which is repugnant to American ideals of individual self-reliance." In emphasizing work, the New Dealers operated under a framework altogether different from that of President Johnson's War on Poverty and the welfare rights movement of the 1960s. Roosevelt sought the right to basic opportunity and to an economic system that would enable people to work. From education and employment, he thought, almost everything else would follow. But he insisted that the opportunity to work could not be simply assumed. It required a great deal of effort from government at the national, state, and local levels. To some degree, Roosevelt did endorse rights to material assistance. But he did so to protect those who were unable to work, principally as a result of accident, disease, or old age. His basic account was not complicated: first, opportunities for those who are able to take advantage of them; second, material necessities, provided as a matter of entitlement, for everyone else. This account could not possibly harm human character. On the contrary, it should improve it.

Roosevelt did not say that people should be given resources if they were able-bodied but refused to work. Since the New Deal, nations have learned a great deal about how to provide good initiatives while also helping those who need it. The most general principle is that government should rely on market-friendly, incentive-based programs, rather than on centralized national controls. As an illustration of a less-than-ideal plan, one unfortunately favored by Roosevelt himself, consider efforts to increase the minimum wage. The first problem is that large increases in the minimum wage decrease employment because employers are less willing to hire people if they must pay them a statutory minimum. An employer who is required to pay workers more than the market rate may well bring fewer workers on board. The second problem is that many of those who benefit from minimum wage increases have other sources of income and are not really poor. If we want to help working people who really need assistance, we will be suspicious of minimum wage increases, simply because they are not specifically targeted to those in need. The popular movement for a "living wage" requires employers to pay specified amounts in excess of the federal minimum (e.g., the amount necessary to lift a family of four above the federal poverty level). The living wage increases the income of many poor people, but it also increases the income of many people who are not poor. Like the minimum wage, it has the unfortunate effect of throwing people out of work.

As an illustration of what really works, consider the earned income tax credit (EITC), now used by many countries, including the United States. Under this approach, low-wage workers obtain a tax credit from the government, sufficient to raise their total compensation to a decent ("remunerative") level. In the United States, for example, someone who earns an income of about $10,000 receives about $3,800 at tax time; a mother and father who earn $25,000 receive about $1,200 at tax time. In this country, the EITC has been a terrific success, lifting millions of people from poverty. In recent years, it has helped as many as 5 million people, including over 2 million children, to receive incomes in excess of the poverty line.

There are three large advantages to the EITC approach. First, it does not make labor more costly for employers and thus does not decrease employers' desire to hire people. Second, it increases people's incentive to work by making work more remunerative. Third, it is specifically directed to people in need. Creative policymakers have built on this model to protect other aspects of the second bill. They have sought, for example, to provide housing vouchers to poor people and to provide food stamps to those who are unable to buy enough to eat. I do not attempt to design policy initiatives here. I am suggesting that those who believe in the second bill are not committed to approaches that would undermine incentives or cause serious dislocations in the economy. They are committed to certain goals or principles. The means for achieving those goals should attempt to use rather than displace markets, and they should be closely attuned to the harmful effects of certain kinds of government guarantees. It is fully possible to embrace the second bill while also encouraging self-help.

NEGATIVE RIGHTS AND POSITIVE RIGHTS

Many people believe they support "negative rights," or rights against government interference, but not "positive rights," or rights to government help. If this distinction is meaningful, then the second bill might be criticized on the ground that it creates an affirmative right to public assistance and is foreign to our traditional understanding of rights. Perhaps liberal democracies should restrict themselves to protection against government itself. At a minimum, perhaps the right to protection against government has a special status. Perhaps the second bill protects interests rather than rights, and perhaps we would cheapen the category of rights by including entitlements to positive protection by government. Perhaps the framers of the Constitution wisely understood a bill of rights as a place for preventing government overreaching and oppression.

Even if the rights included in the second bill are positive and those in the original bill are negative, it would not follow that the second bill should be rejected. Many people contend that the negative catalog should be supplemented with a positive one. If, for example, we believe in the distinction between negative rights and positive rights but insist that rights are efforts to protect human capabilities, we will embrace some negative rights and some positive ones. But the more serious problem is that the argument is rooted in a false distinction. The so-called negative rights are rights to government help too. This point is a natural implication of the realist attack on laissez-faire sketched in Chapter 2. It is no less important today than it was then, and the failure to appreciate it leads to mass confusion.

To see the point, begin with the two foundations of a market economy: private property and freedom of contract. Because they require government assistance, they cannot be guaranteed by laissez-faire. Private property depends on property rights, which do not exist without government and law. Those rights and everything that accompanies them are created by the legal system. Government is needed both to create the system of property rights and to police it. Without trespass laws and a police force, property could not exist. As Walter Lippmann wrote in 1937, "While the theorists were talking about laissez faire, men were buying and selling legal titles to property, were chartering corporations, were making and enforcing contracts, were suing for damages. In these transactions, by means of which the work of society was carried on, the state was implicated at every point." In the aftermath of communism, nations in Eastern Europe and the former Soviet Union have learned this lesson all too well. If Americans are able to neglect it, it is only because the affirmative acts of government in creating and enforcing property rights are so pervasive and so taken for granted that they do not seem to be acts at all.

In fact government is "implicated" in everything people own. When a company owns a broadcasting station or a number of broadcasting stations, this is possible only because the government creates a right of ownership—not only in the station's building and equipment but in the content the station broadcasts and even in the particular frequency on which it does so—and is prepared to back up that right with the law. If rich people have a great deal of money, it is because the government furnishes a system in which they are entitled to have and keep that money. Of course this is not to deny that many people work very hard for what they earn. But without government, people would face a free-for-all, a test of strength. Who knows what would emerge from that test? In the absence of an active government creating and policing property rights, ownership (to the extent that it exists at all) is a product of private power, meaning that it may be quite insecure. The resulting system has been well described as a kind of institutionalized black market, in which property rights depend on recognition by the powerful, including local leaders—village elders, warlords, Mafia heads, or anyone strong enough to fight well. In such a system, property is likely to be fragile and cannot easily be leveraged to create more wealth.

What is true of property is no less true of contracts. For free markets to work, governments cannot possibly stand aside. They need to set out a great deal of contract law. They also need to hold buyers and sellers to their contractual obligations, through courts and possibly the police; otherwise, too many people will fail to carry out their promises. If contractual commitments cannot be enforced by government, free markets will not operate. A strong and active government is indispensable. The supposedly negative right to contractual liberty is positive in character, requiring governmental involvement rather than absence.

The same points hold for all of our so-called negative liberties. Consider freedom of speech. In the United States, as in most democracies, free speech requires the streets and parks to be open and safe for political dissent. For streets and parks to be open, government must act; it is not enough to abstain. It is expensive to maintain public streets and parks. But government must do even more; it must expend effort to protect and manage public protests. In fact the most negative of liberties require an affirmative government. The basic right to be free from torture and police abuse requires that government take action to monitor the acts of its own agents to ensure that torture and abuse do not occur. If they do, government must prosecute the torturers as criminals. We can describe the right to be free from government abuse as a "negative" right if we wish, and in a sense the description is intelligible. But we should not overlook the extent to which protection of this "negative" right requires an array of (well-funded) "positive" protections.

The protection of other "negative" rights costs money too. The Fifth, Sixth, Seventh, and Eighth Amendments—a significant part of the original bill of rights—regulate the systems of criminal and civil justice. They require jury trials, fair hearings, rules of evidence, and bail. By doing this and more, they require taxpayers to devote a great deal of money to the administration of justice. Consider the suggestion, from a commentator in 1946, that it "is only because we are born into this mechanism as we are born into our homes that we take it for granted and fail to realize . . . what an immensity of daily effort on the part of government is required to keep it running. In terms of mechanism and trained personnel, a system of social security is child's play in comparison with the system that gives effect to due process of law." And this is simply the tip of the iceberg. To monitor its own agents, and thus to protect negative liberty, the government must spend hundreds of millions of dollars every year. Property and contract rights are more expensive still. They require a police force and a system of national defense; and now we are speaking of a significant fraction of the federal budget.

Hence it is a huge blunder to suggest, as many do, that for the old-style rights, the "government apparatus required is relatively small. . . .

The only significant expense is that of the military, to protect against foreign aggression." To protect the first bill, government must do far more than provide a military. Its apparatus must be very large indeed.

In these circumstances it is almost comically implausible to find so many people complaining that taxes take some portion of "their" money. A monthly paycheck, dividends from stocks, and interest on investments exist only because of a legal order and a set of policies from which people benefit. That order and those policies cost a great deal of money. When some money counts as "ours," it is not because nature so decreed it. It is because of an apparatus of rules involving ownership and contract. If an accompanying set of rules, called the rules of taxation, reduce the relevant amount, it is silly to try to complain about "government intrusion." Government intrusion is what makes paychecks, stocks, and investment interest possible in the first place. Of course some taxes are too high. But the objection to high taxes cannot possibly rest on a general complaint about "government."

Once these points are understood, it becomes impossible to oppose the second bill on the ground that rights are properly limited to protection "against" government. Even for those who reject the second bill, freedom requires government's presence, not absence.

We might go further still. Can those deprived of housing, food, and clothing complain that government has interfered with their "negative" rights? Certainly they can. Those who lack housing do so because other people's property is protected by the law of trespass. To recognize this point is not to complain about property rights, which are indispensable, but simply to say that homelessness is a legal status, produced partly by government and having nothing to do with nature. Recall Amartya Sen's emphasis on the role of "legal rights" in producing famines. "Other relevant factors, for example market forces, can be seen as operating *through* a system of legal relations (ownership rights, contractual obligations, legal exchanges, etc.). The law stands between food availability and food entitlement. Starvation deaths can reflect legality with a vengeance." Whether people are able to eat depends on their legal entitlements, particularly their legal rights to food and the things that make it possible for people to eat. The point holds for not only starvation deaths but a wide range of deprivations for which the second bill is meant as a remedy.

OF RIGHTS AND INTERESTS

Some people might concede this point and yet insist that there can be no "right" to government assistance—employment, food, shelter, clothing, housing, or medical care. In their view, citizens have a "right" to freedom of speech, religious liberty, or property, but not to government help. These claims need not depend on confused notions about negative and positive rights. They might depend on a principled position about what a right really is.

The term "right" is used in many different ways. In religious communities, it often refers to what is conferred by God, as distinct from human institutions. Perhaps the original bill of rights refers to God-given rights; perhaps the second bill is quite different on this score. The Declaration of Independence proclaims, "We hold these truths to be self-evident, that all men are created equal, that they are endowed by their Creator with certain unalienable Rights . . ." For many people, the rights listed in the second bill cannot plausibly be described in these terms. In the natural law tradition, overlapping with religious ones, the notion of rights usually refers to what people have or deserve by virtue of their humanity; sometimes this notion is mixed with an idea of what people had in the state of nature before government was instituted. Perhaps the second bill enumerates rights that cannot plausibly be justified by reference to natural law. In the social contract tradition, rights are sometimes conceived on the basis of an inquiry into what people gave up, and what they retained, by virtue of their movement from the state of nature into civil society. Perhaps social contract theories can support civil and political liberties but not a right to education or employment.

I do not intend to engage these approaches here or say anything controversial about the nature or foundation of rights. Following Roosevelt, I mean to understand rights in an essentially pragmatic way, one that brackets and does not contest the views just described. On the pragmatic approach, rights should be understood as *instruments for protecting important human interests*. This is a definition meant for certain purposes, not an argument; it does not accept or reject any large-scale theoretical claims. To accept the definition for certain purposes, one need not reject any particular account of the foundation of rights; one need not reject theology, social contract theory, or natural law. If we are asking about the theoretical foundations of rights, or using the term "rights" in a way that distinguishes them from mere interests, we would need to venture into more controversial territory. But for those who are thinking about a nation's basic commitments, the pragmatic approach will certainly do.

In this respect, the best response to those who believe that the second bill does not protect rights at all is just this: unembarrassed evasion. Perhaps the second bill does not protect rights in the sense in which the critics understand that idea. Perhaps the rights in the second bill do not have the status or foundations of the rights of the original bill. But an understanding of rights in that particular sense is irrelevant to the pragmatic goals of Roosevelt and others who endorsed the second bill. To share their endorsement, it is necessary only to say that the second bill recognizes important human interests and is a useful instrument for ensuring their realization. Can those points be reasonably disputed? On what ground?

SECURITY AND SCLEROSIS

A less high-flown objection would argue that the second bill would be systematically perverse or self-defeating. To see the objection, we might compare American law and policy with that of European nations having a full-blown commitment to a welfare state—say, France, Germany, and Austria. In those nations, a skeptic might insist that a cultural commitment to security and a decent social minimum has produced outcomes that Roosevelt himself might abhor. In some nations, millions of workers receive guarantees of job security, a short work week, and significant periods of vacation. But at the same time, millions of others are chronically unemployed and live off the dole, in the sense that Roosevelt believed to be destructive to the human spirit. The problem, in short, is economic sclerosis, stemming from the harmful effects of stringent regulation of the kind that seems broadly compatible with the New Deal. Policies that stem from a second bill threaten to redistribute the opportunity to work not from rich to poor, but from the unemployed poor to the employed middle class. Efforts to promote security might be self-defeating, not in the sense that they undermine incentives but because they create a patchwork of controls that increase both unemployment and dependency.

Let us take these points as objections to a European-style regulatory and welfare state, and as a plea for a more flexible system of labor and employment law. So taken, I do not mean to take a stand on them here. Many policies, nominally designed to protect the well-being of workers, end up increasing unemployment, if only because they increase the cost of hiring people. European labor markets, as well as European workers, have been badly hurt by rigid forms of regulation. But the problem lies in wrong-headed policies, not underlying goals. An aphorism attributed to law professor Karl Llewellyn is apt: "Technique without morals is a menace; but morals without technique is a mess." Much harmful regulation is a mess because it lacks technique. But the second bill specifies certain ends; it is agnostic about how to achieve them. A culture that is committed to the second bill would do well to choose means that are effective and do not produced harmful side effects. I have mentioned the earned income tax credit as an example. Creative policymakers can undoubtedly think of many others. The experience in Europe, to the extent that it has been unsuccessful, offers a warning about means; it does not draw Roosevelt's ends into the slightest doubt.

TAXES AND TAKINGS

A more severe objection would be that rights to decent minimum conditions are actually violative of rights, simply because they call for redistribution of resources. On this view, the second bill should be rejected because it compromises rights, properly conceived. The second bill would force some people to assist others through the coercive taking of their resources. To ensure that everyone has a "useful and remunerative job," "adequate food and clothing and recreation," or "a decent home," it will be necessary for many Americans to pay for others. Perhaps this is a violation of rights. In the words of one critic, the first bill "reflects an individualist political philosophy that prizes freedom, welfare rights a communitarian or collectivist one that is willing to sacrifice freedom." A similar point was lightly suggested in a *Wall Street Journal* editorial the day after Roosevelt's speech:

> We hope—indeed we assume—that the new bill would be in addition to and not a replacement of the existing one; yet the President discussed the existing one in the past tense. "They *were* [emphasis supplied] our rights to life and liberty," Mr. Roosevelt said.
> *Are*, not *were*, Mr. President.

It is important to be careful with this objection. The second bill is proposed in the name of liberty, not equality. Many people have made claims for basic equality of income and wealth, but Roosevelt was hardly in favor of that. Those who seek a decent floor need not seek equality; the second bill certainly does not. Roosevelt emphasized government efforts to ensure that the private economy would enable people to earn what they need. But unquestionably Roosevelt sought to "take" from those with large amounts of resources enough to ensure decent amounts for those who would otherwise be in desperate need.

Does this violate rights? Is taxation in the interest of the second bill a form of theft? To answer yes to these questions, we would have to believe that people have a right to their current holdings, so that any diminution of those holdings amounts to a violation of their rights. But I hope that I have said enough to show that this is an utterly implausible position. Those who possess a great deal do so because laws and institutions, including public institutions, make their holdings possible. Without public support, wealthy people could not possibly have what they own. Their holdings are protected by taxpayer-funded agencies, including the police and the courts. The same is true of liberty itself. In the state of nature—freed from the protection of law and government—how well would wealthy people fare?

What we earn is, in an important sense, ours. But what we *have* is made possible by an elaborate system of affirmative government. Those who denounce government largesse as a violation of rights disregard the extent to which their own rights are a product of government action and largesse.

Perhaps the real complaint about the second bill of rights as a rights violation does not involve the transfer of resources. Perhaps the fear is that the second bill would require an elaborate governmental apparatus that would pave the way toward a form of tyranny. Certainly this fear has played a role in stopping movements for health care reform in the United States. Perhaps the fear is well placed in this context. In the New Deal period, objections to the creation of new regulatory institutions, equipped with governmental power and sometimes insufficiently controlled by the democratic process, were quite common. Since then, the nation has had many unfortunate experiences with bureaucratic institutions. Consider the late, unlamented Interstate Commerce Commission—responsible, in its last decades, for high prices and little good in the transportation industry in the United States. Readers can no doubt think of their own examples.

It is important to create safeguards against bureaucratic error and abuse. Wherever possible, private, market-friendly approaches should be used to implement policies and protect rights. But as an objection to the second bill, the fear of tyranny is jejune. The rights to education and freedom from monopoly should not raise this concern at all. All over the world, governments provide protection in the event of old age, sickness, accident, and unemployment without creating tyranny. In the United States, far more could be done to protect basic security. Any such efforts must be carefully designed to avoid the risks of mistake and overreaching. But there is every reason to think that careful design is possible. Here again the earned income tax credit provides a useful model.

I have stressed my belief that Roosevelt was correct to contend that the second bill should be taken not as part of the written constitution, but as embodying principles to which the nation is fundamentally committed. But many people in many nations believe that something like the second bill should be a part of the formal constitution; and for other people in other nations this belief might be justified. Those who hold it must answer an objection that I have mentioned at several places—that the second bill could not possibly be enforced by courts. It is now time to explore that objection in detail.

12

The Question
of Enforcement

Better the occasional faults of a government that lives in a
spirit of charity than the consistent omissions of a
government frozen in the ice of its own indifference.

Franklin Delano Roosevelt

I HAVE ALREADY REFERRED to the question whether courts
could enforce the second bill of rights. If we conclude that judicial enforcement is impossible, we will not have defeated the argument for the second bill. On the contrary, we will have moved
some way toward Roosevelt's own position. Those who think that the
second bill is unenforceable might believe, with Roosevelt, that its
enumerated rights should count as constitutive commitments to be
protected democratically rather than judicially. Or they might urge a
path like that set out in the International Covenant on Economic,
Social, and Cultural Rights, where violations are monitored and
publicized but not addressed by courts.

In many nations, however, those who accept the second bill have
been arguing for judicial enforcement. Nor is the question irrelevant
in the United States. To a limited extent, aspects of the second bill are
recognized as parts of the existing Constitution, and courts continue
to play a role. State constitutions protect some aspects of the second

bill, and there are continuing arguments on behalf of a stronger place for state courts in protecting the relevant rights. Can they do so? This question is an intensely pragmatic one.

Skeptics are easy to find. In their view, courts could not possibly require governments to provide education, "adequate food and clothing and recreation," freedom from monopoly, or health care; requirements of this kind would be well beyond judicial capacities. But it is not clear that the skepticism is warranted. Why, exactly, would such requirements exceed judicial capacities? One possibility is that any "right to health care" is impossibly vague and courts lack the tools to say, specifically, what such a right entails. As we have seen, many old-fashioned rights seem equally vague. The right to "freedom of speech" could mean any number of things. Does free speech encompass commercial advertising, libel, sexually explicit speech, bribery, criminal solicitation, and nude dancing? Courts try to answer this question notwithstanding the vagueness of the text, and in doing so, they typically concede that the right itself is far from self-defining. Or consider the right to be free from "unreasonable searches and seizures." Is that right really more vague than the right to health care? The same question can be asked about most of the original bill of rights.

With respect to judicial enforcement, the difficulty with the second bill does not lie in ambiguity or vagueness but in the limited resources of government and the extreme difficulty of ensuring that the rights in the second bill are respected in practice. This is a particular problem in poor nations that cannot come close to ensuring that every citizen has health care, employment, or even food and shelter. For wealthy countries like the United States, it might be possible, in practice, to guarantee that almost all citizens have some of the rights in the second bill, such as a minimum level of education and social security. But even these countries would find it difficult to guarantee all of the rights listed in the second bill. No nation can ensure that every citizen has a job; a certain level of unemployment is inevitable. Even in the most generous nation, some citizens are likely to lack shelter some of the time. Homelessness cannot be eliminated even by the most effective housing programs. The broader problem is that in order to implement the second bill, government officials have to engage in resource allocation and program management. Courts are not in a good position to oversee those tasks.

Does this mean that courts can play no role at all? Does it follow that the second bill could not be enforced by the judiciary? My aim in this chapter is to shed light on this question, largely by discussing the constitution of South Africa and two extraordinary decisions by its Constitutional Court. Against its experience of apartheid, South Africa devoted a great deal of thought to social and economic rights in designing its new constitution. Its national debate on that topic was probably the most sophisticated in the history of the world, and the resulting constitution embodies an intriguing and ingenious solution to the puzzle of whether and how to place something like the second bill in a founding document. As we shall see, what makes the solution so promising is that it recognizes the relevant rights in a way that squarely acknowledges the budgetary problem.

The Constitutional Court of South Africa has issued two important opinions involving social and economic rights. The first of these involved the right to shelter; the second, the right to health care. In both decisions, the Constitutional Court concluded that courts could and should protect social and economic rights. And in both, the court ruled that the nation's government had failed to comply with its constitutional obligations. In *Government of the Republic of South Africa v. Grootboom*, the court said that the government was required to come up with a program of emergency housing for those in need of it. In *Minister of Health v. Treatment Action Campaign*, it ruled that the government was required to allow HIV-positive citizens access to drugs that promised to help them. The court did not say that every person in South Africa had an individual right to decent shelter or appropriate health care. But it did say that the government is under an obligation to take the two rights seriously and adopt programs that attempt to ensure them.

In my view, the Constitutional Court set out a fresh and promising approach to judicial protection of social and economic rights that directly addresses the most serious concerns of those who believe that such rights cannot be enforced by courts. The court's rulings require close attention to the human interests at stake and sensible priority setting, but they do not mandate protection of each person whose economic needs are at risk. They suggest that the underlying rights can serve, not to preempt democratic deliberation, but to ensure democratic attention to important interests that might otherwise be neglected in ordinary debate. This has large implications for how we think about citizenship, democracy, and minimal social and economic needs.

PRIORITY SETTING, WITH A GLANCE AT NEW YORK

Courts protecting the rights recognized by the second bill might interfere with sensible priority setting. A state that provides too little help to those who seek housing may be boosting employment or expending its resources on public health programs or educating children. Is a court supposed to oversee the full range of government programs to ensure that the state is emphasizing the right areas? How could a court possibly acquire the knowledge or make the value judgments that would enable it to do that? There is a related point. A judicial effort to protect social and economic rights might seem to preempt democratic deliberation on crucial issues. It would undermine the capacity of citizens to choose, in accordance with their own judgments, the kinds of welfare and employment programs that they favor. Of course some of these points hold for conventional rights as well. For instance, decisions designed to ensure a system of one person–one vote have required courts to involve themselves in electoral issues ordinarily resolved by elected representatives. Social and economic rights might be especially troublesome on this count if they put courts in the position of overseeing large-scale bureaucratic institutions.

We have seen that it would be possible to respond to these concerns in various ways. Perhaps constitutions should not include social and economic rights at all; perhaps the second bill should be treated as a set of constitutive commitments without legal status. Or perhaps such rights should be included in the Constitution, but with the explicit understanding that the legislature, not the courts, will be entrusted with their enforcement. Section IV of the Indian constitution expressly follows this route, offering judicially unenforceable "directive principles" and attempting to encourage legislative attention to these rights without involving the judiciary. The Indian constitution follows Roosevelt's basic plan—insisting that the second bill contains rights, real ones, but without entangling courts in the process of enforcement. If courts are not involved, there is a risk that the rights will be meaningless. But constitutional recognition of those rights might well prompt serious democratic attention to them.

We do not have to look outside of the United States to investigate the enforcement question. Many state constitutions guarantee social and economic rights. The right to education is especially popular, finding some kind of recognition in almost every state's founding document. Several state constitutions refer specifically to public assistance in a way that might well be taken to create rights. New York is a typical example. Article XVII, section 1 of the New York constitution declares: "The aid, care and support of the needy are public concerns and shall be provided by the state and by such of its subdivisions, and in such manner and by such means, as the legislature may from time to time determine." This provision was ratified in 1938, fresh on the heels of the Great Depression. It had two purposes. The first was to establish the legitimacy of social welfare programs and thus insulate them from constitutional attack. The second, more important for my purposes, was to establish that the state had a positive duty to assist those in need. Hence the highest court in New York declared that "assistance to the needy is not a matter of legislative grace; it is specifically mandated by our Constitution" and is "a fundamental part of the social contract."

But what, specifically, does this provision mean? We could understand it as expressing an aspiration rather than establishing any kind of right. Support for the needy is to be provided only "in such manner and by such means, as the legislature may from time to time determine." Perhaps courts have no business assessing the legislature's determinations. But in *Tucker v. Toia*, decided in 1971, the Court of Appeals of New York went much further, using the constitutional provision to strike down a state law. The relevant law restricted welfare payments, saying that they would not go to people under twenty-one who lived apart from a married person or a spouse *unless* the would-be beneficiary had first brought a lawsuit against any legally responsible relative to contribute to their support or care. The obvious purpose of this law was to ensure that legally responsible relatives, rather than taxpayers, paid for people's needs.

The court found that this provision violated the constitutional rights of young people. It ruled that the provision "would effectively deny public assistance to persons under the age of 21 who are concededly needy, often through no fault of their own, who meet all the criteria . . . for determining need," solely because they have not obtained a final disposition in a support proceeding. Some needy minors, the court reasoned, might not know the whereabouts of their parents, who might not be located in the state. The court agreed that the New York legislature has "great discretion in this area" but insisted that it could not "shirk its responsibility which is as fundamental as any responsibility of government."

In a more recent case, the same court went further, concluding that the state could not deny Medicaid benefits to legal immigrants. The case was brought by twelve aliens lawfully residing in New York. Under New York law, people entering the United States after August 22, 1996, could not receive state Medicaid benefits for five years after they established U.S. residency. The court acknowledged that the state "is not required to meet every legitimate need of every needy person," and that it had a great deal of discretion "to determine who is 'needy' and allocate the public dollar accordingly." But in this case, the state had imposed "an overly burdensome eligibility condition having nothing to do with need, depriving them of an entire category of otherwise available basic necessity benefits."

Notwithstanding these decisions, New York courts have been reluctant to intervene aggressively into state welfare programs. In one case, for example, welfare support was denied to people who refused, apparently without adequate justification, to accept employment. The court upheld the denial of support, concluding that such people could reasonably be deemed not to be "needy." The court also upheld a statute saying that when infant children were living with grandparents, a portion of their grandparents' income would be "deemed" available to them for purposes of calculating their welfare payments. The court said that this statute was a reasonable way of defining need even if, in individual cases, the grandparents' income was sometimes unavailable for the child.

The situation in New York is highly illuminating. It suggests that a degree of judicial enforcement of the second bill is indeed possible—that courts can take some steps toward protecting desperate needs while also respecting reasonable judgments by the legislature.

Rights and Resources

A great deal of litigation on these issues has come from Europe, especially Eastern Europe, where courts have actively protected social and economic rights. For example, the Constitutional Court of Latvia, invoking the right to social insurance, ruled that foreign nationals working in Latvia under temporary residence permits have the right to unemployment benefits under the Constitution. The same court struck down a law allowing employers extra time to make their contributions to social security for employees. The Supreme Court of Estonia struck down a law making grants of public assistance conditional on the recipient's ownership of or legal right to use a dwelling. The court saw the law as unduly restricting the fundamental right to subsistence benefits.

In an especially striking decision, the European Union ruled that a prisoner had an absolute right under the European Human Rights Convention to government provision of adequate food; this right could not be restricted for any reason. It followed that government could not reduce a prisoner's meals from three per day to one as punishment for his refusal to wear prison clothing. The Polish Constitutional Court invoked the right to housing to invalidate an eviction law that did not guarantee poor people adequate replacement housing. The High Court of Romania relied on the right to unemployment benefits to strike down a law that denied such benefits to workers who lost their jobs while attending institutions of higher education.

All over the world, courts are developing principles to adjudicate claims that the government has failed to respect social and economic guarantees. The most detailed of these rulings have come from South Africa.

The appropriate approach to social and economic rights was intensely debated before ratification of the South African constitution. The idea of including such economic rights was greatly spurred by their recognition in international law, and above all by the International Covenant on Economic, Social, and Cultural Rights. This in itself is a testimony to Roosevelt's influence. Without his advocacy of freedom from want and his plea for a second bill of rights, it is most doubtful that social and economic guarantees would have the status they do. As a matter of principle, few South Africans argued that shelter, food, and decent health care did not belong on the list of important human interests. Nor were these kinds of rights given less importance than conventional civil and political rights. The argument against including them in the constitution was made on pragmatic grounds: Were they really subject to judicial enforcement? Could they be protected in the same way more conventional rights are? In the end, the argument for social and economic rights was irresistible, in large part because such guarantees seemed an indispensable way of expressing a commitment to overcome the legacy of apartheid—the overriding goal of the new South African constitution.

I should emphasize here a general point about constitutionalism. Some constitutions are *preservative*; they seek to maintain existing practices to ensure that things do not get worse. Other constitutions are *transformative*; they set out certain aspirations that are emphatically understood as a challenge to long-standing practices. They are defined in opposition to those practices. The American Constitution combines preservative and transformative features. Some of its provisions look backward. Consider, for example, the due process clause of the Fifth and Fourteenth Amendments, which forbids government from taking life, liberty, or property without due process of law. The due process clause has often been understood as an effort to protect long-standing traditions; it ensures that government does not violate Anglo-American rights as understood for generations. But other provisions of the American Constitution look forward. The equal protection clause of the Fourteenth Amendment, for example, was designed as an attack on racial discrimination. It was directed against practices of discrimination that had been long-standing and that many feared would endure. Not surprisingly, when the American Constitution has been used to create social and economic guarantees, it has been through interpretation of the equal protection clause.

The South African constitution is the world's leading example of a transformative constitution. A great deal of the document is an effort to eliminate apartheid "root and branch." The presence of social and economic rights in its text is best understood as an effort to ensure that future governments do not fall prey to anything like the evils of the apartheid era. The central goal was to ensure that no class of people would live in desperate conditions and that government would promise to take steps to ensure against extreme deprivation.

But what is the relationship among social and economic rights, available resources, courts, and legislatures? The authors of the South African constitution were aware that the new government could not guarantee a comfortable minimum to every citizen of the nation. They were therefore presented with a choice. Having decided to include some aspects of the second bill, they could have followed the Indian approach and adopted "directive principles" not subject to judicial enforcement. Alternatively, they could have followed an approach that has also proved popular in international documents, in which social and economic rights are guaranteed only "within the available resources" of the nation. This wording leaves considerable ambiguity: What does "within the available resources" mean? At a minimum, this qualification is a recognition that limited resources will force the government to do less than it might in principle.

The South African constitution embodies the latter course. The rights in question typically take the following form:

1. Everyone has the right to [the relevant good].
2. The state must take reasonable legislative and other measures, within its available resources, to achieve the progressive realization of this right.

This is the basic form of constitutional rights to housing, health care services, sufficient food and water, and social security. But some aspects of the second bill seem more firmly protected. Thus the constitution says simply and directly: "No one may be refused emergency medical treatment." It also gives everyone the right "to a basic education, including adult basic education." With respect to children, the constitution says without qualification that every child has the right "to basic nutrition, shelter, basic health care, services, and social services," and also "to be protected from maltreatment, neglect, abuse or degradation." In some ways, the South African constitution goes well beyond the second bill. It gives everyone the right "to an environment that is not harmful to their health or well-being." It also recognizes a right "to have the environment protected" via "reasonable legislative and other measures" that prevent pollution, promote conservation, and secure ecologically sustainable development.

At first glance, this constitution appears to guarantee many of the rights recognized by the second bill and make them enforceable by courts. But for most of the social and economic rights, the reference to "available resources" renders the document unclear on enforcement. Who decides what is available? On the basis of the text alone, we could imagine a judicial ruling to the effect that courts can play no role at all—that elected officials alone can decide whether and what resources are "available." On this view, the South African constitution is, with respect to judicial enforcement, closely akin to the Indian constitution. But we could also imagine a ruling to the effect that courts are required to protect the relevant rights—by ensuring that the state has taken "reasonable legislative and other measures, within its available resources, to achieve progressive realisation" of those rights. If, for example, the state does little to provide people with decent food and health care, and if it is financially able to do much more, it would seem that the state has violated the constitutional guarantee.

In an early judgment certifying the constitution, the Constitutional Court of South Africa wrote an opinion on several of these issues. In speaking of social and economic rights, the court said that these rights are indeed subject to judicial enforcement. The court concluded that such rights "are, at least to some extent, justiciable." The fact that resources would have to be expended on them was hardly decisive, for this was true of "many of the civil and political rights entrenched" in the constitution. Many rights, including so-called negative rights, "will give rise to similar budgetary implications without compromising their justiciability."

So far, the court seemed to be suggesting that in South Africa, the second bill would not be treated differently from the first. But in a final sentence, it added fresh confusion by suggesting that at "the very minimum, socio-economic rights can be protected negatively from improper invasion." The court did not say whether and when courts could go beyond the "minimum" to protect rights "positively"; nor did it clarify what it would mean to invade socio-economic rights "negatively." Perhaps the court meant to say that when the state, or someone else, actually deprived someone of (for example) shelter, say by evicting them from the only available source of housing, judicial enforcement would be appropriate. This might be a case of "improper invasion" of a right. It would not be trivial to recognize a constitutional right to be free of such invasions. But compared to what is imaginable, this would be a narrow use of judicial authority in overseeing the relevant rights. It would not obligate the government to provide food, shelter, or health care.

The first important decision from South Africa's highest court was about the right to shelter.

SHELTER

The *Grootboom* case was brought by nine hundred plaintiffs, of whom 510 were children. The plaintiffs had lived for a long period in an informal squatter settlement named Wallacedene, near the Western Cape. Most of the people there were desperately poor; they lived in shacks without water, sewage, or refuse removal services. Only one in twenty had electricity. The lead plaintiff, Irene Grootboom, lived with her own family and her sister's family in a shack of about twenty square meters.

Numerous people in the Wallacedene settlement had applied for low-cost housing. Many had been placed on a waiting list, where they remained for a number of years. In late 1998, frustrated by the intolerable conditions at Wallacedene, they moved out and put up shacks and shelters on vacant land that was privately owned and earmarked for formal low-cost housing. A few months later, the owner obtained an ejectment order against them. But Grootboom and others refused to leave. They contended that their previous sites were now occupied and they had nowhere else to go. Eventually they were forcibly evicted, their homes burned and bulldozed, and their possessions destroyed. At this point they found shelter on a sports field in Wallacedene, under temporary structures consisting of plastic sheets. At this stage they contended that their constitutional rights had been violated.

Two constitutional provisions were central to the plaintiffs' claim. The first was section 26, which provides:

> (1) Everyone has the right to have access to adequate housing.
> (2) The State must take reasonable legislative and other measures, within its available resources, to achieve the progressive realisation of this right.

(3) No one may be evicted from their home, or have their home demolished, without an order of court made after considering all the relevant circumstances. No legislation may permit arbitrary evictions.

The second was section 28(1)(c), limited to children. That section reads:

28 Every child has the right—. . .
   . . . to family care or parental care, or to appropriate alternative care when removed from the family environment:
   . . . to basic nutrition, shelter, basic health care services and social services.

For purposes of constitutional interpretation, the largest puzzle had to do with the relationship between section 26 and section 28. As I have suggested, section 28 could easily be read as giving children an unqualified right to various goods and imposing on the government an absolute obligation, even if resources are scarce, to ensure that children eat, are housed, and receive health care and social services. Under this interpretation, section 26 creates a qualified right for everyone ("progressive realisation"), whereas section 28 creates an unqualified right for children in particular. The lower court reasoned in exactly this way, holding that section 28 creates a freestanding, absolute right on the part of children to the constitutional protections. On this interpretation, the rights of children are not qualified by "available resources" or by the "progressive realisation" clause.

The Court Speaks

In 2000 the Constitutional Court rejected this interpretation. It refused to say that children have unqualified rights of any kind. At the same time, it concluded that social and economic rights would be enforced by courts. More particularly, it concluded that the constitution imposes a judicially enforceable duty on government; that what is required is "reasonableness"; and that the plaintiffs' constitutional rights had been violated by the absence of a program to provide "temporary relief" for those without shelter. The court held that the constitution required not only a long-term plan to provide low-income shelter but also a system to ensure short-term help for people with no place to live. This is the first time the high court of any nation issued a ruling with this degree of ambition. What is most striking about the ruling is the distinctive and novel approach to social and economic rights, requiring not shelter for everyone but sensible priority setting with particular attention to the plight of the neediest.

The court's analysis began by noting that all people have a right to legislative and other measures designed to achieve "the progressive realization of this right" to shelter, not to shelter regardless of financial constraints. At the same time, the state and "all other entities and persons" are constitutionally required "to desist from preventing or impairing the right of access to adequate housing." By itself this idea is quite ambiguous. What counts as prevention or impairment?

To implement the right to shelter, the court said that the state faced two kinds of duties. With respect to "those who can afford to pay for adequate housing," the state's duty is to "unlock the system, providing access to housing stock and a legislative framework to facilitate self-built houses through planning laws and access to finance." Notice the court's emphasis on the "unlocking" role of the constitution. On one interpretation, the court is stressing that free markets in housing can actually promote the right to shelter. On that interpretation, the state has a duty to ban a system of monopoly in housing— to create markets sufficiently free and flexible to provide housing to those who can pay for it. If a nation has free markets in shelter, the system of competition should make a great deal of housing available and some of it at low prices. A free market system is to a large extent an ally, rather than an enemy, of shelter for all.

For the poorest people, the state's obligation is different. Here its duty might be discharged through "programmes to provide adequate social assistance to those who are otherwise unable to support themselves and their dependents." In *Grootboom*, the central issue was whether the government had taken "reasonable" measures to ensure progressive realization of the right. The court concluded that it had not, despite the extensive public apparatus to facilitate access to housing. The reason for this conclusion was simple: The state had not provided emergency assistance for those in need. The real problem was that "there is no express provision to facilitate access to temporary relief for people who have no access to land, no roof over their heads, for people who are living in intolerable conditions and for people who are in crisis because of natural disasters such as floods or fires, or because their homes are under threat of demolition."

The court acknowledged that the government need not make provision for those in desperate need "if the nationwide housing programme would result in affordable houses for most people within a reasonably short time." Note that "most people" does not mean all people; the clear implication is that a lack of housing for some would not necessarily be unreasonable or inconsistent with the constitutional plan. The government is constitutionally obligated to maintain a *system* of a certain kind rather than fully individual protections. But under the existing national program, "most people" would not have "affordable houses" within a reasonably short time. Hence the nation's housing program is constitutionally unacceptable insofar as "it fails to recognize that the state must provide for relief for those in desperate need. . . . It is essential that a reasonable part of the national housing budget be devoted to this, but the precise allocation is for the national government to decide in the first instance."

In the court's view, the constitution did not create a right to "shelter or housing immediately upon demand." But it did create a right to a "coherent, co-ordinated programme designed to meet" constitutional obligations. The state was therefore required to create such a program, including reasonable measures specifically designed "to provide relief for people who have no access to land, no roof over their heads, and who are living in intolerable conditions or crisis situations." Here we can find a novel, distinctive, and promising approach to a democratic constitution's social and economic rights.

HEALTH

Should other aspects of the second bill be understood under a similar framework? The South African Constitutional Court gave a partial answer in an extraordinary context: that nation's AIDS crisis. At first glance, the constitutional right to "health care services" would seem to give a great deal to citizens of South African.

In the *Treatment Action Campaign* case, decided in 2002, the specific question was whether the government had adequately responded to the risk that HIV-positive mothers would transmit the virus to their newborn infants. The government had adopted an unusually restrictive policy requiring each of the nation's nine provinces to establish two research centers for testing and counseling and for the administration of the antiviral drug nevirapine. Except in these centers, however, the government prohibited the administration of nevirapine, even when doctors believed it medically appropriate. The Treatment Action Campaign, concerned to protect citizens against AIDS, claimed that the government's policy violated the constitution. It argued that nevirapine had to be made available in the public health sector whenever the attending doctor favored its use. The treatment action campaign also claimed that the government had violated its constitutional obligations in failing to establish a time frame for the creation of a national program designed to prevent mother-to-child transmission of HIV. These were extraordinary claims. The plaintiffs were asking the Constitutional Court to scrutinize the government's operation of an exceedingly complex health care system.

The governing constitutional provisions were sections 27 and 28. Section 27 grants "everyone" the right of access to "health care services, including reproductive health care," with the qualification that the state "must take reasonable legislative and other measures, within its available resources, to achieve the progressive realisation of" these rights. Here we find a clear echo of the second bill. Section 28, it will be recalled, grants every child the right to "basic nutrition, shelter, basic health care services and social services." The government justified its policies by pointing out that nevirapine required a substitution of bottle-feeding for breast-feeding, which could prove confusing for poorly educated mothers. In any case, the government argued that it wanted, in the long run, to develop a "comprehensive package" for testing and counseling, which would include dispensing nevirapine. The government contended that without this comprehensive package, doctors at public health hospitals could not provide the appropriate advice, counseling, and follow-up care. Without these ancillary services, the government argued that nevirapine might not provide the promised benefits. To this the government added its fear that the drug carried a set of potentially harmful side effects.

The court accepted one of the government's central claims. It acknowledged that "the socio-economic rights should not be construed as entitling everyone to demand that the minimum core be provided to them." Thus the court rejected the suggestion that every citizen should enjoy, independently of resources, a minimal level of health care protection. What is required is that the state "provide access" to these rights "on a progressive basis." Hence the constitution required the state to undertake reasonable measures designed "to eliminate or reduce the large areas of severe deprivation that afflict our society." But on this count, the court was entirely unconvinced by the government's effort to defend its program. Its central conclusion was captured in a question: "What is to happen to those mothers and their babies who cannot afford access to private health care and do not have access to the research and training sites?"

On the facts, the court found that the government's arguments were not reasonable. "It is clear from the evidence that the provision of Nevirapine will save the lives of a significant number of infants even if it is administered without the full package and support services." Scientific studies had shown that nevirapine could combat mother-to-child transmission even if the mother breast-fed her baby. No solid evidence supported the claim that low doses of nevirapine would produce resistant strains of HIV. Even if this was a risk, the benefits of the same doses were likely to be far greater. "The prospects of the child surviving if infected are so slim and the nature of the suffering so grave that the risk of some resistance manifesting at some time in the future is well worth running." As for safety, the court found too little evidence of potential harm to justify the government's concern. Of course budgetary constraints were relevant and justified the absence of a "comprehensive package" everywhere. But they did not justify limiting the availability of a life-saving drug.

The court concluded that the government was obliged to "devise and implement within its available resources a comprehensive and coordinated programme to realise progressively the rights of pregnant women to have access to health services to combat mother-to-child transmission of HIV." The program had to include "reasonable measures for counselling and testing pregnant women for HIV, counselling HIV-positive pregnant women on the options open to them to reduce the risk of mother-to-child transmission of HIV, and making appropriate treatment available to them for such purposes." The court ordered the government to remove the restrictions on the availability of nevirapine; to permit and facilitate the use of the drug, with appropriate testing and counseling; to make provision for training counselors in its use; and to take reasonable steps to extend testing and counseling facilities throughout the public health sector to facilitate the use of nevirapine.

This is a truly remarkable opinion. The Constitutional Court essentially monitored government efforts to address the AIDS crisis. In the process it rejected a policy judgment that seemed, on its face, to have at least some logical foundation. It is hard to imagine a similar decision from an American court. The U.S. Constitution has played no role in the many debates about speeding up government approval of drugs to control AIDS. Confronted with a challenge to government decisions, American courts would undoubtedly say that the Constitution provides no right to health care. The American Constitution bears on at least one medical procedure—abortion—but the Court has made it clear that the government is under no obligation to subsidize abortion, even when it is medically necessary for poor women.

QUESTIONS ANSWERED

The South African Constitutional Court's decisions cast new light on the proper relationship among the second bill, constitutional law, and democratic deliberation. In poor nations, and even in wealthy ones, governments cannot possibly ensure that everyone lives in decent conditions. If courts cannot say that "everyone" will have housing or adequate health care, what can they say in response to an objection that a government program is inadequate?

All rights have costs. The right to free speech will not be protected unless taxpayers fund a judicial system willing and able to protect that right. A system committed to free speech will also require taxpayer resources to be devoted to keeping open certain arenas where speech can occur, such as streets and parks. In protecting the most conventional rights, the government cannot avoid setting priorities. But when cases go to court, the conventional rights are and can be fully protected at the individual level. Most of the time, courts can say that an official is censoring speech or restricting freedom of religion, and they can insist that the misconduct stop. Courts do not need to ask government to create some kind of "reasonable" overall system for safeguarding these rights.

By their very nature, social and economic rights are different. No one thinks that every individual has an enforceable right to full protection of the interests cataloged on the second bill. In making clear that the state need not give every citizen a home, the South African court stressed that the right to housing is not absolute. For the second bill, the difficult task is to identify an approach that avoids two extreme options: judicial protection of fully individual rights or a conclusion that courts cannot play a role at all. But the South African court has marked out a third path. What the court calls for is some sort of reasonable plan designed to ensure that relief will be forthcoming to a significant percentage of poor people. On this view, the South African constitution constrains government not by ensuring that everyone receives shelter but by requiring government to devote a reasonable level of resources, more than it otherwise would, to the problem of insufficient housing for the poor. That in effect is what the court held in *Grootboom*. It required government to develop and fund a program by which a large number of poor people are given access to emergency housing. Of course the idea of reasonableness is not self-defining, and here the government has a good deal of discretion. But whatever its discretion, it did not act reasonably in the *Grootboom* case itself.

In *Treatment Action Campaign*, the court refused to hold that every individual must receive adequate health care. Instead it banned the government from utterly neglecting a large-scale problem, and it reviewed the reasonableness of government's central choices. This decision must be understood in the context of the South African government's palpably inadequate response to the HIV crisis—a response bred partly by the irresponsible denial, among high-level officials, that HIV is responsible for AIDS at all. In these circumstances, it made sense for the court to do something other than rubber-stamp the government's failure to make a life-saving medicine available to young children. What the constitutional right requires is not housing or health care on demand, but a reasonable effort at ensuring both. This approach ensures respect for sensible priority setting and close attention to particular needs, without displacing democratic judgments about how to set priorities. This is now the prevailing approach in South Africa.

The broader point is that a constitutional right to shelter or health care can strengthen the hand of those who might be unable to make much progress in the political arena, perhaps because they are unsympathetic figures or are disorganized and lack political power. Provisions in the second bill of rights can promote democratic deliberation, not preempt it, by directing political attention to interests that would otherwise be disregarded in ordinary political life. By requiring reasonable programs, with respect for limited budgets, the court has found a way of assessing claims of constitutional violations without requiring more than existing resources will allow. In so doing, the court has provided the most convincing rebuttal yet to the claim that judicial protection of the second bill could not possibly work in practice. We now have reason to believe that a democratic constitution, even in a poor nation, is able to protect those rights without placing an undue strain on judicial capacities.

By itself, this point does not demonstrate that the second bill belongs in a constitution, or that the United States should amend its founding document in order to include it. For America, the simpler and better course seems to be Roosevelt's own: to treat the second bill as a set of constitutive commitments, helping define the nation's deepest principles. But the South African experience shows that some of the strongest objections to constitutionalizing the second bill are misconceived. If courts are asked to protect the rights that Roosevelt identified, they have sensible ways to do so.

Epilogue

Roosevelt's Incomplete Triumph

America is new. It is in the process of change and development. It has the great potentialities of youth.

Franklin Delano Roosevelt

I'm sorry, I have to run.

Franklin Delano Roosevelt

FRANKLIN DELANO ROOSEVELT wrote or contributed to countless articles, essays, and speeches, but he produced only one book before he became president. In 1926, at the age of forty-four, Roosevelt lectured at Milton Academy in Massachusetts. The slim volume that resulted from his lectures is called *Whither Bound?*

Much of the book is devoted to an account of the likely future and the need for an optimistic attitude toward it. Roosevelt speaks disapprovingly of an imaginary "citizen of this land" who is "sorely troubled . . . of gloomy religion, of copybook sentiment, of life by precept," who "lived as had his fathers before him." This imaginary citizen is hostile to social and scientific change; he is alarmed by technology and even more by challenges to the existing social structure. "Women—think of it, Women!—were commencing to take positions in offices and industrial plants, and demanding—a very few of them—things called political rights." For Roosevelt, the coming changes should be seen as opportunities, full of promise. But "some among us would stop the clock, call a halt to all this change, and then in some well-thought-out way bring back an orderly, defined way of life . . . the 'good old days' restored."

Roosevelt ridicules this position. He predicts that medicine will conquer many old forms of disease, with the result that "we begin to expect to live to a ripe old age by right, and not by mere chance." He foresees changes in transportation that will make current capacities appear "childish within our own lives." More remarkably, he contemplates a future "when any two persons on earth will be able to be completely present to one another" in less than a second. "I wonder, indeed, if the thought of this probability is one whit more startling to us to-night than the thought of the human voice carried over the telephone was to our grandfathers." All the trends, Roosevelt suggests, are "toward the greater unification of mankind." Human diseases are increasingly spreading from one nation to another. "Power is exported. Capital is international." As a result, isolation "of individual nations will be as difficult in this future as would be the isolation of New England or the South to-day." This is true in economics, science, and even law, where experiments in one national unit "are influenced by experiments in other units."

In his last few pages, Roosevelt turns from prognostication to political and moral issues. Here he offers a plea. The idea of "service of mankind," he urges, while much discussed, is "still in its infancy of development. True service will not come until all the world recognizes all the rest of the world as one big family." It is not enough to help a fellow human being out of a sense of duty. Assistance should be provided not from duty but "as an interest. How many of us lend helping hands to people we do not like, people who do not 'belong to our crowd,' people whom we subconsciously hope we may never see again?" Increasingly, Roosevelt contends, "we become interdependent. Communities merge into states, states into nations, nations into families of peoples." The real task is to "take our part positively and not negatively."

In the decade that followed, America's public institutions were radically transformed under Roosevelt's leadership. The federal government assumed powers formerly believed to rest with the states. The presidency grew dramatically in stature and importance; it became the principal seat of American democracy. A newly developed bureaucracy, including independent regulatory commissions, was put in place. The foundations of the transformation are best captured in a changing understanding of rights, often requiring helping hands. In Roosevelt's view, desperate conditions are not inescapable by-products of our economic order; they are preventable by a decent and alert government. "The laws of economics are not made by na ture; they are made by human beings." Roosevelt insisted on opportu-nities for all and a cushion for those at the bottom of this "man-made world of ours." He organized his claims under the rubric of security, which he saw as indispensable to freedom. Eventually these claims were thoroughly internationalized, with the insistence that each of the four freedoms should be enjoyed "everywhere in the world."

Roosevelt believed that by 1944 the United States had "come to ac-cept" the second bill of rights. Badly scarred by the Great Depression and a world war, the nation was now committed to freedom from want and freedom from fear, which it saw as inextricably intertwined. The second bill was necessary to achieve both forms of freedom. Following James Madison's aspirations for the original bill of rights, Roosevelt hoped that the second bill would play a large role in poli-tics and even culture. Americans had come to understand that what-ever their rhetoric, no one is against government intervention, and the idea of laissez-faire is a misleading description of their system. Those with wealth and property are advantaged, every day of every year, by government and law. The people who complain most vocifer-ously about "government interference" are already benefiting from it. Far from being self-sufficient, they owe their own well-being in large part to government assistance. By 1944, Roosevelt argued, the real task was to implement the second bill.

Well over a half century later, this task remains badly incomplete. To be sure, the second bill helps account for central features of modern American government. The right to education is firmly entrenched at the state level and receives explicit recognition in many state constitutions. The Supreme Court has said that the fed-eral Constitution itself gives some protection to this right, and the national government is committed in principle to ensuring a decent education for all. In the same vein, the right to be free from monop-oly is a firmly established part of contemporary government. The laws forbidding conspiracy in restraint of trade are nearly as secure as the right to free speech itself. So too the Social Security Act has the essen-tial characteristics of a constitutive commitment. In public life, no serious person can argue for its abolition. Reasonable politicians differ about how, exactly, to keep that commitment. But when officials are seen to question the commitment itself, the public reacts as if a fundamental principle were at stake. Large-scale national programs do a great deal to provide food, housing, employment, and even health care. In all of these ways, we live under Roosevelt's Constitution whether we know it or not. The American Constitution has become, in crucial respects, his own.

But Roosevelt's triumph is only partial. The second bill of rights is not implemented. Twenty percent of American children live in poverty—the highest rate of any industrialized nation in the world. Millions of young Americans receive an inadequate education. Millions of Americans are unemployed. Millions experience serious hunger. Millions lack health insurance—and as a result, thousands of Americans die prematurely each year.

The numbers mask larger issues. Too many of the nation's citizens neglect the extent to which their own well-being is a product of a system of government that benefits them every day. Too many Americans complain about government intervention without understanding that the wealth and opportunities they enjoy exist only because of that intervention—aggressive, pervasive, coercive, and well funded. In a society that purports to prize opportunity for all, too many citizens lack a minimally fair chance. In the past decades, we have disregarded some of our deepest ideals, with roots not merely in the New Deal but in the Civil War and the founding period itself. The second bill of rights is largely unknown.

America now celebrates what it calls the Greatest Generation, the victors in World War II. Because of its achievements, its sacrifices, and its valor, the World War II generation deserves the celebration. But it does not deserve sentimentality, romanticism, or ancestor worship. These could not be farther from its pragmatic and forward-looking spirit. In the midst of World War II, the greatest leader of that generation believed it had a project, one that was radically incomplete. The project is best captured in the second bill of rights.

Freedom from fear is inextricably linked to freedom from want. Liberty and citizenship are rooted in opportunity and security. In a sense, America lives under the second bill. But in another sense, we have lost sight of it. The second bill of rights should be reclaimed in its nation of origin.

APPENDIX I

Message to the Congress on the State of the Union

JANUARY 11, 1944

To the Congress:

This Nation in the past two years has become an active partner in the world's greatest war against human slavery.

We have joined with like-minded people in order to defend ourselves in a world that has been gravely threatened with gangster rule.

But I do not think that any of us Americans can be content with mere survival. Sacrifices that we and our allies are making impose upon us all a sacred obligation to see to it that out of this war we and our children will gain something better than mere survival.

We are united in determination that this war shall not be followed by another interim which leads to new disaster—that we shall not repeat the tragic errors of ostrich isolationism—that we shall not repeat the excesses of the wild twenties when this Nation went for a joy ride on a roller coaster which ended in a tragic crash.

When Mr. Hull went to Moscow in October, and when I went to Cairo and Teheran in November, we knew that we were in agreement with our allies in our common determination to fight and win this war. But there were many vital questions concerning the future peace, and they were discussed in an atmosphere of complete candor and harmony.

In the last war such discussions, such meetings, did not even begin until the shooting had stopped and the delegates began to assemble at the peace table. There had been no previous opportunities for man-to-man discussions which lead to meetings of minds. The result was a peace which was not a peace.

That was a mistake which we are not repeating in this war.

And right here I want to address a word or two to some suspicious souls who are fearful that Mr. Hull or I have made "commitments" for the future which might pledge this Nation to secret treaties, or to enacting the role of Santa Claus.

To such suspicious souls—using a polite terminology—I wish to say that Mr. Churchill, and Marshal Stalin, and Generalissimo Chiang Kai-shek are all thoroughly conversant with the provisions of our Constitution. And so is Mr. Hull. And so am I.

Of course we made some commitments. We most certainly committed ourselves to very large and very specific military plans which require the use of all Allied forces to bring about the defeat of our enemies at the earliest possible time.

But there were no secret treaties or political or financial commitments.

The one supreme objective for the future, which we discussed for each Nation individually, and for all the United Nations, can be summed up in one word: Security.

And that means not only physical security which provides safety from attacks by aggressors. It means also economic security, social security, moral security—in a family of Nations.

In the plain down-to-earth talks that I had with the Generalissimo and Marshal Stalin and Prime Minister Churchill, it was abundantly clear that they are all most deeply interested in the resumption of peaceful progress by their own peoples—progress toward a better life. All our allies want freedom to develop their lands and resources, to build up industry, to increase education and individual opportunity, and to raise standards of living.

All our allies have learned by bitter experience that real development will not be possible if they are to be diverted from their purpose by repeated wars—or even threats of war.

China and Russia are truly united with Britain and America in recognition of this essential fact:

The best interests of each Nation, large and small, demand that all freedom-loving Nations shall join together in a just and durable system of peace. In the present world situation, evidenced by the actions of Germany, Italy, and Japan, unquestioned military control over disturbers of the peace is as necessary among Nations as it is among citizens in a community. And an equally basic essential to peace is a decent standard of living for all individual men and women and children in all Nations. Freedom from fear is eternally linked with freedom from want.

There are people who burrow through our Nation like unseeing moles, and attempt to spread the suspicion that if other Nations are encouraged to raise their standards of living, our own American standard of living must of necessity be depressed.

The fact is the very contrary. It has been shown time and again that if the standard of living of any country goes up, so does its purchasing power—and that such a rise encourages a better standard of living in neighboring countries with whom it trades. That is just plain common sense—and it is the kind of plain common sense that provided the basis for our discussions at Moscow, Cairo, and Teheran.

Returning from my journeyings, I must confess to a sense of "letdown" when I found many evidences of faulty perspective here in Washington. The faulty perspective consists in overemphasizing lesser problems and thereby underemphasizing the first and greatest problem.

The overwhelming majority of our people have met the demands of this war with magnificent courage and understanding. They have accepted inconveniences; they have accepted hardships; they have accepted tragic sacrifices. And they are ready and eager to make whatever further contributions are needed to win the war as quickly as possible—if only they are given the chance to know what is required of them.

However, while the majority goes on about its great work without complaint, a noisy minority maintains an uproar of demands for special favors for special groups. There are pests who swarm through the lobbies of the Congress and the cocktail bars of Washington, representing these special groups as opposed to the basic interests of the Nation as a whole. They have come to look upon the war primarily as a chance to make profits for themselves at the expense of their neighbors—profits in money or in terms of political or social preferment.

Such selfish agitation can be highly dangerous in wartime. It creates confusion. It damages morale. It hampers our national effort. It muddies the waters and therefore prolongs the war.

If we analyze American history impartially, we cannot escape the fact that in our past we have not always forgotten individual and selfish and partisan interests in time of war—we have not always been united in purpose and direction. We cannot overlook the serious dissensions and the lack of unity in our war of the Revolution, in our War of 1812, or in our War Between the States, when the survival of the Union itself was at stake.

In the first World War we came closer to national unity than in any previous war. But that war lasted only a year and a half, and increasing signs of disunity began to appear during the final months of the conflict.

In this war, we have been compelled to learn how interdependent upon each other are all groups and sections of the population of America.

Increased food costs, for example, will bring new demands for wage increases from all war workers, which will in turn raise all prices of all things including those things which the farmers themselves have to buy. Increased wages or prices will each in turn produce the same results. They all have a particularly disastrous result on all fixed income groups.

And I hope you will remember that all of us in this Government represent the fixed income group just as much as we represent business owners, workers, and farmers. This group of fixed-income people includes: teachers, clergy, policemen, firemen, widows and minors on fixed incomes, wives and dependents of our soldiers and sailors, and old-age pensioners. They and their families add up to one-quarter of our one hundred and thirty million people. They have few or no high pressure representatives at the Capitol. In a period of gross inflation they would be the worst sufferers.

If ever there was a time to subordinate individual or group selfishness to the national good, that time is now. Disunity at home—bickerings, self-seeking partisanship, stoppages of work, inflation, business as usual, politics as usual, luxury as usual—these are the influences which can undermine the morale of the brave men ready to die at the front for us here.

Those who are doing most of the complaining are not deliberately striving to sabotage the national war effort. They are laboring under the delusion that the time is past when we must make prodigious sacrifices—that the war is already won and we can begin to slacken off. But the dangerous folly of that point of view can be measured by the distance that separates our troops from their ultimate objectives in Berlin and Tokyo—and by the sum of all the perils that lie along the way.

Overconfidence and complacency are among our deadliest enemies. Last spring—after notable victories at Stalingrad and in Tunisia and against the U-boats on the high seas—overconfidence became so pronounced that war production fell off. In two months, June and July, 1943, more than a thousand airplanes that could have been made and should have been made were not made. Those who failed to make them were not on strike. They were merely saying, "The war's in the bag—so let's relax."

That attitude on the part of anyone—Government or management or labor—can lengthen this war. It can kill American boys.

Let us remember the lessons of 1918. In the summer of that year the tide turned in favor of the allies. But this Government did not relax. In fact, our national effort was stepped up. In August, 1918, the draft age limits were broadened from 21–31 to 18–45. The President called for "force to the utmost," and his call was heeded. And in November, only three months later, Germany surrendered.

That is the way to fight and win a war—all out—and not with half-an-eye on the battlefronts abroad and the other eye-and-a-half on personal, selfish, or political interests here at home.

Therefore, in order to concentrate all our energies and resources on winning the war, and to maintain a fair and stable economy at home, I recommend that the Congress adopt:

- A realistic tax law—which will tax all unreasonable profits, both individual and corporate, and reduce the ultimate cost of the war to our sons and daughters. The tax bill now under consideration by the Congress does not begin to meet this test.
- A continuation of the law for the renegotiation of war contracts—which will prevent exorbitant profits and assure fair prices to the Government. For two long years I have pleaded with the Congress to take undue profits out of war.
- A cost of food law—which will enable the Government (a) to place a reasonable floor under the prices the farmer may expect for his production; and (b) to place a ceiling on the prices a consumer will have to pay for the food he buys. This should apply to necessities only; and will require public funds to carry out. It will cost in appropriations about one percent of the present annual cost of the war.

Early reenactment of the stabilization statute of October, 1942. This expires June 30, 1944, and if it is not extended well in advance, the country might just as well expect price chaos by summer.

We cannot have stabilization by wishful thinking. We must take positive action to maintain the integrity of the American dollar.

A national service law—which, for the duration of the war, will prevent strikes, and, with certain appropriate exceptions, will make available for war production or for any other essential services every able-bodied adult in this Nation.

These five measures together form a just and equitable whole. I would not recommend a national service law unless the other laws were passed to keep down the cost of living, to share equitably the burdens of taxation, to hold the stabilization line, and to prevent undue profits.

The Federal Government already has the basic power to draft capital and property of all kinds for war purposes on a basis of just compensation.

As you know, I have for three years hesitated to recommend a national service act. Today, however, I am convinced of its necessity. Although I believe that we and our allies can win the war without such a measure, I am certain that nothing less than total mobilization of all our resources of manpower and capital will guarantee an earlier victory, and reduce the toll of suffering and sorrow and blood.

I have received a joint recommendation for this law from the heads of the War Department, the Navy Department, and the Maritime Commission. These are the men who bear responsibility for the procurement of the necessary arms and equipment, and for the successful prosecution of the war in the field. They say:

> When the very life of the Nation is in peril the responsibility for service is common to all men and women. In such a time there can be no discrimination between the men and women who are assigned by the Government to its defense at the battlefront and the men and women assigned to producing the vital materials essential to successful military operations. A prompt enactment of a National Service Law would be merely an expression of the universality of this responsibility.

I believe the country will agree that those statements are the solemn truth.

National service is the most democratic way to wage a war. Like selective service for the armed forces, it rests on the obligation of each citizen to serve his Nation to his utmost where he is best qualified.

It does not mean reduction in wages. It does not mean loss of retirement and seniority rights and benefits. It does not mean that any substantial numbers of war workers will be disturbed in their present jobs. Let these facts be wholly clear.

Experience in other democratic Nations at war—Britain, Canada, Australia, and New Zealand—has shown that the very existence of national service makes unnecessary the widespread use of compulsory power. National service has proven to be a unifying moral force—based on an equal and comprehensive legal obligation of all people in a Nation at war.

There are millions of American men and women who are not in this war at all. It is not because they do not want to be in it. But they want to know where they can best do their share. National service provides that direction. It will be a means by which every man and woman can find that inner satisfaction which comes from making the fullest possible contribution to victory.

I know that all civilian war workers will be glad to be able to say many years hence to their grandchildren: "Yes, I, too, was in service in the great war. I was on duty in an airplane factory, and I helped make hundreds of fighting planes. The Government told me that in doing that I was performing my most useful work in the service of my country."

It is argued that we have passed the stage in the war where national service is necessary. But our soldiers and sailors know that this is not true. We are going forward on a long, rough road—and, in all journeys, the last miles are the hardest. And it is for that final effort—for the total defeat of our enemies—that we must mobilize our total resources. The national war program calls for the employment of more people in 1944 than in 1943.

It is my conviction that the American people will welcome this win-the-war measure which is based on the eternally just principle of "fair for one, fair for all."

It will give our people at home the assurance that they are standing four-square behind our soldiers and sailors. And it will give our enemies demoralizing assurance that we mean business—that we, 130,000,000 Americans, are on the march to Rome, Berlin, and Tokyo.

I hope that the Congress will recognize that, although this is a political year, national service is an issue which transcends politics. Great power must be used for great purposes.

As to the machinery for this measure, the Congress itself should determine its nature—but it should be wholly nonpartisan in its make-up.

Our armed forces are valiantly fulfilling their responsibilities to our country and our people. Now the Congress faces the responsibility for taking those measures which are essential to national security in this the most decisive phase of the Nation's greatest war.

Several alleged reasons have prevented the enactment of legislation which would preserve for our soldiers and sailors and marines the fundamental prerogative of citizenship—the right to vote. No amount of legalistic argument can becloud this issue in the eyes of these ten million American citizens. Surely the signers of the Constitution did not intend a document which, even in wartime, would be construed to take away the franchise of any of those who are fighting to preserve the Constitution itself.

Our soldiers and sailors and marines know that the overwhelming majority of them will be deprived of the opportunity to vote, if the voting machinery is left exclusively to the States under existing State laws—and that there is no likelihood of these laws being changed in time to enable them to vote at the next election. The Army and Navy have reported that it will be impossible effectively to administer forty-eight different soldier-voting laws. It is the duty of the Congress to remove this unjustifiable discrimination against the men and women in our armed forces—and to do it as quickly as possible.

It is our duty now to begin to lay the plans and determine the strategy for the winning of a lasting peace and the establishment of an American standard of living higher than ever before known. We cannot be content, no matter how high that general standard of living may be, if some fraction of our people—whether it be one-third or one-fifth or one-tenth—is ill-fed, ill-clothed, ill-housed, and insecure.

This Republic had its beginning, and grew to its present strength, under the protection of certain inalienable political rights—among them the right of free speech, free press, free worship, trial by jury, freedom from unreasonable searches and seizures. They were our rights to life and liberty.

As our Nation has grown in size and stature, however—as our industrial economy expanded—these political rights proved inadequate to assure equality in the pursuit of happiness.

We have come to a clear realization of the fact that true individual freedom cannot exist without economic security and independence. "Necessitous men are not free men." People who are hungry and out of a job are the stuff of which dictatorships are made.

In our day these economic truths have become accepted as self-evident. We have accepted, so to speak, a second Bill of Rights under which a new basis of security and prosperity can be established for all—regardless of station, race, or creed.

Among these are:

- The right to a useful and remunerative job in the industries or shops or farms or mines of the Nation;
- The right to earn enough to provide adequate food and clothing and recreation;
- The right of every farmer to raise and sell his products at a return which will give him and his family a decent living;
- The right of every businessman, large and small, to trade in an atmosphere of freedom from unfair competition and domination by monopolies at home or abroad;
- The right of every family to a decent home;
- The right to adequate medical care and the opportunity to achieve and enjoy good health;
- The right to adequate protection from the economic fears of old age, sickness, accident, and unemployment;
- The right to a good education.

All of these rights spell security. And after this war is won we must be prepared to move forward, in the implementation of these rights, to new goals of human happiness and well-being.

America's own rightful place in the world depends in large part upon how fully these and similar rights have been carried into practice for our citizens. For unless there is security here at home there cannot be lasting peace in the world.

One of the great American industrialists of our day—a man who has rendered yeoman service to his country in this crisis—recently emphasized the grave dangers of "rightist reaction" in this Nation. All clear-thinking businessmen share his concern. Indeed, if such reaction should develop—if history were to repeat itself and we were to return to the so-called "normalcy" of the 1920's—then it is certain that even though we shall have conquered our enemies on the battlefields abroad, we shall have yielded to the spirit of Fascism here at home.

I ask the Congress to explore the means for implementing this economic bill of rights—for it is definitely the responsibility of the Congress so to do. Many of these problems are already before committees of the Congress in the form of proposed legislation. I shall from time to time communicate with the Congress with respect to these and further proposals. In the event that no adequate program of progress is evolved, I am certain that the Nation will be conscious of the fact.

Our fighting men abroad—and their families at home—expect such a program and have the right to insist upon it. It is to their demands that this Government should pay heed rather than to the whining demands of selfish pressure groups who seek to feather their nests while young Americans are dying.

The foreign policy that we have been following—the policy that guided us at Moscow, Cairo, and Teheran—is based on the common sense principle which was best expressed by Benjamin Franklin on July 4, 1776: "We must all hang together, or assuredly we shall all hang separately."

I have often said that there are no two fronts for America in this war. There is only one front. There is one line of unity which extends from the hearts of the people at home to the men of our attacking forces in our farthest outposts. When we speak of our total effort, we speak of the factory and the field, and the mine as well as of the battleground—we speak of the soldier and the civilian, the citizen and his Government.

Each and every one of us has a solemn obligation under God to serve this Nation in its most critical hour—to keep this Nation great—to make this Nation greater in a better world.

APPENDIX II

The Universal Declaration of Human Rights (excerpts)

ARTICLE 22

Everyone, as a member of society, has the right to social security and is entitled to realization, through national effort and international co-operation and in accordance with the organization and resources of each State, of the economic, social and cultural rights indispensable for his dignity and the free development of his personality.

ARTICLE 23

(1) Everyone has the right to work, to free choice of employment, to just and favourable conditions of work and to protection against unemployment.

(2) Everyone, without any discrimination, has the right to equal pay for equal work.

(3) Everyone who works has the right to just and favourable remuneration ensuring for himself and his family an existence worthy of human dignity, and supplemented, if necessary, by other means of social protection.

(4) Everyone has the right to form and to join trade unions for the protection of his interests.

ARTICLE 24

Everyone has the right to rest and leisure, including reasonable limitation of working hours and periodic holidays with pay.

Article 25

(1) Everyone has the right to a standard of living adequate for the health and well-being of himself and of his family, including food, clothing, housing and medical care and necessary social services, and the right to security in the event of unemployment, sickness, disability, widowhood, old age or other lack of livelihood in circumstances beyond his control.

(2) Motherhood and childhood are entitled to special care and assistance. All children, whether born in or out of wedlock, shall enjoy the same social protection.

Article 26

(1) Everyone has the right to education. Education shall be free, at least in the elementary and fundamental stages. Elementary education shall be compulsory. Technical and professional education shall be made generally available and higher education shall be equally accessible to all on the basis of merit.

(2) Education shall be directed to the full development of the human personality and to the strengthening of respect for human rights and fundamental freedoms. It shall promote understanding, tolerance and friendship among all nations, racial or religious groups, and shall further the activities of the United Nations for the maintenance of peace.

(3) Parents have a prior right to choose the kind of education that shall be given to their children.

International Covenant on Economic, Social, and Cultural Rights (excerpts)

ARTICLE 2

1. Each State Party to the present Covenant undertakes to take steps, individually and through international assistance and co-operation, especially economic and technical, to the maximum of its available resources, with a view to achieving progressively the full realization of the rights recognized in the present Covenant by all appropriate means, including particularly the adoption of legislative measures.

2. The States Parties to the present Covenant undertake to guarantee that the rights enunciated in the present Covenant will be exercised without discrimination of any kind as to race, colour, sex, language, religion, political or other opinion, national or social origin, property, birth or other status.

ARTICLE 3

The States Parties to the present Covenant undertake to ensure the equal right of men and women to the enjoyment of all economic, social and cultural rights set forth in the present Covenant.

ARTICLE 4

The States Parties to the present Covenant recognize that, in the enjoyment of those rights provided by the State in conformity with the present Covenant, the State may subject such rights only to such limitations as are determined by law only in so far as this may be compatible with the nature of these rights and solely for the purpose of promoting the general welfare in a democratic society.

ARTICLE 5

1. Nothing in the present Covenant may be interpreted as implying for any State, group or person any right to engage in any activity or to perform any act aimed at the destruction of any of the rights or freedoms recognized herein, or at their limitation to a greater extent than is provided for in the present Covenant.

2. No restriction upon or derogation from any of the fundamental human rights recognized or existing in any country in virtue of law, conventions, regulations or custom shall be admitted on the pretext that the present Covenant does not recognize such rights or that it recognizes them to a lesser extent.

ARTICLE 6

1. The States Parties to the present Covenant recognize the right to work, which includes the right of everyone to the opportunity to gain his living by work which he freely chooses or accepts, and will take appropriate steps to safeguard this right.

2. The steps to be taken by a State Party to the present Covenant to achieve the full realization of this right shall include technical and vocational guidance and training programmes, policies and techniques to achieve steady economic, social and cultural development and full and productive employment under conditions safeguarding fundamental political and economic freedoms to the individual.

ARTICLE 7

The States Parties to the present Covenant recognize the right of everyone to the enjoyment of just and favourable conditions of work which ensure, in particular:

(a) Remuneration which provides all workers, as a minimum, with:
  (i) Fair wages and equal remuneration for work of equal value without distinction of any kind, in particular women being guaranteed conditions of work not inferior to those enjoyed by men, with equal pay for equal work;
  (ii) A decent living for themselves and their families in accordance with the provisions of the present Covenant;

(b) Safe and healthy working conditions;
(c) Equal opportunity for everyone to be promoted in his employment to an appropriate higher level, subject to no considerations other than those of seniority and competence;
(d) Rest, leisure and reasonable limitation of working hours and periodic holidays with pay, as well as remuneration for public holidays

ARTICLE 9

The States Parties to the present Covenant recognize the right of everyone to social security, including social insurance.

ARTICLE 11

1. The States Parties to the present Covenant recognize the right of everyone to an adequate standard of living for himself and his family, including adequate food, clothing and housing, and to the continuous improvement of living conditions. The States Parties will take appropriate steps to ensure the realization of this right, recognizing to this effect the essential importance of international co-operation based on free consent.

2. The States Parties to the present Covenant, recognizing the fundamental right of everyone to be free from hunger, shall take, individually and through international co-operation, the measures, including specific programmes, which are needed:

(a) To improve methods of production, conservation and distribution of food by making full use of technical and scientific knowledge, by disseminating knowledge of the principles of nutrition and by developing or reforming agrarian systems in such a way as to achieve the most efficient development and utilization of natural resources;

(b) Taking into account the problems of both food-importing and food-exporting countries, to ensure an equitable distribution of world food supplies in relation to need.

ARTICLE 12

1. The States Parties to the present Covenant recognize the right of everyone to the enjoyment of the highest attainable standard of physical and mental health.

2. The steps to be taken by the States Parties to the present Covenant to achieve the full realization of this right shall include those necessary for:

(a) The provision for the reduction of the stillbirth-rate and of infant mortality and for the healthy development of the child;

(b) The improvement of all aspects of environmental and industrial hygiene;

(c) The prevention, treatment and control of epidemic, endemic, occupational and other diseases;

(d) The creation of conditions which would assure to all medical service and medical attention in the event of sickness.

ARTICLE 13

1. The States Parties to the present Covenant recognize the right of everyone to education. They agree that education shall be directed to the full development of the human personality and the sense of its dignity, and shall strengthen the respect for human rights and fundamental freedoms. They further agree that education shall enable all persons to participate effectively in a free society, promote understanding, tolerance and friendship among all nations and all racial, ethnic or religious groups, and further the activities of the United Nations for the maintenance of peace.

2. The States Parties to the present Covenant recognize that, with a view to achieving the full realization of this right:

(a) Primary education shall be compulsory and available free to all;

(b) Secondary education in its different forms, including technical and vocational secondary education, shall be made generally available and accessible to all by every appropriate means,
and in particular by the progressive introduction of free education;

(c) Higher education shall be made equally accessible to all, on
the basis of capacity, by every appropriate means, and in particular by the progressive introduction of free education;

(d) Fundamental education shall be encouraged or intensified as
far as possible for those persons who have not received or
completed the whole period of their primary education;

(e) The development of a system of schools at all levels shall be actively pursued, an adequate fellowship system shall be established, and the material conditions of teaching staff shall be
continuously improved. . . .

Article 16

1. The States Parties to the present Covenant undertake to submit in
conformity with this part of the Covenant reports on the measures which
they have adopted and the progress made in achieving the observance of
the rights recognized herein.

2. All reports shall be submitted to the Secretary-General of the
United Nations, who shall transmit copies to the Economic and Social
Council for consideration in accordance with the provisions of the pres-
ent Covenant.

Excerpts from Various Constitutions

Constitution of South Africa (excerpts)

Section 26 Housing

(1) Everyone has the right to have access to adequate housing.

(2) The state must take reasonable legislative and other measures, within its available resources, to achieve the progressive realisation of this right.

(3) No one may be evicted from their home, or have their home demolished, without an order of court made after considering all the relevant circumstances. No legislation may permit arbitrary evictions.

Section 27 Health care, food, water and social security

(1) Everyone has the right to have access to -

  (a) health care services, including reproductive health care;

  (b) sufficient food and water; and

  (c) social security, including, if they are unable to support themselves and their dependants, appropriate social assistance.

(2) The state must take reasonable legislative and other measures, within its available resources, to achieve the progressive realisation of each of these rights.

(3 No one may be refused emergency medical treatment.

Section 28 Children

(1) Every child has the right -

    (a) to a name and a nationality from birth;

    (b) to family care or parental care, or to appropriate alternative care when removed from the family environment;

    (c) to basic nutrition, shelter, basic health care services and social services;

    (d) to be protected from maltreatment, neglect, abuse or degradation;

    (e) to be protected from exploitative labour practices;

    (f) not to be required or permitted to perform work or provide services that -

        (i) are inappropriate for a person of that child's age; or

        (ii) place at risk the child's well-being, education, physical or mental health or spiritual, moral or social development;

    (g) not to be detained except as a measure of last resort, in which case, in addition to the rights a child enjoys under sections 12 and 35, the child may be detained only for the shortest appropriate period of time, and has the right to be

        (i) kept separately from detained persons over the age of 18 years; and

        (ii) treated in a manner, and kept in conditions, that take account of the child's age;

    (h) to have a legal practitioner assigned to the child by the state, and at state expense, in civil proceedings affecting the child, if substantial injustice would otherwise result; and

        (i) not to be used directly in armed conflict, and to be protected in times of armed conflict.

(2) A child's best interests are of paramount importance in every matter concerning the child.

(3) In this section "child" means a person under the age of 18 years.

Section 29 Education

(1) Everyone has the right -

    (a) to a basic education, including adult basic education; and

    (b) to further education, which the state, through reasonable measures, must make progressively available and accessible.

(2) Everyone has the right to receive education in the official language or languages of their choice in public educational institutions where that education is reasonably practicable. In order to ensure the effective access to, and implementation of, this right, the state must consider all reasonable educational alternatives, including single medium institutions, taking into account -

(a) equity;
(b) practicability; and
(c) the need to redress the results of past racially discriminatory laws and practices.

(3) Everyone has the right to establish and maintain, at their own expense, independent educational institutions that -

(a) do not discriminate on the basis of race;
(b) are registered with the state; and
(c) maintain standards that are not inferior to standards at comparable public educational institutions.

(4) Subsection (3) does not preclude state subsidies for independent educational institutions.

Constitution of India (excerpts)
Part IV Directive Principles of State Policy

Article 37

Application of the principles contained in this Part

The provisions contained in this Part shall not be enforced by any court, but the principles therein laid down are nevertheless fundamental in the governance of the country and it shall be the duty of the State to apply these principles in making laws.

Article 38

State to secure a social order for the promotion of welfare of the people

(1) The State shall strive to promote the welfare of the people by securing and protecting as effectively as it may a social order in which justice, social, economic and political, shall inform all the institutions of the national life.

(2) The State shall, in particular, strive to minimise the inequalities in income, and endeavour to eliminate inequalities in status, facilities and opportunities, not only amongst individuals but also amongst groups of people residing in different areas or engaged in different vocations.

Article 39

Certain principles of policy to be followed by the State

The State shall, in particular, direct its policy towards securing -

(a) that the citizens, men and women equally, have the right to an adequate means of livelihood;

(b) that the ownership and control of the material resources of the community are so distributed as best to subserve the common good;

(c) that the operation of the economic system does not result in the concentration of wealth and means of production to the common detriment;

(d) that there is equal pay for equal work for both men and women;

(e) that the health and strength of workers, men and women, and the tender age of children are not abused and that citizens are not forced by economic necessity to enter avocations unsuited to their age or strength;

(f) that children are given opportunities and facilities to develop in a healthy manner and in conditions of freedom and dignity and that childhood and youth are protected against exploitation and against moral and material abandonment.

Article 41

Right to work, to education and to public assistance in certain cases

The State shall, within the limits of its economic capacity and development, make effective provision for securing the right to work, to education and to public assistance in cases of unemployment, old age, sickness and disablement, and in other cases of undeserved want.

Article 45

Provision for free and compulsory education for children

The State shall endeavor to provide, within a period of ten years from the commencement of this Constitution, for free and compulsory education for all children until they complete the age of fourteen years.

Article 47

Duty of the State to raise the level of nutrition and the standard of living and to improve public health

The State shall regard the raising of the level of nutrition and the standard of living of its people and the improvement of public health as among its primary duties and, in particular, the State shall endeavour to bring about prohibition of the consumption except for medicinal purpose of intoxicating drinks and of drugs which are injurious to health.

EUROPEAN SOCIAL CHARTER (EXCERPTS)

PREAMBLE

The governments signatory hereto, being members of the Council of Europe,

Considering that the aim of the Council of Europe is the achievement of greater unity between its members for the purpose of safeguarding and realising the ideals and principles which are their common heritage and of facilitating their economic and social progress, in particular by the maintenance and further realisation of human rights and fundamental freedoms;

Considering that in the Convention for the Protection of Human Rights and Fundamental Freedoms signed at Rome on 4th November 1950, and the Protocol thereto signed at Paris on 20th March 1952, the member States of the Council of Europe agreed to secure to their populations the civil and political rights and freedoms therein specified;

Considering that the enjoyment of social rights should be secured without discrimination on grounds of race, colour, sex, religion, political opinion, national extraction or social origin;

Being resolved to make every effort in common to improve the standard of living and to promote the social well-being of both their urban and rural populations by means of appropriate institutions and action,

Have agreed as follows:

Part I

The Contracting Parties accept as the aim of their policy, to be pursued by all appropriate means, both national and international in character, the attainment of conditions in which the following rights and principles may be effectively realised:

1. Everyone shall have the opportunity to earn his living in an occupation freely entered upon.
2. All workers have the right to just conditions of work.
3. All workers have the right to safe and healthy working conditions.
4. All workers have the right to a fair remuneration sufficient for a decent standard of living for themselves and their families.
5. All workers and employers have the right to freedom of association in national or international organisations for the protection of their economic and social interests.
6. All workers and employers have the right to bargain collectively.
7. Children and young persons have the right to a special protection against the physical and moral hazards to which they are exposed.
8. Employed women, in case of maternity, and other employed women as appropriate, have the right to a special protection in their work.
9. Everyone has the right to appropriate facilities for vocational guidance with a view to helping him choose an occupation suited to his personal aptitude and interests.
10. Everyone has the right to appropriate facilities for vocational training.
11. Everyone has the right to benefit from any measures enabling him to enjoy the highest possible standard of health attainable.
12. All workers and their dependents have the right to social security.
13. Anyone without adequate resources has the right to social and medical assistance.
14. Everyone has the right to benefit from social welfare services.
15. Disabled persons have the right to vocational training, rehabilitation and resettlement, whatever the origin and nature of their disability.
16. The family as a fundamental unit of society has the right to appropriate social, legal and economic protection to ensure its full development.
17. Mothers and children, irrespective of marital status and family relations, have the right to appropriate social and economic protection.

18. The nationals of any one of the Contracting Parties have the right to engage in any gainful occupation in the territory of any one of the others on a footing of equality with the nationals of the latter, subject to restrictions based on cogent economic or social reasons.

19. Migrant workers who are nationals of a Contracting Party and their families have the right to protection and assistance in the territory of any other Contracting Party.

Part II

The Contracting Parties undertake, as provided for in Part III, to consider themselves bound by the obligations laid down in the following articles and paragraphs.

Article 1—The right to work. With a view to ensuring the effective exercise of the right to work, the Contracting Parties undertake:

1. to accept as one of their primary aims and responsibilities the achievement and maintenance of as high and stable a level of employment as possible, with a view to the attainment of full employment;

2. to protect effectively the right of the worker to earn his living in an occupation freely entered upon;

3. to establish or maintain free employment services for all workers;

4. to provide or promote appropriate vocational guidance, training and rehabilitation.

Article 2—The right to just conditions of work. With a view to ensuring the effective exercise of the right to just conditions of work, the Contracting Parties undertake:

1. to provide for reasonable daily and weekly working hours, the working week to be progressively reduced to the extent that the increase of productivity and other relevant factors permit;

2. to provide for public holidays with pay;

3. to provide for a minimum of two weeks annual holiday with pay;

4. to provide for additional paid holidays or reduced working hours for workers engaged in dangerous or unhealthy occupations as prescribed;

5. to ensure a weekly rest period which shall, as far as possible, coincide with the day recognised by tradition or custom in the country or region concerned as a day of rest.

Article 3—The right to safe and healthy working conditions.   With a view to ensuring the effective exercise of the right to safe and healthy working conditions, the Contracting Parties undertake:

1. to issue safety and health regulations;
2. to provide for the enforcement of such regulations by measures of supervision;
3. to consult, as appropriate, employers' and workers' organisations on measures intended to improve industrial safety and health.

Article 4—The right to a fair remuneration.   With a view to ensuring the effective exercise of the right to a fair remuneration, the Contracting Parties undertake:

1. to recognise the right of workers to a remuneration such as will give them and their families a decent standard of living;
2. to recognise the right of workers to an increased rate of remuneration for overtime work, subject to exceptions in particular cases;
3. to recognise the right of men and women workers to equal pay for work of equal value;
4. to recognise the right of all workers to a reasonable period of notice for termination of employment;
5. to permit deductions from wages only under conditions and to the extent prescribed by national laws or regulations or fixed by collective agreements or arbitration awards.

The exercise of these rights shall be achieved by freely concluded collective agreements, by statutory wage-fixing machinery, or by other means appropriate to national conditions.

[. . .]

Article 10—The right to vocational training.   With a view to ensuring the effective exercise of the right to vocational training, the Contracting Parties undertake:

1. to provide or promote, as necessary, the technical and vocational training of all persons, including the handicapped, in consultation with employers' and workers' organisations, and to grant facilities for access to higher technical and university education, based solely on individual aptitude;
2. to provide or promote a system of apprenticeship and other systematic arrangements for training young boys and girls in their various employments;

3. to provide or promote, as necessary:

   a. adequate and readily available training facilities for adult workers;
   b. special facilities for the re-training of adult workers needed as a result of technological development or new trends in employment;

4 to encourage the full utilisation of the facilities provided by appropriate measures such as:

   a. reducing or abolishing any fees or charges;
   b. granting financial assistance in appropriate cases;
   c. including in the normal working hours time spent on supplementary training taken by the worker, at the request of his employer, during employment;
   d. ensuring, through adequate supervision, in consultation with the employers' and workers' organisations, the efficiency of apprenticeship and other training arrangements for young workers, and the adequate protection of young workers generally.

Article 11—The right to protection of health. With a view to ensuring the effective exercise of the right to protection of health, the Contracting Parties undertake, either directly or in co-operation with public or private organisations, to take appropriate measures designed inter alia:

1. to remove as far as possible the causes of ill-health;
2. to provide advisory and educational facilities for the promotion of health and the encouragement of individual responsibility in matters of health;
3. to prevent as far as possible epidemic, endemic and other diseases.

Article 12—The right to social security. With a view to ensuring the effective exercise of the right to social security, the Contracting Parties undertake:

1. to establish or maintain a system of social security;
2. to maintain the social security system at a satisfactory level at least equal to that required for ratification of International Labour Convention No. 102 Concerning Minimum Standards of Social Security;
3. to endeavour to raise progressively the system of social security to a higher level;

4. to take steps, by the conclusion of appropriate bilateral and multilateral agreements, or by other means, and subject to the conditions laid down in such agreements, in order to ensure:

  a. equal treatment with their own nationals of the nationals of other Contracting Parties in respect of social security rights, including the retention of benefits arising out of social security legislation, whatever movements the persons protected may undertake between the territories of the Contracting Parties;
  b. the granting, maintenance and resumption of social security rights by such means as the accumulation of insurance or employment periods completed under the legislation of each of the Contracting Parties.

Article 13—The right to social and medical assistance.   With a view to ensuring the effective exercise of the right to social and medical assistance, the Contracting Parties undertake:

1. to ensure that any person who is without adequate resources and who is unable to secure such resources either by his own efforts or from other sources, in particular by benefits under a social security scheme, be granted adequate assistance, and, in case of sickness, the care necessitated by his condition;

2. to ensure that persons receiving such assistance shall not, for that reason, suffer from a diminution of their political or social rights;

3. to provide that everyone may receive by appropriate public or private services such advice and personal help as may be required to prevent, to remove, or to alleviate personal or family want.

Notes

Front Matter

vii   **alms given:** Baron de Montesquieu, *The Spirit of the Laws,* trans. Thomas Nugent (New York: Hafner, 1949), 23.29.25.

vii   **I ask Congress:** See eleventh annual message to Congress in *The Essential Franklin Delano Roosevelt* (Avenel, N.J.: Gramercy, 1995), 290, 295.

vii   **Those who denounce:** Lester Ward, "Plutocracy and Paternalism," *Forum,* November 1885, 304–309; quoted in Sidney Fine, *Laissez Faire and the General Welfare State* (Ann Arbor: University of Michigan Press, 1964), 262.

Introduction

2   **largely unknown:** In specialized circles, of course, the second bill has been discussed, albeit briefly. See, e.g., the illuminating but brisk treatment in David M. Kennedy, *Freedom from Fear: The American People in Depression and War, 1929–1945* (New York: Oxford University Press, 1999), 784–786.

3   **most Americans support:** Relevant data can be found at www.orspub.com.

Chapter 1

9   **"he's hard-boiled":** Robert Sherwood, *Roosevelt and Hopkins* (New York: Enigma, 2001), 266.

10   **speech wasn't elegant:** *The Public Papers and Addresses of Franklin D. Roosevelt,* ed. Samuel Rosenman, 13 vols. (New York: Harper, 1950), 4:40–42.

10   **"the production people can do it":** Doris Kearns Goodwin, *No Ordinary Time: Franklin and Eleanor Roosevelt: The Home Front in World War II* (New York: Simon & Schuster, 1994), 313.

12   **necessitous men:** Here Roosevelt was quoting, not for the first time, from a British judge: "Necessitous men," wrote the Lord Chancellor, in *Vernon v.*

Bethell, Eden 2 (1762): 113, "are not, truly speaking, free men; but, to answer a present emergency, will submit to any terms that the crafty may impose on them."

14   **strategies of the first doctor:** *New York Times,* December 29, 1943, 8.

15   **"Dr. New Deal":** *Time,* January 24, 1944, 12–14.

15   **array of . . . benefits:** See David M. Kennedy, *Freedom from Fear: The American People in Depression and War* (New York: Oxford University Press, 1999), 786–787.

15   **"altered their own lives":** Kennedy, *Freedom from Fear,* 787.

16   **"time has come":** See Lawrence W. Levine and Cornelia R. Levine, *The People and the President: America's Conversation with FDR* (Boston: Beacon, 2002), 524.

CHAPTER 2

17   **"We know now":** Campaign address at Madison Square Garden, in *Public Papers and Addresses of Franklin D. Roosevelt,* 5:566, 568–569.

17   **"foolish traditions":** Speech before the 1932 Democratic National Convention, in *Essential Franklin Delano Roosevelt,* 17.

18   **"two monosyllables":** See Samuel I. Rosenman, *Working with Roosevelt* (New York: Harper, 1952), 71.

18   **"existing dispensation":** *Public Papers and Addresses of Franklin D. Roosevelt,* 2:5.

19   **"not a government program":** See Matthew Miller, *The 2 Percent Solution: Fixing America's Problems in Ways Liberals and Conservatives Can Love* (New York: PublicAffairs, 2003), 30.

19   **"the New Bill of Rights":** Goodwin, *No Ordinary Time,* 485.

20   **"the creature of law":** Jeremy Bentham, *Principles of the Civil Code,* in *The Works of Jeremy Bentham* (Edinburgh: Simpkin, Marshall, 1898), 1:307–308.

20   **Robert Hale and Morris Cohen:** See Robert Hale, "Coercion and Distribution in a Supposedly Non-Coercive State," *Pol. Sci. Q.* 38 (1923): 470; Morris Cohen, "Property and Sovereignty," *Cornell L.Q.* 13 (1927): 8.

20   **For the realists:** In this section I draw from Cass R. Sunstein, *The Partial Constitution* (Cambridge: Harvard University Press, 1993).

20   **"utopian dream":** Robert Hale, *Am. Bar Assn. J.* 8 (1922): 638.

20   **"a creation of law":** *International News Service v. Associated Press,* 248 US 215, 246 (1918) (Holmes, J., concurring).

21   **"absolutely unavoidable":** Robert Hale, "Coercion and Distribution in a Supposedly Non-Coercive State," *Pol. Sci. Q.* 38 (1923): 470–471.

22   **"government neutrality"**: Hale, "Coercion and Distribution," 214; Robert Hale, unpublished manuscript, quoted in Barbara Fried, *The Progressive Assault on Laissez Faire: Robert Hale and the First Law and Economics Movement* (Cambridge: Harvard University Press, 2001), p. 89; Robert Hale, *Am. Bar Assn. J.* 8 (1922): 638-639.

22   **"ownership of some such equipment"**: *Am. Bar Assn. J.* 8 at 639. A similar point was made by Gerald Henderson in 1920; see Gerald Henderson, "Railway Valuation and the Courts," *Harv. L. Rev.* 33 (1920): 902. Henderson describes a situation in which a company lawyer argues to a rate-setting commission that the company should "be allowed always a certain percentage on the value of the property. If value goes up, rates should go on proportionately." But an economist, Henderson notes, could respond "that the only accepted and sensible meaning of the word 'value' is 'value in exchange.'" And "value in exchange" is a function of "what we allow you gentlemen to charge the public. If we reduce your rates, your value goes down. . . . Obviously we cannot measure rates by value, if value is itself a function of rates." In this way Henderson made the point—all over the legal culture in the period—that property rights and economic values were a creature of regulatory decisions.

23   **"discretionary power over the rights and duties of others"**: Robert Hale, "Rate Making and the Revision of the Property Concept," *Colum. L. Rev.* 22 (1922): 209, 214 (emphasis added).

23   **"properly subject to government control"**: Note, *Colum. L. Rev.* 35 (1935): 1090 (emphasis added).

23   **"wealth-absorbing power"**: Ward, "Plutocracy and Paternalism," 304-309; quoted in Fine, *Laissez Faire and the General Welfare State*, 262. An excellent discussion of this period is Fried, *Progressive Assault on Laissez Faire.*

24   **"legal framework"**: See F. A. Hayek, *The Road to Serfdom* (Chicago: University of Chicago Press), 43-45.

24   **famines and poverty**: Amartya Sen, *Poverty and Famines* (Oxford: Oxford University Press, 1981), 165-166.

25   **"any one of us"**: Kennedy, *Freedom from Fear,* 116.

25   **Commonwealth Club address**: Franklin D. Roosevelt, "Campaign Address on Progressive Government at the Commonwealth Club," in *Public Papers and Addresses of Franklin D. Roosevelt,* 1:742-756.

26   **"this man-made world of ours"**: *Public Papers and Addresses of Franklin D. Roosevelt,* 1:657, 855; Franklin D. Roosevelt, Message to Congress, June 8, 1934; reprinted in *Statutory History of the United States: Income Security,* ed. Robert B. Stevens (New York: Chelsea House 1970), 61. See also Morris Cohen, "Property and Sovereignty," *Cornell L.Q.* 13 (1927): 8, which makes similar points.

26   **"terms and conditions of employment"**: 29 USC § 102 (1994) (emphasis added).

26   **property rights:** In *Poverty and Famines*, Amartya Sen presents a striking contemporary illustration of similar ideas, demonstrating that famines do not result from a decreased food supply but from social choices, particularly legal ones deciding who is entitled to what. This claim can be seen as a special case of the New Deal understanding of laissez-faire. See also Jean Dreze and Amartya Sen, *Hunger and Public Action* (Oxford: Oxford University Press, 1991), demonstrating that both famines and entrenched hunger are artifacts of identifiable social policies, rather than a consequence of nature.

27   **"any just form of government"**: Robert Hale, unpublished manuscript, quoted in Fried, *Progressive Assault on Laissez Faire*; Morris Cohen, "Property and Sovereignty," *Cornell L.Q.* 13 (1927): 8, 14.

27   **"farm bill":** *Public Papers and Addresses of Franklin D. Roosevelt*, 2:72.

28   **"industrial system":** *Public Papers and Addresses of Franklin D. Roosevelt*, 1:778.

28   **important set of decisions:** *Lochner v. New York*, 198 US 45 (1905).

29   *Adkins v. Children's Hospital:* 261 US 525 (1923).

29   *West Coast Hotel v. Parrish:* 300 US 379 (1937).

31   **"excesses of the majority":** *Federalist* no. 72.

32   **"calculated to mislead the people":** *Annals of Cong.*, ed. Joseph Gale (1789), 733–745.

33   **"truly man-made":** See Gordon Wood, *The Radicalism of the American Revolution* (New York: Random House, 1993), 272.

33   **"political autocracy":** See speech before the 1936 Democratic National Convention, in *Essential Franklin Delano Roosevelt*, 114.

34   **"economic declaration of rights":** Franklin D. Roosevelt, "Campaign Address on Progressive Government at the Commonwealth Club," in *Public Papers and Addresses of Franklin D. Roosevelt*, 1:742–756.

Chapter 3

35   **"I see"** Second Inaugural Address, in *The Essential Franklin Delano Roosevelt*, 127, 131.

37   **one-third of family heads:** *Anthony Badger, The New Deal: The Depression Years, 1933–1940* (New York: Ivan R. Dee, 1989), 12.

38   **$2.39 per family:** See Arthur M. Schlesinger Jr., *The Crisis of the Old Order* (1957; New York: Houghton Mifflin, 2002), 250.

38   **"scraps of food"**: Quoted in F. L. Allen, *Since Yesterday* (New York: Perennial, 1986), 64.

38   **"smelly pile"**: Allen, *Since Yesterday,* 13.

39   **"garbage dumps"**: David E. Kyvig, *Daily Life in the United States, 1920–1939* (New York: Greenwood, 2001), 191.

39   **wild onions**: Schlesinger, *Crisis of the Old Order,* 250.

39   **"Fifty four men"**: See David F. Burg, *The Great Depression: An Eyewitness History* (New York: Facts on File, 1996), 101.

39   **"Middle West Drought"**: Burg, *Great Depression,* 145.

40   **"fog of despair"**: Schlesinger, *Crisis of the Old Order,* 3.

40   **federal troops**: Schlesinger, *Crisis of the Old Order,* 250.

40   **"I would steal"**: Schlesinger, *Crisis of the Old Order,* 250.

40   **"revolution in the countryside"**: Schlesinger, *Crisis of the Old Order,* 3.

40   **"needed a Mussolini"**: Schlesinger, *Crisis of the Old Order,* 268.

40   **"An economic Mussolini"**: Schlesinger, *Crisis of the Old Order,* 268.

40   **"capitalism is dying"**: Schlesinger, *Crisis of the Old Order,* 5.

40   **dangerous bitterness**: Schlesinger, *Crisis of the Old Order,* 252.

41   **"this is our hour"**: George McJimsey, *Harry Hopkins: Ally of the Poor and Defender of Democracy* (Cambridge: Harvard University Press, 1987), 77.

42   **peacetime allocation**: Roger Biles, *A New Deal for the American People* (DeKalb: Northern Illinois University Press 1991), 127.

42   **"assembly of movements"**: Robert Jackson, *That Man* (New York: Oxford University Press, 2003), 111.

42   **"New Deal began"**: Ellis Hawley, *The New Deal and the Problem of Monopoly* (Princeton: Princeton University Press, 1966), 15.

42   **fiscal policy**: An excellent discussion is Alan Brinkley, "The New Deal and the Idea of the State," in *The Rise and Fall of the New Deal Order, 1930–1980,* ed. Steve Fraser and Gary Gerstle (Princeton: Princeton University Press, 1989), 85–98.

42   **"try something"**: Fraser and Gerstle, *Rise and Fall of the New Deal Order,* 335.

42   **"half-and-half affair"**: Speech before the 1936 Democratic National Convention, in *The Essential Franklin Delano Roosevelt,* 114.

43   **"enlightened administration"**: Franklin D. Roosevelt, Campaign Address on Progressive Government, September 13, 1932; reprinted in *Public Papers and Addresses of Franklin D. Roosevelt,* 1:752.

44   **"three great objectives"**: *Public Papers and Addresses of Franklin D. Roosevelt,* 1:288.

45   **"self-reliance":** *Public Papers and Addresses of Franklin D. Roosevelt*, 2:110.

45   **"destitute workers":** *Public Papers and Addresses of Franklin D. Roosevelt*, 4:19–20.

45   **"insecurities":** See Anthony Badger, *The New Deal: The Depression Years, 1933–1940* (New York: Hill & Wang, 1989), 242.

45   **Civilian Conservation Corps:** Ted Morgan, *FDR* (New York: Simon & Schuster, 1985), 379.

47   **work crews . . . discharged:** Biles, *New Deal*, 97–98, 102–107.

47   **powerful example:** Morgan, *FDR*, 222–223 n. 5.

47   **"subtle destroyer":** Biles, *New Deal*, 104 n. 14.

48   **Hopkins:** Biles, *New Deal*, 104–105.

48   **WPA jobs:** Biles, *New Deal*, 105.

48   **African American youth:** Biles, *New Deal*, 238.

48   **2 million young people:** Biles, *New Deal*, 108.

48   **funds to small farmers:** Paul Conkin, *The New Deal* (London: Routledge & Kegan Paul, 1967), 60 n. 39.

49   **Farm Credit Administration:** Conkin, *New Deal*, 48.

49   **Farmers Home Administration:** Conkin, *New Deal*, 60.

49   **support private industry:** George Fort Milton, *The Use of Presidential Power, 1789–1943* (New York: Octagon, 1965), 266.

50   **clearance of slums:** Conkin, *New Deal*, 62 n. 39.

50   **rural areas:** Biles, *New Deal*, 73 n. 14.

50   **low-interest loans:** Conkin, *New Deal*, 67 n. 39.

51   **old age insurance:** Conkin, *New Deal*, 118–120 n. 25.

51   **avoid a loss:** Conkin, *New Deal*, 48.

51   **"mortgage-ridden home owners":** James MacGregor Burns, *Roosevelt: The Lion and the Fox* (San Diego: Harcourt, 1986), 267.

52   **significant jumps in spending:** See Frederick Hosen, *The Great Depression and the New Deal* (Jefferson, N.C.: McFarland, 1992), 252.

52   **"relieve the suffering":** Biles, *New Deal*, 1.

53   **recession in 1937:** See Alan Brinkley, "The New Deal and the Idea of the State," in Fraser and Gerstle, *Rise and Fall of the New Deal Order, 1930–1980*, 85–98.

55   **have interstate effects:** These developments are traced in Geoffrey Stone et al., *Constitutional Law* (Boston: Aspen, 2002).

55   **commerce clause:** See *United States v. Lopez*, 514 US 549 (1995).

55   **"constitutional moments":** See Bruce A. Ackerman, *We the People: Foundations* (Cambridge: Harvard University Press, 1993).

56   **"Constitution as written":** Douglas H. Ginsburg, "On Constitutionalism," *Cato Supreme Court Review* 7 (2003): 15.

Chapter 4

61   **"two years in bed":** Schlesinger, *Crisis of the Old Order,* 406.

63   **"entitlement and right":** Henry J. Steiner and Philip Alston, *International Human Rights in Context* (Oxford: Oxford University Press, 2000), 251.

63   "collect their pensions": Arthur Schlesinger Jr., *The Age of Roosevelt: The Coming of the New Deal* (New York: Houghton Mifflin, 1956), 308–309.

63   **"a privilege . . . or a right":** See www.orspub.com.

64   **"complementary rights":** Charles Merriam, "The Content of an International Bill of Rights," *Annals of the American Academy* 243 (1946): 11, 15.

65   **"I'll hit it hard":** Joseph P. Lash, *Eleanor and Franklin* (New York: Norton, 1971), 135.

66   **"Your President abhors":** Arthur M. Schlesinger Jr., *The Politics of Upheaval* (Boston: Houghton Mifflin, 1960), 651.

66   **"Results were his only tests":** Joseph Alsop, *FDR: A Centenary Remembrance* (New York: Viking, 1982), 111.

66   **"preconceived theoretical position":** Frances Perkins, *The Roosevelt I Knew* (New York: Viking, 1946), 166–167.

67   **themes of the second bill:** Franklin D. Roosevelt, "Campaign Address on Progressive Government at the Commonwealth Club," in *Public Papers and Addresses of Franklin D. Roosevelt,* 1:742–756.

67   **corporate power:** See Adolf A. Berle Jr. and Gardiner C. Means, *The Modern Corporation and Private Property* (1932; New Brunswick, N.J.: Transaction, 1991), for the classic statement.

67   **"economic power versus political power":** Berle and Means, *Modern Corporation and Private Property,* 357.

67   **widely read book:** Herbert Croly, *The Promise of American Life* (1909; Boston: Northeastern University Press, 1989).

68   **high degree of optimism:** An illuminating statement is Franklin D. Roosevelt, *Whither Bound?* (New York: Houghton Mifflin, 1926), briefly discussed in the conclusion.

71   **"necessities of life":** *Public Papers and Addresses of Franklin D. Roosevelt,* 1:645.

71   **"spiritual values":** *Public Papers and Addresses of Franklin D. Roosevelt,* 1:647, 657.

72   **"modern society":** See *Public Papers and Addresses of Franklin D. Roosevelt,* 1:788.

72   **"willing to work":** *Public Papers and Addresses of Franklin D. Roosevelt,* 3:291–292.

73   **"extend the Bill of Rights":** *Cong. Rec.* 79 (1935): 14, 212 (statement by Rep. Maverick).

73   **"both an industrial democracy and a political democracy":** Statement by Rep. Hildebrandt.

73   **"a Great and Precious Form of Government":** *Public Papers and Addresses of Franklin D. Roosevelt,* 5:230.

73   **"a crusade":** Burns, *Roosevelt,* 266.

74   **"election of Governor Landon":** Arthur Schlesinger Jr., *The Age of Roosevelt: The Politics of Upheaval* (1960; New York: Houghton Mifflin, 2003), 547.

74   **Industrial production nearly doubled:** Burns, *Roosevelt,* 266–267.

74   **National income had increased dramatically:** Schlesinger, *Age of Roosevelt,* 571.

74   **"equality and dignity":** Schlesinger, *Age of Roosevelt,* 268.

74   **"alternative to the New Deal":** Schlesinger, *Age of Roosevelt,* 575.

75   **Roosevelt's popularity:** See Burns, *Roosevelt,* 269–272.

75   **"platform":** Schlesinger, *Age of Roosevelt,* 581.

77   **"greatest political speech":** Schlesinger, *Age of Roosevelt,* 581.

77   **"objectives":** *Public Papers and Addresses of Franklin D. Roosevelt,* 2:9.

78   **July 5:** The 658th press conference, Hyde Park, New York, July 5, 1940, in *Public Papers and Addresses of Franklin D. Roosevelt,* 9:281.

79   **fascism appealed:** See Lawrence Dennis, *The Coming American Fascism* (1937; New York: Gordon, 1994).

80   **four freedoms speech:** See the annual message to the Congress, January 4, 1941, in *Public Papers and Addresses of Franklin Delano Roosevelt,* 9:663.

82   **"Justice for all":** Goodwin, *No Ordinary Time,* 201.

83   **Eleanor['s] . . . ideas:** Goodwin, *No Ordinary Time,* 201.

83   **"long pause":** See Rosenman, *Working with Roosevelt,* 263.

83   **"economic . . . democracy":** Rosenman, *Working with Roosevelt,* 264.

83   **"renewed summation":** Rosenman, *Working with Roosevelt,* 264.

84   **"principles and aspirations":** Goodwin, *No Ordinary Time,* 266.

84   **"smile":** Goodwin, *No Ordinary Time,* 265.

85   **National Resources Planning Board:** A good overview can be found in Marion Clawson, *New Deal Planning: The National Resources Planning Board* (Baltimore: Johns Hopkins University Press, 1981).

86   **"expanding the Bill of Rights":** See Patrick Reagan, *Designing a New America: The Origins of New Deal Planning, 1890–1943* (Amherst: University of Massachusetts Press, 1999), 218.

86   **list:** NRPB, *National Resources Development Report for 1943,* pt. 1, *Post-War Plan and Program* (Washington, D.C., 1943), 3.

87   **"American ideals"**: Reagan, *Designing a New America*, 219.

87   **skeptical legislature**: See Clawson, *New Deal Planning*, 225–226.

87   **Atlantic Charter**: Rosenman, *Working with Roosevelt*, 425.

87   **governing ideas**: See Rosenman, *Working with Roosevelt*, 425–427.

87   **"domestic agenda"**: This exchange of letters is available at the Franklin Delano Roosevelt Library in Hyde Park, New York, and copies are on file with the author.

88   **catalog of rights**: Rosenman, *Working with Roosevelt*, 426.

88   **second bill of rights**: *Public Papers and Addresses of Franklin D. Roosevelt*, 13:369–370.

91   **"these chances"**: Schlesinger, *Age of Roosevelt*, 652–653.

91   **"poverty is preventable"**: Perkins, *The Roosevelt I Knew*, 18.

91   **"courage"**: Burns, *Roosevelt*, 88.

92   **severe pain**: Alsop, *FDR*, 95.

92   **"inflamed"**: Alsop, *FDR*, 95.

92   **"crippled"**: Perkins, *The Roosevelt I Knew*, 30.

92   **"twice-born man"**: Schlesinger, *Crisis of the Old Order*, 406.

92   **"complained as little"**: Schlesinger, *Crisis of the Old Order*, 406.

92   **"paralyzed legs"**: Alsop, *FDR*, 96.

93   **"wiggle your big toe"**: Schlesinger, *Crisis of the Old Order*, 406.

93   **"crutch"**: Schlesinger, *Crisis of the Old Order*, 407.

93   **"serenity"**: Schlesinger, *Crisis of the Old Order*, 407.

93   **"public life"**: Schlesinger, *Crisis of the Old Order*, 409.

93   **"completely calm"**: Goodwin, *No Ordinary Time*, 289.

93   **"no fear at all of the future"**: Isaiah Berlin, *Personal Impressions* (Princeton: Princeton University Press, 2001).

94   **"human frailty"**: Perkins, *The Roosevelt I Knew*, 30.

94   **"he was smiling"**: Perkins, *The Roosevelt I Knew*, 36.

94   **"visit the hospital wards"**: Perkins, *The Roosevelt I Knew*, 37.

94   **"chiselers and cheats"**: See William E. Leuchtenburg, *The FDR Years* (New York: Columbia University Press, 1995), 254–255.

Chapter 5

101   **illuminating**: See Mary Ann Glendon, *A World Made New: Eleanor Roosevelt and the Universal Declaration of Human Rights* (New York: Random House, 2002), for an excellent discussion.

102   **effective enforcement**: For an overview, see David Harris and John Darcy, *The European Social Charter* (New York: Transnational, 2001).

102   **domestic remedies:** Harris and Darcy, *European Social Charter*, 30.

104   **Australian government:** See Dianne Otto, "Addressing Homelessness: Does Australia's Indirect Implementation of Human Rights Comply with its International Obligations?" Available at: ssrn.com/abstract=423321.

104   **careful study:** See Avi Ben-Bassat and Momi Dahan, "Social Rights in the Constitution and in Practice" 2003. Available at: papers.ssrn.com/sol3/papers.cfm?abstract_id=407260.

105   **democratic nations:** Ben-Bassat and Dahan, "Social Rights in the Constitution," 13.

CHAPTER 6

109   **"laws of property":** Thomas Jefferson, *The Papers of Thomas Jefferson* (1953), 8:681–683.

109   **social and economic rights:** See Ben-Bassat and Dahan, "Social Rights in the Constitution and in Practice."

110   **"A BILL OF RIGHTS":** *Federalist* no. 84.

111   **"popular Governments":** Marvin Meyers, ed., *The Mind of the Founder* (Boston: University Press of New England, 1981), 156–160.

111   **"public sentiment":** See *The Papers of James Madison*, ed. R. Rutland and W. Rachal (Charlottesville: University of Virginia Press, 1975), 14:162–163. A valuable discussion is Jack Rakove, "Parchment Barriers and the Politics of Rights," in *A Culture of Rights: The Bill of Rights in Philosophy, Politics and Law, 1791 and 1991*, ed. Michael J. Lacey and Knrd Haakonssen (Cambridge: Cambridge University Press, 1993), 98, 124–142.

112   **"educative value":** Lacey and Haakonssen, *Culture of Rights*, 142.

112   **popular sovereignty:** See Akhil Amar, *The Bill of Rights* (New Haven: Yale University Press, 2000).

113   **connection between the right to bear arms and popular sovereignty:** Amar, *Bill of Rights*, 47.

113   **democratic branch of judicial power:** Amar, *Bill of Rights*, 95.

116   **"state of comfort":** James Madison, *The Papers of James Madison*, ed. R. Rutland and W. Rachal (Charlottesville: University of Virginia Press, 1975), 14:197–198.

116   **"equal division of property":** *The Papers of Thomas Jefferson*, 8:681–683.

117   **"a certain subsistence":** Montesquieu, *Spirit of the Laws*, bk. 23.

117   **"subsist otherwise":** John Locke, *Two Treatises on Government*, bk. 1, chap. 4.

118 **200,000 copies:** See Paul Hunt, *Reclaiming Social Rights* (Brookfield, Vt.: Dartmouth 1996), 6.

118 **"not charity but a right":** See Hunt, *Reclaiming Social Rights*, 7.

118 **help for the destitute:** For an overview, see Michael B. Katz, *In the Shadow of the Poorhouse: A Social History of Welfare in America*, 2d ed. (New York: Basic, 1996).

118 **"their idleness":** Katz, *In the Shadow of the Poorhouse*, 17.

120 **"maintain ourselves":** William Forbath, "Caste, Class, and Equal Citizenship," *Mich. L. Rev.* 98 (1999): 1, 32.

121 **freedom and citizenship:** Forbath, "Caste, Class, and Equal Citizenship," 33.

121 **"we want Homesteads":** Forbath, "Caste, Class, and Equal Citizenship," 33.

122 **"aid, care, and support":** Art. 17, sec. 1 of the New York State Constitution.

124 **"th 'ilection returns":** Peter Dunne, "The Supreme Court's Decisions," *Mr. Dooley's Opinions* 26 (1900).

124 **national consensus:** Robert Dahl made this argument nearly a half century ago, before much of the work of the Warren Court. Notwithstanding the passage of decades, his argument stands up well. See Robert Dahl, "Decision-Making in a Democracy: The Supreme Court as a National Policy-Maker," *Journal of Public Law* 6 (1957): 279.

124 *Griswold v. Connecticut:* 381 US 479 (1965).

125 *Brown v. Board of Education:* 347 US 483 (1954).

125 *Roe v. Wade:* 410 US 113 (1973).

CHAPTER 7

127 **"meaningful involvement and worth":** Conkin, *New Deal.*

127 **"it didn't happen here":** See Seymour Martin Lipset and Gary Marks, *It Didn't Happen Here* (New York: Norton 1990).

128 **"suicide":** Biles, *New Deal.*

128 **"unemployed":** See Karlyn Keene and Everett Carll Ladd, "America: A Unique Outlook?" *American Enterprise* 1 (1990): 118.

129 **"major forces":** Lipset and Marks, *It Didn't Happen Here*, 9.

129 **"very poor people":** Lipset and Marks, *It Didn't Happen Here*, 288.

130 **decent standard of living:** Keene and Ladd, "America: A Unique Outlook?"

131 **reduce inequality:** See Robert Goodin et al., *The Real Worlds of Welfare Capitalism* (Cambridge: Cambridge University Press, 1999).

132 **less mobility:** Carol Graham and Stefano Pettinato, *Happiness and Hardship: Opportunity and Insecurity in New Market Economies* (Washington, D.C.: Brookings Institution, 2002).

133 **"preserve capitalism":** Lipset and Marks, *It Didn't Happen Here,* 73.

133 **"United Mine Workers":** Quoted in Lipset and Marks, *It Didn't Happen Here,* 211.

134 **large differences:** Albert Asesina et al., "Why Doesn't the U.S. Have a European-Style Welfare State?" unpublished manuscript, Harvard University, 2001.

134 **Full Employment Act:** See Stephen Kemp Bailey, *Congress Makes a Law: The Story Behind the Employment Act of 1946* (New York: Greenwood, 1980).

135 **different racial group:** Alesina, "Why Doesn't the U.S. Have a European-Style Welfare State?" 29–30.

135 **hostility to welfare:** Alesina, "Why Doesn't the U.S. Have a European-Style Welfare State?" 39.

CHAPTER 8

139 **"concrete achievements":** Burns, *Roosevelt,* 244.

142 **real effects:** See Ben-Bassat and Dahan, "Social Rights in the Constitution and in Practice."

146 **state constitutions:** See *Tucker v. Toia,* 43 NY2d 1, 371 NE2d 449 (1977).

CHAPTER 9

149 **civil rights:** *Edwards v. California,* 314 US 160, 173 (1941) (Jackson, J., concurring).

149 **Barbara K. Olson Memorial Lecture:** Olson's speech can be found at: www.fed-soc.org/BKOlsonMemorialLecture/bkolsonlecture–111601.htm.

150 *Plyler v. Doe:* 457 US 202 (1982).

152 **form of common law:** See David A. Strauss, "Common Law Constitutional Interpretation," *U. Chi. L. Rev.* 63 (1996): 877.

153 **"consequences of poverty":** Frank I. Michelman, foreword to "On Protecting the Poor Through the Fourteenth Amendment," *Harv. L. Rev.* 83 (1969): 7, 9.

154 **obscure Supreme Court decision:** *Edwards v. California,* 314 US 160 (1941).

156   *Griffen v. Illinois:* 351 US 12 (1956).

157   *Douglas v. California:* 372 US 353 (1963).

157   *Boddie v. Connecticut:* 401 US 371 (1971).

158   **context of marriage:** The best discussion is Frank I. Michelman, "The Supreme Court and Litigation Access Fees: The Right to Protect One's Rights, Part II," 1974 *Duke L.J.,* 1974, 527.

158   **striking down a state poll tax:** *Harper v. Virginia Bd. of Elections,* 383 US 663 (1966).

159   *Shapiro v. Thompson:* 394 US 618 (1969).

160   *Memorial Hospital v. Maricopa County:* 415 US 250 (1974).

161   *Goldberg v. Kelly:* 397 US 254 (1997).

162   **social and economic rights:** See Frank I. Michelman, Foreword to "On Protecting the Poor Through the Fourteenth Amendment," *Harv. L. Rev.* 83 (1969): 7.

163   *Dandridge v. Williams:* 397 US 471 (1970).

165   *Lindsay v. Normet:* 405 US 56 (1972).

165   *San Antonio School v. Rodriguez:* 411 US 1 (1973).

168   **desperate poverty and acknowledged rights:** See Michael Heise, "State Constitutions, School Finance Litigation, and the 'Third Wave': From Equity to Adequacy," *Temple L. Rev.* 68 (1995): 1151. As Heise shows, it is unclear whether children in poor districts have been helped by state court decisions that build on Justice Marshall's rationale in *Rodriguez.* The history and results here offer strong cautionary notes about judicial protection of social and economic rights.

170   *US Department of Ag. v. Moreno:* 413 US 528 (1973).

170   *Papasan v. Allain:* 478 US 265 (1986).

Chapter 10

175   **"a solution":** Burns, *Roosevelt,* 245.

176   **society with free speech:** See Cass R. Sunstein, *Why Societies Need Dissent* (Cambridge: Harvard University Press, 2003).

177   **treated respectfully:** See Thomas Scanlon, "A Theory of Freedom of Expression," *Phil. & Pub. Aff.* 1 (1972): 204; David A. Strauss, "Persuasion, Autonomy, and Freedom of Expression," *Colum. L. Rev.* 91 (1991): 334–346.

177   **human capabilities:** See Martha Nussbaum, *Women and Human Development* (New York: Cambridge University Press, 2000); Amartya Sen, *Development as Freedom* (New York: Anchor, 1999).

177   **deepest disputes:** This theme is developed in Cass R. Sunstein, *Legal Reasoning and Political Conflict* (New York: Oxford University Press, 1996).

178   **"no one asks us why":** Jacques Maritain, *Human Rights: Comments and Interpretations* (London: Wingate, 1949), 9.

178   **"single body of beliefs":** Maritain, *Human Rights*, 10.

178   **"social-mindedness":** Schlesinger, *Age of Roosevelt*, 653.

184   **free press and democratic elections:** See Amartya Sen, *Poverty and Famines* (Oxford: Oxford University Press, 1981).

184   **"early warning system":** Amartya Sen, "Freedoms and Needs," *New Republic*, January 10, 17, 1994, 32.

185   **"general knowledge":** See Erika De Wet, *The Constitutional Enforceability of Economic and Social Rights* (London: Butterworth-Heinemann, 1996).

189   **fifty-five-hour week:** Schlesinger, *Crisis of the Old Order*, 249.

189   **"fitting response":** See annual message to the Congress, January 3, 1938, in *Public Papers and Addresses of Franklin D. Roosevelt*, 7:1, 14.

190   **accidents and catastrophes:** An intriguing general discussion of how to build on insurance models to reduce risk is Robert Shiller, *The New Financial Order: Risk in the Twenty-first Century* (Princeton: Princeton University Press, 2003).

190   **"social functioning":** Sen, *Development as Freedom*, 89.

190   **"bundle of goods and services":** Amartya Sen, *The Standard of Living* (Oxford: Oxford University Press, 1994), 18.

190   **"relatively poor person in a rich country":** Sen, *Standard of Living*, 89–90.

191   **bottom 10 percent:** See Goodin et al., *Real Worlds of Welfare Capitalism*.

191   **"humanity, which was a faith":** Schlesinger, *Age of Roosevelt*, 654.

CHAPTER 11

193   **first-class temperament:** Burns, *Roosevelt*, 157.

193   **intellectual radicalism:** Burns, *Roosevelt*, 244.

195   **emphasizing work:** William E. Forbath, "Constitutional Welfare Rights: A History, Critique, and Reconstruction," *Fordham L. Rev.* 69 (2001): 1821.

197   **poverty line:** Benjamin Aldrich-Moodie, "The Earned Income Tax Credit," Issue Brief no. 1, *The Century Foundation*, September 1999.

199   **the state was implicated:** Walter Lippman, *An Inquiry into the Principles of the Good Society* (1937; New York: Greenwood, 1973), 187.

199   **black market:** See Hernando de Soto, *The Mystery of Capital* (New York: Basic, 2001).

200   **"due process of law":** John R. Ellingston, "The Right to Work," *Annals of the American Academy* 243 (1946): 27, 33.

201   **"foreign aggression":** David Kelley, *A Life of One's Own: Individual Rights and the Welfare State* (Washington: Cato Institute, 1998), 1.

201   **homelessness is a legal status:** See Jeremy Waldron, *Homelessness and the Issue of Freedom in Liberal Rights* (Oxford: Oxford University Press, 1993).

201   **"starvation deaths":** Sen, *Poverty and Famines,* 165–166

205   **"sacrifice freedom":** Kelley, *A Life of One's Own,* 1.

205   ***Are,* not *were,* Mr. President":** *Wall Street Journal,* January 12, 1944, 4.

CHAPTER 12

209   **"a government that lives in a spirit of charity":** Speech before the 1936 Democratic National Convention, in *The Essential Franklin Delano Roosevelt,* 113, 118.

210   **Skeptics:** See Dennis Davis, "The Case Against Inclusion of Socioeconomic Rights in a Bill of Rights Except As Directive Principles," *South African Journal of Human Rights* 8 (1992): 475.

211   ***Government of the Republic of South Africa v. Grootboom:*** 11 BCLR 1169 (CC) (2000).

211   ***Minister of Health v. Treatment Action Campaign:*** 10 BCLR 1033 (CC) (2002).

213   **"fundamental part of the social contract":** *Tucker v. Toia,* 43 NY2d 1, 371 NE2d 449 (1977).

214   **benefits to legal immigrants:** *Mahamed Aliessa v. Novello,* 96 NY2d 418, 754 NE2d 1085 (2001).

215   **denial of support:** *Barie v. Lavine,* 40 NY 2d 665.

215   **welfare payments:** *Loveland v. Gross,* 80 NY2d 419, 605 NE2d 339 (1992).

215   **reasonable judgments:** In the educational context, however, the results of intervention by state courts are quite mixed. See Michael Heise, "State Constitutions, School Finance Litigation, and the 'Third Wave': From Equity to Adequacy," *Temple L. Rev.* 68 (1995): 1151.

215   **Constitutional Court of Latvia:** *On the Compliance of the Requirement Incorporated into the First Part of Article 6 of the Law "On Employment" on the Necessity of Having the Permanent Residence Permit to Obtain the Status of the Unemployed with Articles 91 and 109 of the Constitution of the Republic of Latvia,* Case no. 2001–11–0106 (2002). Available at: www.satv.tiesa.gov.lv/Eng/Spriedumi/02–0106(01).htm.

215   **social security:** *On Compliance of Item 1 of the Transitional Provisions of the Law 'On Social Insurance' with Articles 1 and 109 of the Constitution of the Republic of Latvia,* Case no. 2000–08–0109 (2001). Available at: www.satv.tiesa.gov.lv/Eng/Spriedumi/08–0109(00).htm.

215 **subsistence payments:** *Petition of Tartu City Council to Review the Constitutionality of §22¹(4) of the Social Welfare Act*, Case no. 3–4–1–2–03 (Supreme Court of Estonia). Available at: www.nc.ee/english.

216 **prison clothing:** *R v. Governor of Frankland Prison Ex p. Russell*, 2000 HRLR 512 (Queens Bench Division 2000).

216 **replacement housing:** *Decision Contract. 11/00*, April 4, 2001. Available at: www.trybunal.gov.pl/eng/Judical_Decisions/2001/K_11_00a.pdf.

216 **higher education:** Decision no. 81, *On the Incident of Unconstitutionality of the Provisions . . . Concerning the Social Assistance of the Unemployed and Their Professional Reinstatement*, republished, May 19, 1998. Available at: www.ccr.ro/Decizii/Engleza/decizii_eng.htm.

216 **constitutionalism:** See Lawrence Lessig, *Code and Other Laws of Cyberspace* (New York: Basic, 2000).

219 **judicial enforcement:** Ex Parte Chairperson of the Constitutional Assembly, 1996 (4) SA 744, 1996 (10) BCLR 1243 (CC) at para 78.

226 **medically necessary:** See *Harris v. McRae*, 448 US 297 (1980).

EPILOGUE

231 **"America is new":** *Public Papers and Addresses of Franklin D. Roosevelt*, 1:743.

231 **"I have to run":** Schlesinger, *Crisis of the Old Order*, 407.

231 **slim volume:** See Franklin Delano Roosevelt, *Whither Bound?* (New York: Houghton Mifflin, 1926).

232 **"the good old days":** Roosevelt, *Whither Bound?* 19.

232 **"unification of mankind":** Roosevelt, *Whither Bound?* 27.

232 **"lend helping hands":** Roosevelt, *Whither Bound?* 31.

Bibliographical Note

There is an immense literature on Franklin Delano Roosevelt and the New Deal, and I list only a small subset of that literature here. For an accessible catalogue of Roosevelt's major speeches, the best source is *The Essential Franklin Delano Roosevelt* (New York: Gramercy, 1995). Invaluable treatments include James MacGregor Burns, *The Lion and the Fox* (San Diego: Harcourt, 1956); Frank Freidel, *Franklin D. Roosevelt: A Rendezvous with Destiny* (New York: Little, Brown, 1965); and the multivolume *The Age of Roosevelt* by Arthur M. Schlesinger Jr., including *The Crisis of the Old Order* (New York: Houghton Mifflin, 1957); *The Coming of the New Deal* (New York: Houghton Mifflin, 1958); and *The Politics of Upheaval* (New York: Houghton Mifflin, 1959). More recent discussions are Conrad Black, *Franklin Delano Roosevelt: Champion of Freedom* (New York: Public Affairs, 2001); David M. Kennedy, *Freedom from Fear: The American People in Depression and War* (New York: Oxford, 1999); Kenneth S. Davis' four volumes, especially (for current purposes) volume 2, *FDR: The New Deal Years, 1933–1937* (New York: Random House, 1986); and volume 4, *FDR: The War President, 1940–1943* (New York: Random House, 2000).

Engaging discussions of Roosevelt can be found in Frances Perkins, *The Roosevelt I Knew* (New York: Viking, 1946); Robert Sherwood, *Roosevelt and Hopkins: An Intimate History* (New York: Grosset & Dunlap, 1948); and Isaiah Berlin, *Personal Impressions* (Princeton: Princeton University Press, 2001). Exceptionally informative is Samuel I. Rosenman, *Working with Roosevelt* (New York: Harper, 1952). On the period in general, an illuminating treatment is Anthony J. Badger, *The New Deal: The Depression Years, 1933–1940* (New York: Hill & Wang, 1989). On the New Deal's institutional innovations, Ellis W.

Hawley, *The New Deal and the Problem of Monopoly* (Princeton: Princeton University Press, 1966), remains invaluable.

On the National Resources Planning Board, helpful discussions are found in Marion Clawson, *New Deal Planning: The Natural Resources Planning Board* (Baltimore: Johns Hopkins University Press, 1981); and Patrick D. Reagan, *Designing a New America: The Origins of New Deal Planning* (Amherst: University of Massachusetts Press, 1999). The latter contains a particularly illuminating account of the origins of the second bill of rights.

On the legal realists and Robert Hale, the best discussion, by far, is Barbara Fried, *The Progressive Assault on Laissez Faire: Robert Hale and the First Law and Economics Movement* (Cambridge: Harvard University Press, 2001). On the Universal Declaration of Human Rights, an exceptional account is Mary Ann Glendon, *A World Made New: Eleanor Roosevelt and the Universal Declaration of Human Rights* (New York: Random House, 2001). On social and economic rights in general, helpful overviews include Matthew Craven, *The International Covenant on Economic, Social, and Cultural Rights: A Perspective on Its Development* (Oxford: Oxford University Press, 1995); Asbjorn Eide et al., eds., *Economic, Social, and Cultural Rights: A Textbook*, 2d ed. (Dordrecht: Maryinus Nijhoff, 2001); and *Paul Hunt, Reclaiming Social Rights: International and Comparative Perspectives* (Brookfield, Vt.: Dartmouth, 1996). On American exceptionalism, a good treatment is Seymour Martin Lipset and Gary Marks, *It Didn't Happen Here: Why Socialism Failed in the United States* (New York: Norton, 2000).

On the American Supreme Court's grappling with the question whether there is a constitutional right to welfare, the classic treatment remains Frank I. Michelman, "Foreword: On Protecting the Poor Through the Fourteenth Amendment," *Harv. L. Rev.* 83 (1969): 7. More recent discussions include William E. Forbath, "Caste, Class, and Equal Citizenship," *Mich. L. Rev.* 98 (1999): 1; William E. Forbath, "Constitutional Welfare Rights: A History, Critique, and Reconstruction," *Fordham L. Rev.* 69 (2001): 1821; Sortiros Barber, *Welfare and the Constitution* (Princeton: Princeton University Press, 2003).

Acknowledgments

This book emerged from three sources. The first was a reading group at Harvard Law School in the late 1980s, including William Forbath, Mary Ann Glendon, Frank Michelman, and Martha Minow; our discussions helped inspire this project, and I am grateful to them. The second was a generous invitation by Michael Ignatieff to explore the question why the United States lacks social and economic guarantees; that invitation pointed the way toward Part II of this book. The third source was a set of conversations with my agent, Sydelle Kramer, whom I thank for help of many different kinds. Thanks too to my editor, William Frucht, who offered wonderful suggestions on substance, structure, and style; the book is much better because of his help. John Donatich, the publisher at Basic Books when I embarked on this project, offered needed encouragement and many good suggestions. I am also grateful to librarians at the Franklin Delano Roosevelt Library, in Hyde Park, New York, particularly Robert Clark, for their generosity and assistance.

For valuable comments on a previous draft, thanks to Bruce Ackerman, William Forbath, Dennis Hutchinson, Martha Nussbaum, Eric Posner, David A. Strauss, and Adrian Vermeule. For encouragement and guidance at an early stage, thanks to David Kennedy and Patrick Reagan. Some parts of this book were presented in remarks to the John F. Kennedy School of Government at Harvard University, the Economic Policy Institute, and the Ford Foundation. I am most grateful to participants in those sessions for their reactions, questions, and suggestions. For superb research assistance, special thanks to Smita Singh and Sarah A. Sulkowski; thanks too to Emily Gavin for helpful work in connection with Chapter 3. For general support and good-will, thanks to Ellen Ruddick-Sunstein.

This book is dedicated to my father, a navy lieutenant who was stationed in the Philippines during World War II. Like countless others who fought in that war, my father escaped several close brushes with death. He returned home to live a good and joyful life. My father was a lifelong Republican, but he admired and loved Franklin Delano Roosevelt. I think that he would be pleased to know that some of his feelings have found their way into his son's book.

Index

Abortion, 226
Accident rights, 13, 86, 195, 243
Ackerman, Bruce, 55–56, 59
Adams, John, 185
Adkins v. Children's Hospital, 29–30
African Americans. *See also* Slavery
　　Constitution, U.S. and, 150–151
　　Full Employment Act and, 134
　　post Civil War, 36, 90, 119–121
　　unemployment in, 37
AIDS/HIV, in South Africa, 211, 224–228
All Out (Grafton), 83
Alsop, Joseph, 66
Amendment(s), Constitution of United States,
　　105, 176. *See also* Bill of Rights (original);
　　Constitution of United States
　　alternative, 183–184
　　Civil War, 119–121
　　Congressional power for, 182, 183
　　Eighth, 200
　　employment, 182
　　Equal Rights, 126, 140
　　Fifth, 64, 114, 200
　　First, 112, 167–185
　　Fourteenth, 152, 158, 217
　　H.J. Res. 35 as proposed, 182–183
　　Second, 113
　　Sixth/Seventh, 113–114, 200
America. *See also* Congress, United States;
　　Constitution of United States; Supreme
　　Court, United States
　　Atlantic Charter signed by, 65, 84–85, 87
　　children in poverty in, 234
　　civil/political liberty in, 128
　　class conflict in, 131
　　commitment to equal opportunity in, 186
　　constitutional law in, 152–153
　　Declaration of Independence for, 5, 75, 141,
　　　175, 179, 202
　　electoral system in, 133, 136, 153
　　end to social/economic rights in, 167,
　　　168–171
　　Europe different from, 129–131, 134–135,
　　　203–204

　　exceptionalism in, 106, 127–138
　　individualism in, 3–4, 87, 106, 134, 137
　　mobility of workers in, 132
　　peaceful revolution in, 82
　　redistribution of wealth/resources in, 27–28,
　　　116, 129–130, 131–132, 134–135, 186,
　　　205–207
　　Republicanism in, 33
　　Roosevelt's transformation of, 232–233
American culture
　　free speech and, 179
　　New Deal and, 135–138
　　social/economic rights and, 105, 106,
　　　128–129, 134–135, 153, 169
American Revolution, 33, 36, 69, 75–76, 111
　　Bill of Rights and, 111, 113, 115
　　Roosevelt on, 238, 244
Antitrust laws. *See* Monopoly
Arizona, *Memorial Hospital v. Maricopa County* in,
　　160–161
Armed forces
　　GI bill of rights for, 14, 15–16
　　right to vote for, 12, 242
Arms, right to bear, 113
Articles of Confederation, 36, 109
Atlantic Charter, 65, 84–85, 87
Australia, 104, 241
Austria, 102
　　constitution of, 105

Banks, during Great Depression, 37
Bentham, Jeremy, 20, 176
Berle, Adolf, 67–68, 70, 73, 76
Biddle, Francis, 93
Bill of Rights (original), 73, 233. *See also*
　　Amendments, Constitution of United
　　States; Constitution of United States;
　　Press, freedom of; Religion, freedom of;
　　Second bill of rights; Speech
　　added to Constitution, U.S., 110–115, 126
　　citizenship protected by, 112–115
　　as constitutive commitments, 179
　　Eighth Amendment of, 200
　　expanding, 73, 86